The Knowledge Industry in the United States, 1960-1980

The Knowledge Industry
in the United States
1960-1980

Michael Rogers Rubin and Mary Taylor Huber

with Elizabeth Lloyd Taylor

PRINCETON UNIVERSITY PRESS

PRINCETON, NEW JERSEY

Copyright © 1986 by Princeton University Press
Published by Princeton University Press, 41 William Street,
Princeton, New Jersey 08540
In the United Kingdom:
Princeton University Press, Guildford, Surrey

ALL RIGHTS RESERVED
Library of Congress Cataloging in Publication Data will be
found on the last printed page of this book
ISBN 0-691-04235-7

This book has been composed in Linotron Electra

Clothbound editions of Princeton University Press books
are printed on acid-free paper, and binding materials
are chosen for strength and durability

Printed in the United States of America by
Princeton University Press
Princeton, New Jersey

Contents

List of Tables

Acknowledgments

Readers who are familiar with the organization of academic research will realize that research assistants and associates are in grave danger of slipping into the institutional equivalent of limbo when their professor, the "principal investigator," leaves or dies. We are most grateful to Professor William Baumol of New York University and Princeton University and to Professor Stephen Goldfeld of Princeton University for their guidance and generosity during this difficult period, and for their critical reading of earlier drafts of this book. The Spencer Foundation, the Earhart Foundation, and the National Science Foundation all allowed grants in progress to continue after Professor Machlup's death, and the latter two foundations made available the additional funds that allowed us to complete this work. We should like to record here as well our thanks to Donald Koepp, the University Librarian at Princeton, who graciously allowed us to maintain Professor Machlup's office throughout the eighteen months during which this book took shape and to Stephan Machlup, Hanna Machlup Hastings, and Mitzi Machlup, whose moral support never flagged.

In the period after Machlup's death, a number of other people provided valuable advice and assistance. Professor James Brown of the Economics Department at Princeton University made critical comments for the section on "Education in the Home"; Dr. Stephen Kagann revised and checked his figures on the foregone earnings of high school and college students for the section on "Neglected Cost Items" in education; and Anthony Rojko checked the many calculations required for the discussion in Chapter IV. Edward Weintraub wrote the initial draft for Chapter IX on "Knowledge Production and Occupational Structure," and Mary Norris contributed significantly to Chapter VIII on "Information Services." Assistance in the beginning of Michael Rubin's statistical work was provided by Eugene Rumer and Susan Sabetti, a task to which Ari Michelson, Susan Colman, and Joan Weintraub also contributed.

No project of the breadth and depth as that planned by Machlup could be undertaken without the assistance of many co-workers. A number of researchers who were involved in the larger project prior to Machlup's death also contributed materials that were of direct assistance to us in writing this book. Stephen Kagann's statistical work facilitated Michael Rubin's task from the start, as did the statistical research on education organized at different times by Richard Sobel and Robert Rockwell. Arthur Rosenzweig's fine report on education in the armed services and Joan Eckstein's reports on education in the church and on training on the job proved especially helpful in our research for the relevant sections of Chapter IV.

The number of persons who participated in Machlup's project over the years is truly staggering. Looking back over the files since 1972, we have counted over ninety individuals who provided services ranging from minor bibliographical assistance to ambitious reports of fifty pages and more. All of these people have contributed indirectly to the present work. We hope that they will forgive us for not listing them all by name. Most of the materials that they collected are now housed, along with Machlup's own notes for the series, in the archives of the Hoover Institution in Stanford, California, where they are now available for future research.

Clearly, generous funding was required to support research on so wide a scale. Between 1972, when Machlup first began work on his "revised edition" of *The Production and Distribution of Knowledge in the United States*, and January 1983 when work on the new series ended, he had received grants for his work on knowledge and knowledge production from the following agencies: The Earhart Foundation, the Exxon Education Foundation, the Ford Foundation, the John and Mary R. Markle Foundation, the National Endowment for the Humanities, the National Institute of Education, the National Science Foundation, the Alfred P. Sloan Foundation, and the Spencer Foundation.

There is one final acknowledgment that we believe Fritz Machlup would like us to make. Princeton University Press, and particularly Herbert Bailey and Sanford Thatcher, remained steadfast in its commitment to publish Machlup's work on knowledge production beginning with *The Production and Distribution of Knowledge in the United States* in 1962, through the initial plan for a one- or two-volume second edition, and through its metamorphosis into a series of ten new volumes. The plan for the series, *Knowledge: Its Creation, Distribution and Economic Significance*, included the volumes published by Princeton University Press,

(I)   *Knowledge and Knowledge Production* (1980);
(II)   *The Branches of Learning* (1982);
(III)   *The Economics of Information and Human Capital* (1984),

and the unfinished volumes

(IV)   *The Disciplines of Information*;
(V)   *Education*;
(VI)   *The Creation of New Knowledge: Research and Art*;
(VII)   *Media of Communication*;
(VIII) *Information Services and Information Machines*;
(IX)   *Knowledge Production: Its Size and Growth*;
(X)   *Knowledge Occupations and the Knowledgeable Society*.

Preliminary research for Volume IV was published in 1983 by John Wiley & Sons in *The Study of Information: Interdisciplinary Messages*, edited by Fritz Machlup and Una Mansfield.

Note to the Reader

In order to make it easier for the reader to compare the tables in this book with the original tables in *The Production and Distribution of Knowledge in the United States*, we have used an unusual numbering scheme. For Chapters IV through VIII tables designated by a roman numeral and an arabic number—unless otherwise marked—are simply updated versions of the identically designated tables in Machlup's original book. Tables that include alphabetic characters in their designations present either new material or material formatted differently from Machlup.

Since Chapters I through III are new and have no analogue in Machlup's original text, roman numerals and arabic numbers are used. The tables in Chapter IX update the tables originally reported by Machlup in Chapter X of his book, but since several of Machlup's original tables are omitted here, there is no correspondence between the table numbers in the old and new chapters. Also summary tables are indicated merely by their respective chapter numbers.

List of Abbreviations

AAFRC	American Association of Fund-Raising Counsel
ASTD	American Society for Training and Development
BEA	Bureau of Economic Analysis
BLS	Bureau of Labor Statistics
GPO	Government Printing Office
NCC	National Council of Churches
NCES	National Center for Education Statistics
OECD	Organization for Economic Cooperation and Development
SEC	Securities and Exchange Commission
SIC	Standard Industrial Classification

The Knowledge Industry, 1960-1980

CHAPTER | Introduction

This is a book of statistics on the role of information in the United States economy. As such, it is yet another contribution to the literature in the growing field of the economics of information.[1] More specifically, it is also an update of *The Production and Distribution of Knowledge in the United States* by Fritz Machlup.

In that book Machlup gathered a statistical profile of a group of industries that he collectively dubbed the "knowledge" industry. According to Machlup the knowledge industry accounted for some 29 percent of Gross National Product (GNP) in the United States in 1958. Machlup further showed that slightly less than 32 percent of the work force was engaged in knowledge-producing activities in 1959 and received a similar share of total employee compensation.[2]

Machlup had promised his readers that the later volumes of his series on *Knowledge: Its Creation, Distribution, and Economic Significance* would update the social and economic statistics that he had presented in *The Production and Distribution of Knowledge in the United States*. Unfortunately, his untimely death prevented him from completing this plan. In his absence we present these tables here and document the growth of the knowledge industry and its various branches over a period of twenty-two years. This book presents measurements of the Machlupian knowledge industry for the intervening years when the United States Bureau of the Census has conducted its in-depth economic censuses. These "census years" include 1963, 1967, 1972, and 1977. Estimates are also presented for the year 1980.

Our results may surprise readers whose expectations are based on the high rate of growth that Machlup documented for knowledge production in the decade before 1958, his benchmark year. Our data show that the proportion of knowledge production in the (adjusted) GNP increased from 29 percent in 1958 to 34 percent in 1980. Compared to some of the extravagant predictions that began to appear after the publication of *The Production and Distribution of Knowledge in the United States*, this represents an extremely modest rate of growth relative to the average rate of growth of other components of total GNP.

[1] Fritz Machlup estimated that the literature on the economics of information comprised perhaps 22,000 titles in 1982, including such topics as advertising, insurance markets, financial markets, product and labor markets, and others. For a further discussion, see Machlup's *The Economics of Information and Human Capital*; the third volume of *Knowledge: Its Creation, Distribution, and Economic Significance* (Princeton, N.J.: Princeton University Press, 1984).

[2] Fritz Machlup, *The Production and Distribution of Knowledge in the United States* (Princeton, N.J.: Princeton University Press, 1962), p. 362 and pp. 382-387.

The intellectual framework for this task has not been varied from the original. Machlup's definition of the knowledge industry has been followed meticulously, as, where possible, has been the selection of data sources to perform the measurements we require. This project was commissioned by Machlup and managed by him until his death. In this sense, then, the authors are acting as Machlup's executors, for we have attempted to complete this work in a fashion consistent with the way Machlup would have prepared it. We have tried to maintain fealty to Machlup's concepts. We are not so presumptuous as to say that this work has been completed "in the same way" as if Machlup had lived, for his unique talents are not ours, but we have tried to produce results consistent with those he might have, given the opportunity.

The present study began in 1972 when Machlup first undertook research for a second edition of his earlier book. By 1978 when Mary Huber became his principal assistant in the field of education, this "second edition" had grown to plans for a series of eight volumes, and by 1981 when Michael Rubin joined the project as chief statistical consultant, the series itself had grown to a plan for ten books. Only three had gone to the publisher when Machlup died in 1983, but the tables that Rubin had prepared under Machlup's direction for Volumes V through X of the new series were virtually complete. By presenting these tables as *The Knowledge Industry, 1960-1980*, we return nearly full-circle to his original plan. We have attempted throughout to highlight this comparative feature of our work.

As closely related as this book is to Machlup's, however, the responsibility for the accuracy of the tables and the aptness of the text is entirely our own. When Machlup died on January 30, 1983, we were left with ninety tables in draft form, two years of correspondence between Machlup and Rubin concerning these tables, and at least twenty large file drawers of material collected by Machlup and his assistants on the development of the various branches of the knowledge industry over a period of twenty-two years. Final decisions on some of the more arcane areas of cost and expenditure, particularly in the field of education, remained to be made, as did the task of sifting through the mountain of material at our disposal for items that could aid our interpretation of the statistical data. Our rough division of labor assigned the long chapter on education to Mary Huber, while Michael Rubin took over the rest of the text, with aid from Elizabeth Taylor throughout.

The remaining chapters of this text are generally structured to allow easy reference to Machlup's original work. Thus, Chapters IV through VIII of this work are on the same topics as chapters IV through VIII of Machlup's 1962 work: Chapter IV on education; Chapter V on research and development; Chapter VI on media of communications; Chapter VII on information machines; and Chapter VIII on information services.

Further, the statistical tables within these chapters follow the same numbering scheme as Machlup's. (Thus, for example, Table VIII-7 in both texts pertains to the purchases of information services by state and local governments.)

Of the remaining chapters of this update, Chapter II, which compares Machlup's statistical approach to that in *The Information Economy*, is new; Chapter III is the GNP study found in Machlup's chapter IX; and Chapter IX can be compared to Machlup's chapter X.

As startling as were the results of the research described in *The Production and Distribution of Knowledge in the United States*, they provoked little further serious research until the publication in 1977—fifteen years later—of *The Information Economy*.[3] This nine-volume report, published by the United States Department of Commerce and authored in part by both Marc U. Porat and Michael R. Rubin, acknowledged its intellectual debt to Machlup. The Department of Commerce report, which will hereafter sometimes be referred to as the Commerce study, made use of the national income accounts published by the Bureau of Economic Analysis to create a computer model of the United States economy for the year 1967. The definition of the information sector used in the Commerce study was similar in many respects to that used by Machlup; however, where Machlup included a number of economic activities that are not part of the national income accounts, the Commerce study adhered strictly to that accounting scheme. The same general classification scheme was also used to measure the participation of the U.S. work force in information activities.

The Commerce study typology made the distinction between the so-called "primary" and "secondary" parts of the information sector. This distinction was based upon the fact that many of the elements of the information sector may be found both as separate industries and as adjuncts to other industries. For example, a print shop may be a separate operation doing business with the public; however, it might also be a component of a larger business that is not part of the information sector. Hence, the print shop, which markets directly to the public, is part of the primary information sector, while a similar shop which is owned by a ball bearing factory, and prints only for that factory, is part of the secondary information sector. This concept is important because a large proportion of information activities are part of the secondary sector and would remain unidentified and hidden if not sought out in the typology.

The Information Economy reported that 25.1 percent of GNP could be attributed to the activities of the primary information sector in 1967 and an additional 21.1 percent of GNP could be attributed to the secondary information sector in the same year. In total the information sector accounted for over 46 percent of GNP, according to the Commerce study.[4]

---

[3] Marc U. Porat and Michael R. Rubin, *The Information Economy*, 9 volumes (Washington, D.C: Government Printing Office, 1977).

[4] *The Information Economy* (1977) was updated by Rubin and Elizabeth Taylor in "The U.S. Information Sector and GNP: An Input-Output Study," *Information Processing and Management*, June 1981, pp. 163-194. Rubin and Taylor found that the primary information sector declined as a percentage of GNP to 24.8 percent in 1972 from the 25.1 percent in 1967 reported in *The Information Economy*.

The response to *The Information Economy* was much more rapid than to Machlup's original work. The Organization for Economic Cooperation and Development (OECD) conducted a study of the information sector of several of its member nations in 1978 and 1979. The results of that study were published by the OECD in 1981 under the title, *Information Activities, Electronics and Telecommunications Activities, Impact on Employment, Growth, and Trade.*[5] Among its findings, the study showed that the size of the primary information sector varied from 14.8 percent of GNP in Australia to 24.8 percent in France and the United States.

The OECD measured the number of information workers (including those in both the primary and secondary information sectors) in the economies of several of its members in the same study. The findings, on a percentage basis across countries, are presented in Table I-1.

Another work following Machlup's intellectual framework is *An Analysis on Information Economy in Japan from 1960 to 1980 (sic)*, published by the Japanese Research Institute of Telecommunications and Economics.[6] This study reports that the knowledge industry, including primary and secondary sectors, accounted for 29.5 percent of Japan's GNP in 1960 and 35.4 percent in 1979. Knowledge workers, again in both the primary and secondary sectors, increased from 21.3 percent of Japan's work force in 1960 to 37.7 percent in 1980. As we shall see, these results are very similar to those obtained here for the United States.

TABLE I-1

PERCENTAGE OF INFORMATION WORKERS IN
VARIOUS OECD MEMBER ECONOMIES

Country	Year	Percent
Austria	1976	32.2
Canada	1971	39.9
Finland	1975	27.5
France	1975	32.1
Japan	1975	29.6
Sweden	1975	34.9
United Kingdom	1975	35.6
United States	1970	41.1
West Germany	1978	33.2

SOURCE: Organization for Economic Cooperation and Development, *Information Activities, Electronics and Telecommunications Activities, Impact on Employment, Growth, and Trade* (Paris, 1981).

[5] (Paris, 1981).

[6] S. Komatsuzakt, T. Tanimitsu, G. Ohira, and K. Yamamoto, "An Analysis of Information Economy in Japan from 1960 to 1980," an undated monograph published by the Research Institute of Telecommunications and Economics, Tokyo, Japan.

CHAPTER **II** Alternative Approaches to
Measuring the Knowledge Industry in
the United States Economy.[1]

Machlup in *The Production and Distribution of Knowledge in the United States* (1962) and the authors of the U.S. Department of Commerce report, *The Information Economy* (1977), devised two similar and yet distinct methods to define and measure the magnitude of the so-called "information sector" in the United States economy. The Commerce study method was then used again in 1981 in the study of member countries of the Organization for Economic Cooperation and Development, *Information Activities, Electronics and Telecommunications Technologies: Impact on Employment, Growth and Trade.*[2]

The two methods each identified the components of the information sector, referred to by Machlup as the "knowledge industry" and by the Commerce study as "information industries." Using their respective definitions of the sector, each then measured its contribution to Gross National Product (GNP). From similar foundations, however, each developed along its own path, diverging in several key respects from the other.

The definitions of the information sector used in the two studies varied in several ways. First of all, the Commerce study adhered rigidly to the National Income Account system maintained by the Bureau of Economic Analysis (BEA) of the U.S. Department of Commerce. Machlup restructured the National Income Accounts. Secondly, as noted earlier, the Commerce study distinguished between "primary" and "secondary" elements of the information sector; no such distinction was made by Machlup. Thirdly, Machlup measured "final demand," whereas the Commerce study used "value added" as the measure of GNP.

[1] A similar version of this chapter, entitled "Alternative Approaches to Measuring the Information Sector of the United States Economy," by Michael R. Rubin and Elizabeth L. Taylor, was prepared under Machlup's direction and was presented to the MIT Workshop on the Measurement of Information and Flows of Communications, July 27 to 30, 1982. This chapter includes revisions of that document prepared by Machlup before his death.

[2] See Fritz Machlup, *The Production and Distribution of Knowledge in the United States* (Princeton, N.J.: Princeton University Press, 1962); also Marc U. Porat and Michael R. Rubin, *The Information Economy*, 9 volumes (Washington, D.C.: Government Printing Office, 1977); and finally, *Information Activities, Electronics and Telecommunications Technologies: Impact on Employment, Growth and Trade* (Paris: Organization for Economic Cooperation and Development, 1981).

Comparing the Alternative Methods

COMPARISON OF THE INDUSTRY BRANCHES

The classifications used in the two studies are similar, but not identical. In a broad generalization, five categories of information activities can be identified: (1) education; (2) media of communication; (3) information machines; (4) information services; and (5) other information activities.

Machlup broke these categories into roughly 50 individual groups or branches, whereas the Commerce study offered a somewhat more detailed breakdown with 115 groups. Each classification system is spelled out in substantial detail by the respective authors. The Commerce study, for example, identified each group by the Standard Industrial Classification (SIC) system. The presentation offered here simplifies the breakdowns used in the two systems in order to facilitate comparisons.

Table II-1 presents a comparison of the two classifications broken down by the five major categories listed above. A discussion of each category follows in turn.

TABLE II-1

Comparison of the Industry Branches

Industry branches	Machlup	Commerce study
Education		
Education in the Home	X	
Training on the Job	X	
Education in the Church	X	
Education in the Armed Services	X	
Elementary and Secondary Education	X	X
Higher Education	X	X
Commercial Schools	X	X
Federal Expenditures	X	X
Public Libraries	X	X
Implicit Cost of Education		
Students' Foregone Earnings	X	
Implicit Rents of Buildings	X	
Media of Communication		
Printing and Publishing	X	X
Photography and Phonography	X	X
Stage Podium and Screen	X	X
Radio and Television	X	X
Other Advertising	X	X
Telecommunications	X	X
Conventions	X	
Information Machines		
Printing Trades Machinery	X	X
Paper Industries Machinery		X
Musical Instruments	X	
Motion Picture Equipment	X	X

TABLE II-1 (con't)

Industry branches	Machlup	Commerce study
Telephone and Telegraph Equipment	X	X
Signaling Services	X	X
Measuring and Controlling Instruments	X	X
Typewriters	X	X
Computers	X	X
Office Machines and Parts	X	X
Semiconductors*		X
Electronic Tubes*		X
Other Electronic Equipment		X
Ink		X
Photographic Equipment and Supplies	X	X
Information Services		
Legal	X	X
Engineering and Architectural	X	X
Accounting and Auditing	X	X
Medical	X	X
Securities Brokers	X	X
Insurance Agents	X	X
Real Estate Agents	X	X
Wholesale Agents	X	X
Retail "Information" Stores		X
Government Activities	X	X
Other Information Activities		
Research and Development	X	X
Construction of Information Buildings		X
Nonprofit Activities	X	X

* Not yet in mass production in 1958, but included in any case by Machlup, as part of the cost of other information machines. As noted in the text, where a product is only an input for another industry branch, Machlup included its cost in the output of that branch.

Education.   The Commerce study offered a substantially more restrictive definition of information/education activities than did Machlup. The Commerce study included only formal education, whereas Machlup went beyond this, including a variety of other ways of teaching and learning. Among the more significant inclusions by Machlup were: (1) education in the church; (2) education in the armed services; (3) foregone earnings of students and of mothers staying home to care for their young children; and (4) implicit rental of education buildings.

Media of Communication.   The two classifications were generally consistent with one another in their definitions of the media of communications. Machlup was somewhat more restrictive than the Commerce study, excluding retail trades that included too large a measure of manual work.

Information Machines.   Wide disparities in the classifications can be found in the respective delimitations of information machines. Although both studies included measuring and controlling instruments, office machines, computers, printing equipment, and telephone and telegraph equipment, the coverage differs in other areas. Machlup included only one element missing from the Commerce study—musical instruments. However, since Machlup was calculating only final demand expenditures for knowledge, in those instances where a product was only an input for another industry branch and made no contribution to final demand, he omitted it. Thus, for example, because semiconductors are included in the cost of other information machines but have no final demand sales, Machlup omitted them for his accounts. On the other hand, the Commerce study included a number of items not found in Machlup, including ink, electronic components, other electronic equipment, and office furniture since the Commerce study was measuring value added. The distinction between the final demand and value added approaches is explained more fully below.

Information Services.   The two classifications were generally consistent with one another in their definitions of information services.

Other Information Activities.   Both studies included research and development expenditures (which in Machlup's arrangement were shown in a separate category). The Commerce study shows outlays for the construction and maintenance of schools and libraries under the heading of "Other Information Activities," whereas Machlup placed them under the heading of "education" (where he also showed the outlays for churches). The Commerce study included, however, the construction cost of office buildings, which Machlup had omitted.

With an understanding of the overall similarities and differences in the two arrangements, we can turn to other differences between the two studies.

UTILIZING NATIONAL INCOME ACCOUNTS

The differences in classification systems described above represent, perhaps, the true watershed that separates the two methods. Many of the differences between the two groupings rest upon Machlup's decision to go beyond the data compiled by the Bureau of Economic Analysis (BEA) in the official National Income Accounts. In contrast, the Commerce study rigidly adhered to the data available in those accounts.

Each study justified its decision in relatively strong terms. Marc U. Porat, for example, writing in volume one of *The Information Economy* states that: "Machlup's accounting scheme innovated rather liberally on the National Income Accounts concepts and practices, whereas this study does not" (p. 44).

He also states "The choice was whether formally to introduce an information sector into the conventional national accounts structure; or whether to innovate both by introducing a new sector *and* by redefining the very concept of

GNP. The decision was reached with caution—that the concept of an information sector was sufficiently new that a simultaneous overhaul of the GNP scheme would confuse and obfuscate more than it would help" (p. 45).

Machlup rebuts: "The drawback [of the Commerce method] is the disregard of implicit cost (which the governmental statistics cannot include but) which is essential in the cost of education. . . . We are interested in the price or cost of information—not only those portions that can be culled from BEA statistics" (letter to Michael Rubin, June 23, 1982).

He also declares, "I submit that for some purposes the concepts and practices of national product accounting have to be departed from; there are questions that require different arrangements of the data."[3]

The choice is between orthodoxy or completeness. The development of alternative systems of national accounting is becoming more widespread, if not more accepted.[4] Nonetheless, conformity has its virtues.

On a practical level the compilation and manipulation of data is significantly easier using a technique that makes use of an existing data base such as the BEA National Income Accounts. The statistics reported in *The Information Economy* were collected, combined into an input-output table, and put into machine-readable form by the Bureau of Economic Analysis. *The Information Economy* was prepared by purchasing a computer tape from the Department of Commerce and by subsequently using a computer program to rearrange the BEA data to fit the new classification. The resulting input-output table was a computer model of the 1967 economy in the United States, which permitted Porat and Rubin to predict changes in output and employment resulting from hypothetical changes in government spending and tax policies. Although the Commerce study method represented the "lazy man's" approach to economic research, the creation of an econometric model, albeit rudimentary, of the information sector nevertheless remains a substantial accomplishment.

If the use of the BEA data offered important benefits in terms of ease of analysis and of the availability of a computer-based econometric model, it nonetheless was a prison that permitted no escape. The problem is that the new model can have no more detail than the original model. An industry omitted from the BEA model, must, of necessity, be omitted from the Commerce study model as well. In measuring the information sector, this proved to be a serious drawback. The Bureau of Economic Analysis collected data largely at the four-digit SIC (Standard Industrial Classification) level. Many of the infor-

[3] Fritz Machlup, *Knowledge and Knowledge Production* (Princeton, N.J.: Princeton University Press, 1981), p. 237.

[4] See, for example, Robert Eisner, "An Extended Measure of Government Product: Preliminary Results for the United States, 1946-76," *Rev. Income and Wealth*, March 1981, pp. 33-64; also, Juster and Land, *Social Accounting Systems* (New York: Academic Press, 1981).

mation activities of the economy can only be identified using a high level of disaggregation; hence, the Commerce study offers relatively little detail; its 115 separate activities aggregate to only 26 separate, measurable industries.

In contrast, the Machlup approach overcomes some of these difficulties, but only at the expense of creating new difficulties. Machlup chose to include a variety of activities in his work that BEA does not consider to be part of the National Income Accounts. These include: (1) earnings foregone by mothers to stay home to train their children; (2) earnings foregone by students; (3) the tax loss from tax-exempt schools; and (4) a variety of others.

The Machlup approach requires a far different research technique. Data must be collected from whatever sources are available. This uses much more labor than the approach used by the Commerce study.

The result, using the Machlup method, is a more detailed picture of the various components of the information sector. The trade-off is the absence of a computer model, more work, and accusations of statistical heresy.

"KNOWLEDGE INDUSTRY" VERSUS "PRIMARY" AND "SECONDARY" SECTORS

The Commerce study introduced the concept of a "primary" and "secondary" information sector. The primary sector comprises those industries that participate directly in the information marketplace and includes virtually all of the information activities listed in Table II-1. The Commerce study, however, noted that some information activities take place outside the marketplace, as part of the manufacturing process for noninformation products. The accounting and legal departments of a ball-bearing manufacturing plant, for example, are part of the secondary information sector.

The secondary information sector is difficult to measure, since that measurement requires dividing "noninformation" firms and industries into two parts, one of which is involved in "pure" noninformation activities and the other of which engages in "pure" information activities. Conceptually, each firm is divided into two "quasi-firms," one of which carries out information activities while the other has no such activities. The various quasi-firms that conduct information activities comprise the secondary information sector. Taking the ball-bearing industry as an example, the measurement of the secondary information sector requires, conceptually, that each ball-bearing firm be broken into two quasi-firms. One quasi-firm produces only ball-bearings, while the other is an information company providing management, legal, and accounting services to the first. The latter quasi-firm is part of the secondary information sector.

In practice, the Commerce study carries out the process described above by splitting each industry's work force into two groups; one of information workers, the other of noninformation workers. The Bureau of the Census periodically compiles data on the occupational distribution of various industries.

These data were used to perform the split. The Commerce study attributed each industry's output to the information and noninformation sectors on the basis of the proportion of the industry's work force engaged in each activity. Thus, the measurement of the secondary information sector used work force data to estimate production data.

In contrast, Machlup argues that the measurement of employment in information activities, the "occupational approach," should be kept separate from the measurement of information goods and services in the national economy, the "industry approach." Machlup states that the Commerce study method "mixes information *inputs* in industries outside the information sector with *outputs* of industries in the information sector." (*Knowledge and Knowledge Production*, p. 240.)

"VALUE ADDED" OR "TOTAL SALES"

Each of the methods discussed here has followed its own path in computing the contribution of the information sector to GNP. The Commerce study uses "value added," whereas Machlup uses "total sales" or "total cost" of output. This difference reflects two distinct methods of measuring GNP; one based upon income (value added), and the other based upon product sales (final demand). The total for each of these measures will be the same for the entire economy; however, the total for individual industries can vary substantially.

Table II-2, an excerpt from *The Information Economy*, shows the relationship of the two accounting conventions.

The rationale for the adoption of either of these accounting methods is described by the authors of the two studies. First, the Commerce study tells us:

> Using the income side of the accounts offers two main advantages. First, it allows the researcher to measure the cost of the secondary information services directly. Second, value added is a more accurate measure of wealth and income originating in the economy since it is insensitive to the cost of goods sold. An item with costly intermediate purchases will "sell" more to final demand since its output price will be correspondingly higher. Two goods with identical wealth-generating attributes could have very different final demand sales, depending on the use of the item. If the goods or service is mainly intermediate in nature (such as advertising), it will slow a zero final demand but a sizable value added. For example, iron ore sells very little of its output to final demand since most sales are to other firms; yet it generates a considerable amount of wages and profits. By contrast, the jewelry industry sells almost all of its output to final consumers.
>
> The omission of value-added estimates from earlier work undoubtedly reflected the state of data processing facilities available at the time. Without fast computers and, more importantly, very extensive interlocked machine-readable data bases, it is doubtful whether a more comprehensive report

TABLE II-2

FACTORS USED TO COMPUTE THE CONTRIBUTION
OF THE INFORMATION SECTOR TO THE GNP

Commerce study (income side-value added)	Machlup study (product side-final demand)
(1) Compensation of employees Wages and salaries Supplements	(1) Personal consumption expenditures
(2) Rental income of persons	(2) Gross private domestic investment Gross domestic private capital formation
(3) Corporate profits & inventory valuation adjustments	(3) Net exports of goods & services
(4) Net interest	(4) Government purchases of goods & services Federal defense purchases Federal nondefense purchases State & local purchases
(5) Business transfer payments	
(6) Indirect business taxes	
(7) Less: Subsidies less current surplus of government enterprise	
(8) Capital consumption allowances	

SOURCE: Marc U. Porat, *Definition and Measurement*, Vol. 1 of *The Information Economy* by Marc U. Porat and Michael R. Rubin (Washington, D.C.: Government Printing Office, 1977), 1:48.

could have been prepared. In the 15 years since Machlup's research, a wealth of information became available and accessible. Hence, the consolidated accounts presented in this chapter look at the information sector from both the final demand and value added perspectives. The two measurements of GNP differ considerably. (*The Information Economy*, 1: 47.)

Machlup, on the other hand, writes:

To use only value added by the producers of the knowledge goods and knowledge services would understate the cost of the product. To use a simple analogy: if we want to know the share of steel production in gross national product, we want not just the value added by steel producers but also all the things they had to purchase from other firms in order to produce the steel. Likewise, if we want to know the total of book production, we must not confine ourselves to the value added by the publishers; we need their sales receipts for the books produced or, if books were produced for free distribution, we would need the full cost of production, including the paper, the printers' bills, and all other intermediate products and services purchased. And if the publishers were working in rent-free offices, provided by governments, foundations, or universities, we would have to add the rental values of these offices as implicit cost of the product. Value-added statistics may provide im-

portant data for the measurement of the output of some knowledge industries, but it is not the appropriate basis for the purposes of our inquiry.
(*Knowledge and Knowledge Production*, p. 240.)

In practical terms, the depth of detail is substantially greater when the
Machlup method is used as we will see in the following sections.

The Machlup method, however, could overstate the size of the knowledge
industries compared to GNP, if care is not taken. In general, only final demand
expenditures can be counted, and intermediate products must be excluded.
This "double-counting" hazard was fully recognized by Machlup, who took
great care to avoid it.

COMPARING THE RESULTS: BASE YEAR 1972

The differences between the two methods become very obvious when they are
used with statistical data. As noted earlier, the Machlup study was conducted
for the base year 1958 and the Commerce study for the year 1967. Hence, no
direct comparison is possible.

Studies using the two methods, however, have now been completed for the
year 1972. Rubin recently completed an update of the Commerce study to the
year 1972.[5] The revisions of the Machlup work are presented in this volume.

A focus on one particular industry may be instructive. The Machlup
method attributes $188.6 billion to expenditures for education in 1972. Of this
amount, $96.7 billion are various imputations to GNP that are not recognized
in the official national income accounts. Since the Commerce study method
relies upon these accounts, the $96.7 billion is omitted from the Commerce
study method. In addition, the Machlup method includes several categories of
expenditures omitted from the Commerce study method, including expenditures for education in the military, and others. These expenditures total $6.0
billion that are present in the Machlup method but absent in the Commerce
study method. Finally, the Machlup method uses slightly different means of
calculating the value of expenditures for preschool, commercial, and religious
education, arriving at a total $3.6 billion greater for these activities than are
reported in the national income accounts and used in the Commerce study
method.

When all of these difficulties are subtracted from the original Machlup
method figure, we are left with $82.3 billion, the amount measured by the
Commerce study method as final demand expenditures for education. The statistics for each method are presented in Table II-3.

As we have noted above, however, the Commerce study method relies upon
the value added side of GNP for its calculations. (Since the Commerce study

[5] See Michael Rubin and Elizabeth Taylor, "The U.S. Information Section and GNP: An Input-Output Study," *Information Processing and Management*, July 1981, pp. 163-194.

TABLE II-3

The Cost of Education in 1972: The Machlup Method and the Commerce Method
(billions of dollars)

	Machlup study	Commerce study
At Home (mothers' foregone earnings)*	9.3	
Preschool	1.4	0.7
Elementary and Secondary		
Monetary Expenses	54.0	54.0
Implicit Expenses*	5.9	
Students' Foregone Earnings*	47.0	
Higher Education		
Monetary Expenses	20.8	20.8
Implicit Expenses*	6.7	
Students' Foregone Earnings*	27.8	
Education in the Church	8.0	6.4
Education in the Military	4.3	
Commercial Education	1.7	0.4
Federal Programs	0.7	
Public Libraries	1.0	
Total	188.6	82.3

Sources: Tables and text within this work for the Machlup method and for the Commerce study, Michael R. Rubin and Elizabeth L. Taylor, "The U.S. Information Sector and GNP: An Input-Output Study," *Information Processing and Management*, July 1981, pp. 160-191.

* Not part of BEA National Income Accounts.

method relies upon an input-output table, the final demand figures cited above are easily available, even though they are not used for any analytic purposes by the Commerce study method.) Although the true figure is undoubtedly much higher, the Commerce study method is able to segregate only $8.2 billion value added for educational services in 1972. The reader should remember that in the value added approach, only several items would be counted, including the profits of for-profit institutions of education; and salaries paid by all educational institutions.

Since the vast majority of educational institutions are nonprofit, the only major entry picked up in the Commerce study method is "employee salaries." Unfortunately for the Commerce study method, the salaries of many teachers are hopelessly entangled in the category "general government" and cannot be identified separately.

The comparison that has been made in this section between methods could be made between each of the other elements of the information sector as well. In the typical case, the Commerce study defines several information activities within an industry, but is not able successfully to measure them. The result is a substantially more aggregated, and less detailed, body of data than is present with the Machlup method.

CHAPTER **III**   Total Production of
Knowledge and the National Product

This chapter summarizes the research findings that are presented in more detail in Chapters IV through VIII and places them within the context of the national economy. For each of the recent economic census years, 1958, 1963, 1967, 1972, and 1977, and for the year 1980, the components of the knowledge industry are measured and compared to total production in the United States. This information is first presented in current dollars and then is repeated in constant 1972 dollars in order to remove the effect of inflation from our calculations.

KNOWLEDGE PRODUCTION, SELECTED YEARS, BY INDUSTRY

The prelude to our analysis and compilation of statistics on the production of the knowledge industry is the calculation of the adjusted Gross National Product (GNP), which is the benchmark of the remainder of the work here. The conventional GNP concept is not suitable for our purposes since many components of knowledge production, as defined by Machlup and as measured here either (1) are treated here as final products even though they enter as a cost of current production or are omitted entirely in the official statistics; or (2) they are treated here as an intermediate product that is a cost of the current production of other goods, even though it is treated as a final product in the official statistics. In the first type of case, the expenditures must be added to the conventional GNP figure; in the second sort of case, the expenditures must be subtracted.

The results of this exercise are presented in Table III-1. Among the additions to GNP are a number of items that we will count in total knowledge production, but that are omitted from the official statistics. Among these are the implicit earnings of high school, college, and university students that are foregone in obtaining an education. Also included are the foregone earnings of mothers who stay at home to educate their young children. Finally, the calculation includes implicit rents of schools, colleges, and universities, expenses that are not paid but that represent the rental value of properties that they would yield were they devoted to other activities.

Other additions to GNP are required for those expenditures that we treat as a final product, but that are treated as a cost of current production in the official statistics. Among these are expenditures by businesses on advertising in news-

TABLE III-1

ADJUSTMENTS TO GNP: 1958, 1963, 1967, 1972, 1977, AND 1980
(millions of dollars)

	1958	1963	1967	1972	1977	1980
(1) GNP, Conventional Concept	448,881	594,738	796,312	1,171,121	1,899,500	2,626,100
(2) Additions to GNP						
Implicit earnings of mothers	4,432	5,273	6,584	9,326	10,475	11,316
Implicit earnings of high school students	15,172	23,813	32,623	46,962	65,578	79,886
Implicit earnings of college and university students	6,380	10,060	16,624	27,849	41,939	52,260
Implicit rents for elementary and secondary schools	1,869	2,672	2,869	3,536	5,157	6,556
Implicit rents of colleges and universities	893	1,705	2,429	4,024	5,679	6,726
Business R & D expenditures	3,707	5,456	8,142	11,710	19,696	30,400
Business expenditures on periodicals	1,056	1,294	1,738	1,889	3,250	4,949
Business expenditures on newspapers	2,479	3,107	4,163	6,048	9,666	13,301
Radio station revenue	521	680	907	1,407	2,275	3,206
Television station revenue	1,030	1,597	2,276	3,179	5,889	8,808
Advertising	5,000	6,000	7,537	10,415	16,774	21,914
Total	42,539	61,657	85,892	126,345	186,378	239,322
(3) Subtractions from GNP						
Government purchases of printing	27	45	89	130	258	470
Government purchases of telephones	1,870	2,281	2,474	8,348	10,581	6,706
Government purchases of telegraph	58	59	55	144	133	77
Government purchases of postal services	52	89	146	294	611	745
Federal government services	1,555	2,655	3,474	5,971	8,870	14,430
State and local government services	2,419	2,850	3,860	7,023	13,754	19,743
Total	5,981	7,979	10,098	21,910	34,207	42,171
(4) Adjusted GNP (1 + 2 − 3)	485,439	648,416	872,106	1,275,556	2,051,651	2,823,251

SOURCES: Summary tables in Chapters IV–VIII of this book.

NOTE: In this and in all subsequent tables, the expenditures reported by Machlup for 1958 have been modified to reflect revisions in the underlying data by their sources.

papers, periodicals, on radio and television, and so on. Also included are business expenditures for research and development.

There must also be subtractions from the conventional GNP figure, corresponding to those items that are treated in the official statistics as a final product, but that we treat as an intermediate product. Included in this category are government expenditures for the purchase of printing, telephone, telegraph, and postal services, and so on.

The result of this exercise is an "adjusted" GNP, which reflects the changes needed to make our statistics comparable with the official national income accounts. With this figure, we may calculate the share of GNP that is produced by the knowledge industry and its various components.

Table III-2 summarizes the major findings of our entire research effort. Drawing upon the detailed reports contained in Chapters IV though VIII, we find that expenditures for knowledge production have increased steadily from 1958 to 1980, rising from $138,825 million in the earlier years to $967,909 million in the most recent years. As a share of adjusted GNP, these expenditures rose steadily from 28.6 percent in 1958 to 31.0 percent in 1963, and 33.3 percent in 1967. That growth, however, ended by 1972, when expenditures for knowledge production accounted for 33.9 percent of GNP. These expenditures have remained roughly 34 percent of GNP in 1977 and 1980.

TABLE III-2

EXPENDITURES FOR KNOWLEDGE PRODUCTION AND COMPARISONS WITH ADJUSTED GNP:
1958, 1963, 1967, 1972, 1977, AND 1980
(millions of dollars)

	1958	1963	1967	1972	1977	1980
Education	57,238	86,334	128,578	188,644	280,187	351,362
Research and development	10,711	17,059	23,146	28,477	42,982	62,222
Media of communications	37,234	48,645	66,991	100,849	166,719	227,135
Information machines	9,878	15,239	22,696	29,149	54,418	90,210
Information services	23,764	33,803	49,398	85,142	156,665	236,980
Total	138,825	201,080	290,809	432,261	700,971	967,909
Adjusted GNP	485,439	648,416	872,106	1,275,556	2,051,671	2,823,251
(percent of adjusted GNP)						
Education	11.8	13.3	14.7	14.8	13.7	12.5
Research and development	2.2	2.6	2.6	2.2	2.1	2.2
Media of communications	7.7	7.5	7.7	7.9	8.1	8.0
Information machines	2.0	2.4	2.6	2.3	2.7	3.2
Information services	4.9	5.2	5.7	6.7	7.6	8.4
Total	28.6	31.0	33.3	33.9	34.2	34.3

SOURCES: Summary tables in Chapters IV-VIII of this book.

In short, the knowledge industry has rested upon a plateau of about 34 percent of adjusted GNP for a full decade.

All, however, is not static. In the decade of the 1970s, expenditures for information machines increased their share of adjusted GNP by nearly 50 percent, rising from 2.3 percent in 1972 to 3.2 percent by 1980. Expenditures for information services increased as a portion of GNP by one-fourth, rising from 6.7 to 8.4 percent. Indeed, the broad pattern of change can best be seen in Table III-3, which shows that expenditures for educational activities had declined almost to their 1958 share of GNP by 1980 (12.5 percent in 1980, and 11.8 percent in 1958) after cresting at 14.8 percent of GNP in 1972. In contrast, the share in GNP of all other knowledge-producing activities, in the aggregate, increased from 16.8 percent to 21.8 percent between 1958 and 1980. The reader should note that the decline in the share of GNP constituted by education reflects a relative slowing in the growth of expenditures in this area; however, the absolute growth in expenditures for education remained substantial, albeit smaller than the growth in GNP.

TABLE III-3

EDUCATION AND OTHER KNOWLEDGE-PRODUCING ACTIVITIES
AS A PERCENT OF GNP: 1958,
1963, 1967, 1972, 1977, AND 1980

	1958	1963	1967	1972	1977	1980
Educational activities	11.8	13.3	14.7	14.8	13.7	12.5
Other knowledge production	16.8	17.7	18.6	19.1	20.5	21.8

SOURCE: Table III-2 of this book.

The causes of these trends can be suggested briefly. Chapter IV documents the demographic developments that resulted in increased school enrollments during most of the 1960s and the early 1970s, and for the declining enrollments in the later 1970s. Technological innovations in information processing and handling, including the computer and the wide new array of capabilities it offers, no doubt have been integral to the steady growth of expenditures for both information machines and information services.

Some further insights into this growth pattern can be gleened from examination of the source of these expenditures. Table III-4 summarizes the expenditures of three groups—governments, businesses, and consumers—for the production and distribution of knowledge. On a percentage basis, business has paid for a steadily increasing share of total knowledge production since the late 1960s, rising from 27.4 percent to 35.1 percent of the total in the years from 1967 to 1980. A parallel decline can be found in consumer and governmental expenditures over the same period. Consumer expenditures dipped from 41.1 percent to 36.7 percent of the total between 1967 and 1980, while government

TABLE III-4

KNOWLEDGE PRODUCTION BY SOURCE OF FUNDS: 1958, 1963, 1967, 1972, 1977, AND 1980
(millions of dollars)

	1958	1963	1967	1972	1977	1980
Government expenditures	35,459	54,352	82,176	117,190	179,572	233,871
Business expenditures	40,444	57,568	79,543	119,174	223,104	339,454
Consumer expenditures	58,647	83,706	119,589	178,562	269,075	354,895
Unallocated	4,275	5,454	9,501	17,335	29,220	39,689
Total	138,825	201,080	290,809	432,261	700,971	967,909
			(percent of total)			
Government expenditures	25.5	27.0	28.2	27.1	25.6	24.1
Business expenditures	29.1	28.6	27.4	27.6	31.8	35.1
Consumer expenditures	42.3	41.6	41.1	41.3	38.4	36.7
Unallocated	3.1	2.7	3.3	4.0	4.2	4.1
Total	100.0	100.0	100.0	100.0	100.0	100.0

SOURCES: Summary tables in Chapters IV-VIII of this book. The allocation among groups is the same as Machlup's.

NOTE: The figures may not add up to 100 percent because they have been rounded off.

expenditures fell from 28.2 percent to 24.1 percent. The most telling aspect of these findings is perhaps the coincidence of timing with the slowdown in the growth of expenditures for education that began in the early 1970s.

Yet another set of insights into our findings are offered by data on the stage of production at which the expenditures were made. Table III-5 reports expenditures for knowledge production, separated into purchases of final product on the one hand and intermediate products that are a cost of current production on the other. The proportion of these expenditures for knowledge production had remained very nearly constant at an 80:20 ratio of final to intermediate product over the period of our study.

KNOWLEDGE PRODUCTION IN CONSTANT 1972 DOLLARS

So far this chapter has reported our findings in "current" dollars, that is, at the actual prices prevailing in each year. No correction has been made for the effects of inflation. More specifically, there has been no adjustment for the fact that the prices of different goods and services rise at different rates over time. Several examples may make this point more clearly. The price of newspapers has roughly tripled in the years of our study so that, if 1958 prices were set to equal 100, 1980 prices would equal exactly 300. The price of admissions to motion pictures rose at a slightly faster rate yet, going from 100 to 310. In sharp contrast, the price of calculators has remained absolutely constant between 1958 and 1980 at our index base of 100. To complicate the situation further,

TABLE III-5

EXPENDITURES FOR KNOWLEDGE PRODUCTION BY STAGE OF PRODUCTION: 1958, 1963, 1967, 1972, 1977, AND 1980
(millions of dollars)

	1958	1963	1967	1972	1977	1980
Intermediate product	25,209	35,544	50,535	77,398	138,442	199,670
Final product	113,616	165,536	240,274	354,863	562,529	768,239
Total	138,825	201,080	290,809	432,261	700,971	967,909
(percent of total)						
Intermediate product	18.2	17.7	17.4	17.9	19.8	20.6
Final product	81.8	82.3	82.6	82.1	80.2	79.4
Total	100.0	100.0	100.0	100.0	100.0	100.0

SOURCES: See text and tables within this book.

the prices of some commodities have dropped over the years of our study so that, for example, the price of radio and TV receivers, set at 100, in 1958, had declined to 88 by 1980.[1]

The difference in the way prices change from product to product can severely distort statistics based upon current prices. What appears to be a dramatic increase in the production of a commodity may instead be nothing more than a rapid increase in the price of that product. To correct this kind of distortion, our statistics on expenditures can be deflated.

In this section, our statistics on expenditures for knowledge production are deflated and expressed in terms of constant 1972 dollars. For this purpose we used the GNP output deflators for various goods and services calculated by the Bureau of Economic Analysis of the U.S. Department of Commerce. In brief, these deflators are derived from yearly statistics on the revenues and production levels of various industries; that is, the increase in an industry's revenue is caused by two factors, increases in production and increases in prices. The output deflators measure the increase in prices for a given level of output. An alternative source used when GNP deflators are not available is the Consumer Price Index (CPI), which is compiled by the Bureau of Labor Statistics of the U.S. Department of Labor. In contrast to the output deflators, which are based on industry-wide revenue and production statistics, the CPI is a monthly survey of prices at the retail level. Many products, however, are not surveyed either by the CPI or its companion survey, the Producer Price Index.

The process of deflating the statistics gives rise to a variety of problems that make the final outcome a matter of art. We will examine the problems inher-

[1] These price deflators are based upon the GNP output deflator for various industries reported by the U.S. Department of Commerce.

ent in deflation of each of the products and services that are part of knowledge production. The appendix to this book contains detailed tables reporting the source and value of each of the deflators used for each individual element of our study, as well as detailed results of the exercise.

No attempt has been made to deflate expenditures for research and development independently. Rather, the generally accepted constant dollar figures for R & D expenditures that are published by the National Science Foundation have been used.

The products and services listed in the categories "media of communications" and "information machines" present fewer difficulties than do the remaining elements of our study. With few exceptions, GNP output deflators are available for each product or service and can be associated unambiguously with that product or service. In a few instances, entries are taken from the producer and consumer price indices. In all instances, however, these "official" numbers may be quite inaccurate due to inadequate treatments of technological or quality change.

The deflation of several information services involves serious conceptual difficulties of which the reader should be aware. Neither the costs of demand deposit accounts nor the cost of credit card handling involve a direct price to the consumer. Although each of these activities may involve some direct charge to the consumer for the "handling," some additional part of the expense is paid for indirectly. This indirect charge may be a surcharge on rates paid by retailers using a credit card or it may take the form of interest on the balance of demand deposits not paid to the consumer. In any event, a surrogate must be employed as a deflator for the "price" of these services. It was decided to use the GNP output deflator for banking to deflate the costs of demand deposits and to use the GNP output deflator for credit agencies and financial brokers to deflate the costs of credit card processing, and also of security and commodity brokerage fees.

Similar conceptual problems are encountered in the various components of education. The foregone earnings of students and stay-at-home mothers are deflated using the Bureau of Labor Statistics wage deflator; the implicit rents of school buildings are deflated using the CPI entry for "residential rents"; and much of the remainder is deflated using the GNP deflator for education. This particular deflator is unsatisfying for a variety of reasons. In terms of coverage, the deflator is defined in terms only of private education. Only because we have no better alternative do we use that deflator for public as well as for private schools. Making the leap of faith that the pace of inflation in public and private schools was comparable is not enough.

No less disturbing, however, is the extremely high rate of inflation implied by the GNP deflator for education. Set at 100 in 1958, this deflator indicated that the "price" of education had risen to 526 in 1980—one of the largest apparent price increases recorded over this period. Nothing is allowed in this rate of increase figure for changes that may have increased the quality (and cost) of education over this period. Improved student-teacher ratios, purchases of better classroom and laboratory equipment, and higher salaries for teachers who may be better qualified, all can contribute to the increased cost of education. To what extent we should attribute higher costs of education to inflation and to what extent to quality improvements in the product is a matter of conjecture.

The difficulties besetting deflation of time series that extend over more than two decades must be made clear. But they need not discourage us. Our findings must be taken with several grains of salt, but they may also be taken as the best estimate available.

Table III-6 reports expenditures for knowledge production for the years of our study in constant 1972 dollars. As a percent of adjusted GNP, these expenditures varied between 33.9 percent (1972) to 36.5 percent (1980). Although there was variation within that range, there was little apparent pattern in the overall fluctuations.

Table III-7 suggests that there were strong internal trends within the aimless overall pattern. Expenditures for education, which in current dollars rose from 12 percent of adjusted GNP to over 14 percent and then returned to 12 percent, in constant dollars rose to a high of 17.4 percent in 1967, before declining steeply to 12.0 percent in 1980. Flaws in the process of deflation may ac-

TABLE III-6

EXPENDITURES FOR KNOWLEDGE PRODUCTION AND COMPARISONS TO ADJUSTED GNP, IN CONSTANT DOLLARS: 1958, 1963, 1967, 1972, 1977, AND 1980
(millions of 1972 dollars)

	1958	1963	1967	1972	1977	1980
Education	121,722	151,980	192,014	188,644	197,669	189,085
Research and development	16,215	23,733	29,241	28,477	30,695	35,114
Media of communications	55,754	64,330	81,061	100,733	127,685	147,223
Information machines	13,349	19,583	26,382	29,149	43,096	62,363
Information services	45,910	53,802	67,948	85,142	111,777	143,679
Total	252,950	313,428	396,646	432,145	510,922	577,464
Adjusted GNP	733,026	903,647	1,101,267	1,275,556	1,475,358	1,579,741
(percent of adjusted GNP)						
Education	16.6	16.8	17.4	14.8	13.4	12.0
Research and development	2.2	2.6	2.7	2.2	2.1	2.2
Media of communications	7.6	7.1	7.4	7.9	8.7	9.3
Information machines	1.8	2.2	2.4	2.3	2.9	3.9
Information services	6.3	6.0	6.2	6.7	7.6	9.1
Total	34.5	34.7	36.1	33.9	34.7	36.5

SOURCES: See Appendix to Chapter III.

TABLE III-7

EDUCATION AND OTHER KNOWLEDGE-PRODUCING ACTIVITIES
AS A PERCENT OF GNP: 1958, 1963, 1967, 1972,
1977, AND 1980
(based on constant 1972 dollars)

	1958	1963	1967	1972	1977	1980
Educational activities	16.6	16.8	17.4	14.8	13.4	12.0
Other knowledge production	17.9	17.9	18.7	19.1	21.3	24.5

SOURCE: Table III-6 in this book.

count for some of this effect, but the overall pattern is consistent with that in the current dollar figures.

Although expenditures for research and development generally maintained a constant proportion of GNP, the products and services subsumed under the categories of media of communications, information machines, and information services all steadily increased their shares of GNP.

CONCLUSIONS

Whether examined in current or constant dollars, expenditures for the production of knowledge in the United States account for roughly one-third of GNP. Whereas the constant dollar analysis suggests that there was a small continuing growth trend, these expenditures have held extremely steady over the last decade in current dollars, at 34 percent of GNP.

CHAPTER **IV** Education

This chapter updates statistics presented in Chapter IV of Machlup's *The Production and Distribution of Knowledge in the United States* (1962) and provides new tables on fields of educational activity that either were not considered in the original text or for which statistics were provided in the narrative alone. Machlup divided his material into separate sections on education "outside" and education "inside" the schools. Because so much statistical information has now become available on contexts outside the conventional realm of kindergarten through college, however, we have decided to present our material in roughly chronological order—from early childhood education to training and education designed for adults. After a brief look at total costs, we will discuss the education of young children in the home and in preschools and then move on to elementary, secondary, and higher education—including important cost items normally neglected in offical statistical reports. Discussions of education in the church, in the armed forces, in commercial vocational schools, and on the job are then followed by brief comments on some additional programs funded by the federal government, and on public libraries.

THE TOTAL COST OF EDUCATION[1]

Our findings on expenditures and implicit costs of educational activities in the United States are summarized for each of the economic census years since 1958 and for 1980 in Summary Table IV. The total amount that we have recorded rose from $57,238 million in 1958 to $351,362 million in 1980, or 6.1 times. This increase exceeds that of expenditures for research and development of 5.8 times and is about the same as the increase in expenditures for media of communication. It is considerably lower, however, than the growth in expenditures for information machines of 9.2 times and for information services of 10.0 times (see Table III-2). As we pointed out in Chapter III, the total costs of education rose from 11.79 percent of adjusted GNP in 1958 to 14.79 percent in 1972, but thereafter declined to 12.45 percent in 1980.

Although the proportion of expenditures paid by government for knowledge production as a whole declined from 1958 to 1980 (see Table III-4), the proportion of educational costs paid for by public funds rose—from 39 percent in 1958 to 42 percent in 1980 (see Summary Table IV). Educational activities

[1] Fritz Machlup, *The Production and Distribution of Knowledge in the United States* (Princeton, N.J.: Princeton University Press, 1962), pp. 103-107 and 353-359.

SUMMARY TABLE IV

EXPENDITURES FOR EDUCATION: 1958, 1963, 1967, 1972, 1977, AND 1980
(millions of dollars)

	1958	1963	1967	1972	1977	1980
In the Home	4,432	5,273	6,584	9,326	10,475	11,316
Preschool			238	1,052	1,985	3,447
Head Start			349	376	475	735
Elementary and Secondary						
Monetary	15,648	24,482	37,008	54,000	85,500	107,100
Implicit rent	1,869	2,672	2,869	3,536	5,157	6,556
Tax exemption	351	468	645	928	1,161	1,475
Students' foregone earnings	15,172	23,813	32,623	46,962	65,578	79,886
Transportation and clothes	455	714	979	1,409	1,967	2,397
Colleges and Universities						
Monetary	4,022	7,950	14,413	20,772	31,473	41,281
Implicit rent	893	1,705	2,429	4,024	5,679	6,726
Tax exemption	168	299	547	1,057	1,732	2,355
Students' foregone earnings	6,380	10,060	16,624	27,849	41,939	52,260
Transportation and clothes	383	604	997	1,671	2,516	3,136
Church	3,320	4,520	5,994	8,016	13,544	17,720
Military	3,410	2,226	3,697	4,257	5,684	7,299
Commercial	253	669	1,088	1,703	2,987	4,809
Federal programs	342	480	835	729	864	901
Public libraries	140	399	659	977	1,471	1,963
Total	57,238	86,334	128,578	188,644	280,187	351,362
Percent of Adjusted GNP	11.79	13.31	14.74	14.79	13.66	12.45
Paid for by						
Government	22,570	33,495	52,960	76,641	118,978	149,145
Consumers	34,668	52,839	75,618	112,003	161,209	202,217

SOURCES: Tables and text within Chapter IV.

paid for by government include the Head Start program; monetary expenditures and implicit rent for public schools and colleges (see Table IV-4, IV-11A, and IV-K); the value of property tax exemptions for both public and private schools and colleges (see Table IV-K); education in the armed forces; other federal programs; and public libraries. The educational activities paid for by consumers include education in the home; preschool; monetary expenditures and implicit rent for private schools and colleges (Tables IV-4, IV-11B, and IV-K); the foregone earnings of students; payments by students for transportation and clothing; education in the church; and education in commercial vocational schools. Clearly this is a rough division, and the reader may care to reread

Machlup's discussion of method (*Production and Distribution of Knowledge*, pp. 353-359).

We have not attempted to estimate the proportion of "consumer" expenditures for education that are actually paid for by business through donations to educational institutions or through tuition assistance programs for employees. Indeed, readers who examine both Table IV-18 in the original text and Summary Table IV here will see that we have omitted all estimates for expenditures by employers for training their employees. As we explain in the section on "Training on the Job," however, most students are convinced that expenditures for education by business are large and have risen rapidly in recent years.

We should emphasize that we use the term "consumer" only to maintain consistency with our analyses of other branches of the knowledge industry. We do not mean to prejudge the issue of whether the costs and expenditures that we report for education should be considered as "consumption" or "investment." We refer the reader to Machlup's discussion of productivity in education in *The Production and Distribution of Knowledge in the United States* (pp. 107-121) and to his discussion of investment in human capital in part 2 of *The Economics of Information and Human Capital* (1984), volume 3 of *Knowledge: Its Creation, Distribution, and Economic Significance*.

EARLY CHILDHOOD EDUCATION: EDUCATION IN THE HOME[2]

In this section we shall present two quite different ways of estimating the value of resources allocated to the education of young children in the home. We shall first update the figures used in *The Production and Distribution of Knowledge in the United States* to compute the earnings foregone by those mothers who have chosen to stay home with their preschool-age youngsters instead of going out to work. We shall then shift our focus from mothers to children and estimate the value of their education in the home by examining the costs of nursery school—a market alternative for which data became available only after Machlup had published the original study.[3]

THE OPPORTUNITY COSTS OF EDUCATION IN THE HOME

Parents do make some direct payments for the education of children in the home—witness, for example, the purchase by parents of "educational" toys and games. Yet the biggest factor in home production, the parent's time, is generally not remunerated. Machlup's approach to estimating the value of educational services provided in the home was to consider the "opportunity costs" to caretaking mothers of the time that they donated to raising their young. It must be emphasized that Machlup was not attempting to assign a

[2] Machlup, *Production and Distribution of Knowledge*, pp. 52-56.

[3] We examine the data on costs and enrollments in nursery school in more detail in the section on "Early Childhood Education: Formal Schooling in the Prekindergarten Years."

money value to all child rearing done by all parents in their homes, but only to that portion that was done at the expense of real money income; i.e., of wages actually foregone.[4]

Machlup's first step toward calculating the earnings foregone by women staying at home to rear young children was to estimate how many of them might be expected to have taken paid jobs if they had no children or only older children. The statistics on women in the labor force presented in Table IV-1 enable us to examine the differences in rates of employment between women with children of different ages. A glance at these figures will show that rates of employment for women in all categories or have increased substantially since 1954, and so dramatically for women with children under six that by 1977 the percentage of working women among them had overtaken that of women with children who were grown. Yet the relevant comparison group cannot be that of women whose children are over the age of eighteen, for these women include the elderly and retired, so we shall choose those women, closer in age to the mothers of preschoolers, whose children are still in school. As Table IV-1 shows, the proportion of working women with school-age children has remained higher than the proportion of working women with children below school age. We shall follow Machlup and attribute this difference to the decision of these younger mothers to stay at home while their children are young.

The annual differences in rates of employment between women with children from six to seventeen and women with children under six years of age can

TABLE IV-1

NUMBER OF WOMEN, TOTAL AND IN LABOR FORCE, BY AGE OF CHILDREN, 1954-1980

	All women age 14 and over	Women ever married		
		Total	No children under 18	Children 6-17	Children under 6
1954					
Population (thousand)	59,542	48,499	25,037	10,354	13,103
Labor force (thousand)	19,726	14,314	8,296	3,795	2,223
Percent of population in labor force	33.1	29.5	33.1	36.7	17.0
1955					
Population (thousand)	60,250	49,288	25,178	10,547	13,564
Labor force (thousand)	20,154	15,066	8,543	4,048	2,474
Percent of population in labor force	33.4	30.6	33.9	38.4	18.2

[4] Machlup's procedure may be understood as a variant of the general "opportunity cost" approach to the valuation of time. Many economists regard as a seminal contribution to recent work in the economics of the household, Gary Becker's article, "A Theory of the Allocation of Time," *The Economic Journal*, Vol. 75, No. 299 (September 1965), pp. 493-517.

TABLE IV-1 (*con't*)

	All women age 14 and over	Women ever married			
		Total	No children under 18	Children 6-17	Children under 6
1956					
Population (thousand)	60,975	49,849	25,327	10,628	13,894
Labor force (thousand)	20,842	15,675	8,942	4,245	2,488
Percent of population in labor force	34.2	31.4	35.3	39.9	17.9
1957					
Population (thousand)	61,863	50,376	25,292	11,011	14,073
Labor force (thousand)	21,524	16,146	9,158	4,401	2,587
Percent of population in labor force	34.8	32.1	36.2	40.0	18.4
1958					
Population (thousand)	62,472	50,962	25,519	11,297	14,146
Labor force (thousand)	22,451	16,636	9,142	4,647	2,847
Percent of population in labor force	36.0	32.6	35.8	41.4	20.1
1959					
Population (thousand)	63,561	51,677	25,741	11,633	14,303
Labor force (thousand)	22,376	17,214	9,250	5,007	2,957
Percent of population in labor force	35.2	33.3	35.9	43.0	20.7
1960					
Population (thousand)	64,607	51,995	25,952	12,037	14,006
Labor force (thousand)	22,516	17,114	9.096	5,120	2,898
Percent of population in labor force	34.9	32.9	35.0	42.5	20.7
1961					
Population (thousand)	65,847	53,083	26,431	12,218	14,434
Labor force (thousand)	24,199	18,536	9,824	5,529	3,183
Percent of population in labor force	36.8	34.9	37.2	45.3	22.1
1962					
Population (thousand)	67,166	54,031	27,143	12,259	14,629
Labor force (thousand)	23,978	18,497	9,662	5,501	3,334
Percent of population in labor force	35.7	34.2	35.6	44.9	22.8
1963					
Population (thousand)	68,392	54,700	27,301	12,813	14,586
Labor force (thousand)	24,675	19,061	9,784	5,718	3,559
Percent of population in labor force	36.1	34.8	35.8	44.6	24.4
1964					
Population (thousand)	69,503	55,371	27,762	12,962	14,657

TABLE IV-1 *(con't)*

	All women age 14 and over	*Women ever married*			
		Total	No children under 18	Children 6-17	Children under 6
Labor force (thousand)	25,399	19,618	10,091	5,934	3,593
Percent of population in labor force	36.5	35.4	36.3	45.8	24.5
1965					
Population (thousand)	70,691	56,084	28,399	13,119	14,566
Labor force (thousand)	25,952	20,040	10,358	6,000	3,682
Percent of population in labor force	36.7	35.7	36.5	45.7	25.3
1966					
Population (thousand)	71,828	56,847	29,340	12,987	14,520
Labor force (thousand)	26,820	20,714	10,864	6,043	3,807
Percent of population in labor force	37.3	36.4	37.0	46.5	26.2

	All Women Age 16 and Over	*Women ever married*			
		Total	No Children under 18	Children 6-17 only	Children under 6
1967					
Population (thousand)	69,410	57,746	30,063	13,264	14,419
Labor force (thousand)	27,545	21,630	11,048	6,443	4,139
Percent of population in labor force	39.7	37.5	36.7	48.6	28.7
1968					
Population (thousand)	70,679	58,298	30,198	13,994	14,106
Labor force (thousand)	28,778	22,421	11,343	6,955	4,123
Percent of population in labor force	40.7	38.5	37.6	49.7	29.2
1969					
Population (thousand)	71,919	59,230	30,809	14,538	13,883
Labor force (thousand)	29,898	23,397	11,798	7,376	4,223
Percent of population in labor force	41.6	39.5	38.3	50.7	30.4
1970					
Population (thousand)	73,261	60,120	31,266	14,692	14,162
Labor force (thousand)	31,233	24,268	12,146	7,567	4,555
Percent of population in labor force	42.6	40.4	38.8	51.5	32.2
1971					
Population (thousand)	74,580	60,948	32.020	15,152	13,776
Labor force (thousand)	31,681	24,494	12,293	7,874	4,327

TABLE IV-1 (con't)

	All Women Age 16 and Over	Women ever married			
		Total	No Children under 18	Children 6-17 only	Children under 6
Percent of population in labor force	42.5	40.2	38.4	52.0	31.4
1972					
Population (thousand)	75,506	61,896	32,319	15,677	13,900
Labor force (thousand)	32,939	25,462	12,780	8,244	4,438
Percent of population in labor force	43.6	41.1	39.5	52.6	31.9
1973					
Population (thousand)	76,850	69,971	33,438	15,619	13,914
Labor force (thousand)	33,904	26,165	13,148	8,253	4,764
Percent of population in labor force	44.1	41.6	39.3	52.8	34.2
1974					
Population (thousand)	78,131	63,742	34,083	15,800	13,859
Labor force (thousand)	35,320	27,090	13,523	8,495	5,072
Percent of population in labor force	45.2	42.5	39.7	53.8	36.6
1975					
Population (thousand)	79,477	64,561	34,739	15,971	13,851
Labor force (thousand)	36,507	28,043	13,896	8,754	5,393
Percent of population in labor force	45.9	43.4	40.0	54.8	38.9
1976					
Population (thousand)	80,834	65,425	35,509	16,434	13,482
Labor force (thousand)	37,817	28,734	14,137	9,239	5,358
Percent of population in labor force	46.8	43.9	39.8	56.2	39.7
1977					
Population (thousand)	82,059	65,982	36,262	16,899	12,821
Labor force (thousand)	39,374	29,904	14,776	9,856	5,272
Percent of population in labor force	48.0	45.3	40.7	58.3	41.1
1978					
Population (thousand)	83,374	66,482	36,910	16,910	12,662
Labor force (thousand)	40,971	30,748	15,077	10,122	5,549
Percent of population in labor force	49.1	46.3	40.8	59.9	43.8
1979					
Population (thousand)	84,686	67,123	37,554	16,864	12,705
Labor force (thousand)	42,971	31,964	15,842	10,379	5,743
Percent of population in labor force	50.7	47.6	42.2	61.5	45.2

TABLE IV-1 (con't)

	All Women Age 16 and Over	Women ever married			
		Total	No Children under 18	Children 6-17 only	Children under 6
1980					
Population (thousand)	87,939	69,665	39,272	17,130	13,263
Labor force (thousand)	44,934	33,692	16,454	11,010	6,228
Percent of population in labor force	51.1	48.4	41.9	64.3	47.0

SOURCES: (1954-1959): U.S. Bureau of the Census, *Current Population Reports: Labor Force*, Series P-50 (Washington, D.C.: Government Printing Office) and U.S. Department of Labor, Women's Bureau, *1958 Handbook on Women Workers*, Bulletin 266, table 25 (Washington, D.C.: Government Printing Office). (1960-1980): U.S. Bureau of Labor Statistics, *Marital and Family Characteristics of the Labor Force* (Washington, D.C.: Government Printing Office).

now be used to estimate how many women of the latter group are actually fore-going income by staying at home. First we calculate how many mothers of pre-school-age children could be expected to hold jobs if they participated in the work force at the same rate as women with school-age children and then we subtract from this hypothetical figure the number of women with preschool-age children already at work. Table IV-2 presents the results of these calcula-tions: It is notable that the number of mothers whom we estimate to have stayed home in order to care for young children is actually less in 1980 than it was in 1958.[5]

The earnings foregone by these women are calculated in Table IV-A. Using the median full- and part-time annual earnings of female workers to estimate the income that mothers of preschool-age children would have earned had they taken jobs, we can see that, in current dollars, the cost to them of staying home was $4,432.3 million in 1958, and $11,316.0 million in 1980. In con-stant 1972 dollars, this actually represents a decrease of $676 million, from $6,414.3 million in 1958 to $5,738.3 million in 1980.[6]

[5] Dr. James Brown has suggested to us that we might expect a higher rate of participation in the labor force for women with younger children than for women with school-age children as it be-comes more common for women to go to work. By adhering to Machlup's method, we may thus have underestimated the number of younger mothers who have chosen to stay home while their children are young.

[6] We have used the Bureau of Labor Statistics wage deflators recorded in the Appendix to Chap-ter III in order to calculate constant 1972 dollars. For 1958 the deflator is 69.1 and for 1980 it is 197.2. It is important to note that our estimates of opportunity costs do not necessarily represent the total opportunity costs to women who choose to stay at home. Recent work on labor markets suggests that women who delay or interrupt their careers suffer future reductions in income as well. See Fritz Machlup, *The Economics of Information and Human Capital* (Princeton: Princeton University Press, 1984), p. 90.

TABLE IV-2

NUMBER OF MOTHERS OF YOUNG CHILDREN STAYING
OUT OF LABOR FORCE, 1954-1980

Year	Labor force partici- pation rate of women with children 6-17 only	Women with children under 6			
		Total population (thousands)	Hypotheti- cally in labor force (thousands)	Actually in labor force (thousands)	Difference (thousands)
1954	36.7	13,103	4,808	2,223	2,585
1955	38.4	13,564	5,209	2,474	2,735
1956	39.9	13,894	5,544	2,488	3,056
1957	40.0	14,073	5,629	2,587	3,042
1958	41.4	14,146	5,856	2,847	3,009
1959	43.0	14,303	6,150	2,957	3,193
1960	42.5	14,006	5,952	2,898	3,054
1961	45.3	14,434	6,539	3,183	3,356
1962	44.9	14,629	6,568	3,334	3,234
1963	44.6	14,586	6,505	3,559	2,946
1964	45.8	14,657	6,713	3,593	3,120
1965	45.7	14,566	6,657	3,682	2,975
1966	46.5	14,520	6,752	3,807	2,945
1967	48.6	14,419	7,008	4,139	2,869
1968	49.7	14,106	7,011	4,123	2,888
1969	50.7	13,883	7,039	4,223	2,816
1970	51.5	14,162	7,293	4,555	2,738
1971	52.0	13,776	7,164	4,327	2,837
1972	52.6	13,900	7,311	4,438	2,873
1973	52.8	13,914	7,347	4,764	2,583
1974	53.8	13,859	7,456	5,072	2,384
1975	54.8	13,851	7,590	5,393	2,197
1976	56.2	13,482	7,577	5,358	2,219
1977	58.3	12,821	7,475	5,272	2,203
1978	59.9	12,662	7,585	5,549	2,036
1979	61.5	12,705	7,814	5,743	2,071
1980	64.3	13,263	8,528	6,228	2,300

SOURCE: Computed from Table IV-1.

THE REPLACEMENT COSTS OF EDUCATION IN THE HOME

Replacement costs have long been recognized as an alternative to opportunity costs by economists concerned with the valuation of household work.[7] Based on the observation that many of the services provided gratis by homemakers are also provided by others for sale, the replacement cost approach values the homemaker's services not by what is given up to perform them, but by

[7] An outline of the varieties of approach using replacement costs, and a discussion of their relation to the opportunity cost approach can be found in Oli Hawrylyshyn, "The Value of Household Services: A Survey of Empirical Estimates," *Review of Income and Wealth*, Vol. 22, No. 2 (June 1976), pp. 101-131.

TABLE IV-A

EARNINGS FOREGONE BY MOTHERS OF SMALL CHILDREN, 1958-1980

Year	Full and part-time median annual wage and salary income of female workers	Full-time median annual wage and salary income of female workers	Excess of women with children under 6, in labor force (thousands) (above the hypothetical)	Foregone earnings using full- and part-time wage (millions of dollars) (1) x (3)	Foregone earnings using full-time wage (millions of dollars) (2) x (3)
	(1)	(2)	(3)	(4)	(5)
1958	1,473		3,009	4,432.3	
1959	1,527		3,193	4,875.7	
1960	1,595		3,054	4,871.1	
1961	1,629		3,356	5,466.9	
1962	1,692		3,234	5,471.9	
1963	1,790		2,946	5,273.3	
1964	1,909		3,120	5,956.1	
1965	2,098		2,975	6,241.6	
1966	2,149		2,945	6,328.8	
1967	2,295	3,900	2,869	6,584.4	11,189.1
1968	2,468		2,888	7,127.6	
1969	2,612	4,300	2,816	7,355.4	12,108.8
1970	2,801	4,700	2,738	7,669.1	12,868.6
1971	3,045	5,000	2,837	8,638.7	14,185.0
1972	3,246	5,300	2,873	9,325.8	15,226.9
1973	3,337	5,800	2,583	8,619.5	14,981.4
1974	3,687	6,200	2,384	8,789.8	14,780.8
1975	4,072	6,850	2,197	8,946.2	15,049.5
1976	4,374	7,250	2,219	9,705.9	16,087.8
1977	4,755	7,800	2,203	10,475.3	17,183.4
1978	4,968	8,300	2,036	10,114.8	16,898.8
1979	4,352	9,150	2,071	9,013.0	18,949.7
1980	4,920	10,000	2,300	11,316.0	23,000.0

SOURCES: Columns (1) and (2): U.S. Bureau of the Census, *Current Population Reports: Consumer Income*, Series P-60 (Washington, D.C.: Government Printing Office). Column (3): From Table IV-2, Column 5.

what is "saved" by performing them oneself. Clearly, the choice of a "market alternative" is critical. Quite different results would be obtained, for example, if one valued a mother's culinary performance by what it would cost for the family to hire a cook rather than by what it would cost for the family to eat out. If our concern is with the education of young children, we could take a generous view of the value of parents' services and examine the costs of private tutors, or we could take a conservative view and use the costs of teen-aged babysitters instead. Although our choice forces us to restrict our analysis to the education of three-, four-, and five-year-olds, we have followed a middle road and chosen nursery school as the most appropriate "market alternative" to education in the home.

The reader may ask why we do not choose to use the day-care arrangements made by actual working mothers as a measuring rod for the value of education in the home. The reason is that data on costs are notoriously difficult to find, presumably because most children of working mothers are, in fact, cared for in a myriad of private homes. In 1965 a survey showed that 47.2 percent of children under six years of age with working mothers were cared for in their own home by a father or sibling and that an additional 37.2 percent were cared for in a relative's or a nonrelative's home. Studies conducted in 1977 and 1982, though not comparable with the earlier survey, also show that home care remained predominant. The proportion of working mothers whose youngest child under the age of five was cared for in their own or in another home fell only slightly, from 72.3 percent in 1977 to 70.8 percent in 1982.[8] Better statistical data are, understandably, more readily available for the more formalized sector of preschool education.

Actually, the best figures on the costs of formal preschool education do not come from conventional nursery schools, but from the federally funded Heard Start program, and thus do not represent actual tuition, or expenditures by the families whose children are enrolled, but costs to the agencies that provide the service instead. As Table IV-B shows, these costs rose from $599 per child in 1966, shortly after Head Start began, to $2,110 per child in 1980. We discuss the special features of Head Start in our section on "Formal Schooling in the Prekindergarten Years." Here we need only note that in lieu of systematic information on the costs of other formal preprimary program for three-, four-, and five-year-olds, we shall assume that the per capita costs of Head Start are representative.

The enrollment data necessary for our calculations are presented in Table IV-B. We can see here that while the number of three-, four-, and five-year-olds in the population decreased between 1966 and 1980, the proportion of these youngsters enrolled in formal schools and programs increased during the same period from 33 to 55 percent. If we assume that those children not enrolled in nursery school or kindergarten were receiving an equivalent education from caretakers in homes, we can proceed—as we have in Table IV-B— to calculate a dollar value for the education that they receive. In 1980, for example, there were 4,144 thousand youngsters aged three, four, and five, who

---

[8] The data for 1965 are from a study on "Child Care Arrangements of Working Mothers in the United States" by Seth Low and Pearl G. Spindler, Children's Bureau Publication 461 (Washington, D.C.: Government Printing Office, 1968), and are summarized in U.S., Congress, Senate, Committee on Finance, *Child Care: Data and Materials* 2nd Sess., October 1974, Appendix A, pp. 151-157. The data for 1977 and 1982 are reported by the Census Bureau in *Child Care Arrangements of Working Mothers: June 1982*, Current Population Reports, Series P-23, No. 129 (Washington, D.C.: Government Printing Office, 1983). It may be worth noting that the earlier survey found that 73.9 percent of the arrangements made by working mothers for the care of children up to thirteen years of age involved no cost to the parent (pp. 156-157 of the summary in the Senate report).

TABLE IV-B

REPLACEMENT VALUE FOR THE EDUCATION OF THREE- TO FIVE-
YEAR-OLDS IN THE HOME, 1966-1980

Year	Population (thousands)	Enrollment in schools (thousands)	Not enrolled (thousands)	Head Start costs per child (dollars)	Replacement value (3) X (4) (millions of dollars)
	(1)	(2)	(3)	(4)	(5)
1966	12,486	4,179	8,307	599	4,975.9
1967	12,242	4,312	7,930	825	6,542.3
1968	11,905	4,372	7,533	983	7,404.9
1969	11,424	4,324	7,100	1,064	7,554.4
1970	10,949	4,516	6,433	1,056	6,793.2
1971	10,610	4,535	6,075	1,109	6,737.2
1972	10,166	4,546	5,620	1,118	6,283.2
1973	10,344	4,580	5,764	1,180	6,801.5
1974	10,393	5,076	5,317	1,203	6,396.4
1975	10,185	5,277	4,908	1,293	6,346.0
1976	9,727	5,161	4,566	1,346	6,145.8
1977	9,249	4,577*	4,672	1,526	7,129.5
1978	9,111	4,584*	4,527	i,664	7,532.9
1979	9,119	4,664*	4,455	1,864	8,304.1
1980	9,284	5,140	4,144	2,110	8,743.8

SOURCES: Columns (1) and (2): National Center for Education Statistics, *Digest of Education Statistics* (Washington, D.C.: Government Printing Office). Column (4): (1969-1974) U.S. Department of Health, Education, and Welfare, *Project Head Start Statistical Fact Sheet* (Washington, D.C.: Government Printing Office); (1979-1980) U.S. Department of Health and Human Services, *Project Head Start Statistical Fact Sheet* (Washington, D.C.: Government Printing Office); (1975-1978) estimated.

* Enrollment figures for 1977, 1978, and 1979 do *not* include five-year-olds enrolled in primary school. In 1976 there were 371,000 five-year-olds enrolled in primary school, and in 1980 there were 262,000 five-year-olds enrolled in primary school. Column 3 thus slightly overestimates the total number of children aged three to five who were not enrolled in school for the years of 1977, 1978, and 1979.

were not enrolled in formal school programs. Multiplying this figure by the per pupil expenditures for Head Start, we obtain an estimate of $8,743.8 million for education in the home.

OPPORTUNITY COSTS VERSUS REPLACEMENT COSTS

As Table IV-C shows, the results of the "opportunity costs" approach differs widely from the results of the "replacements costs" approach. Machlup's method for calculating the opportunity costs to mothers of educating their children in the home yields an estimate of $11,316.0 million for 1980, whereas the data on preschool programs estimate the replacement costs for mothers' educational services to be only $8,743.8 million in the same year. The reader should recall, however, that the first approach measures earnings foregone by mothers of children from infancy through five years of age, while the latter ap-

TABLE IV-C

ALTERNATE METHODS OF COMPUTING THE VALUE OF
EDUCATION IN THE HOME, 1958-1980
(millions of dollars)

Year	Opportunity costs	Replacement value
1958	4,432.3	
1959	4,875.7	
1960	4,871.1	
1961	5,466.9	
1962	5,471.9	
1963	5,273.3	
1964	5,956.1	
1965	6,241.6	
1966	6,328.8	4,975.9
1967	6,584.4	6,542.3
1968	7,127.6	7,404.9
1969	7,355.4	7,554.4
1970	7,669.1	6,793.2
1971	8,638.7	6,737.2
1972	9,325.8	6,283.2
1973	8,619.5	6,801.5
1974	8,789.8	6,396.4
1975	8,946.2	6,346.0
1976	9,705.9	6,145.8
1977	10,475.3	7,129.5
1978	10,114.8	7,532.9
1979	9,013.0	8,304.1
1980	11,316.0	8,743.8

SOURCE: Tables IV-A and IV-B in this book.

proach only considers the value of market alternatives for the education of three-, four,- and five-year-olds.

In a review of *The Production and Distribution of Knowledge in the United States*, the economist Mary Jean Bowman suggested that Machlup had seriously underestimated the value of the education of young children in the home by basing his estimate on the earnings foregone of only a small proportion of the mothers who were staying at home.[9] Machlup's own concern was less that his approach might underestimate the value of education in the home than that it might overestimate this value instead. As he pointed out in a footnote to the text (*Production and Distribution of Knowledge*, pp. 56-57), even those mothers who suffer real losses of income as a result of their decision to stay at home, use their time to cook and clean as well as to instruct or otherwise care for their young.

It is our belief that an approach based on replacement costs rather than op-

[9] Mary Jean Bowman, "Essay Review: Professor Machlup on Knowledge and Reform," *The School Review*, Vol. 71, No. 2 (Summer 1963), pp. 235-245.

portunity costs may address both the questions of overestimation and underestimation at once. As the preschool programs that we have chosen as a "market alternative" are predominantly part-time programs, the figures that we have used "automatically" valuate as a cost of education only part of the time that parents spend at home.[10] Our estimate also, however, places a value on the child-rearing activities of all parents whose children remain at home, without regard to whether the parents are working already, or would be working if their children were not so young.

Economists have observed that one difficulty of the replacement cost approach is that it values services performed in the home by market alternatives that homemakers have explicitly rejected.[11] One may also appreciate the irony of taking the Head Start program, which was designed to make up for perceived deficiencies in the quality of home education, and then using its costs as a yardstick to measure the money value of education in the home. Two other difficulties are the exclusion of children under three years of age from our estimates and the fact that the data on Head Start costs have only been available since 1966. In view of these limitations, we have decided to calculate our final figures using the results from the approach through opportunity costs in order to preserve comparability with Machlup's calculations in 1962.

Early Childhood Education: Formal Schooling in the Prekindergarten Years

It is significant that Machlup's discussion of early childhood education in *The Production and Distribution of Knowledge in the United States* was divided between a section on "Education in the Home" and a proposal for school reform. Although Machlup's suggestion that academic instruction begin when children are four rather than six years of age has not been realized in substance, it has begun to appear in form. As we have already noted, formal schooling for children below the age of six has been one of the principal areas of growth in the field of education in recent years. The statistics on participation in preprimary education presented in Table IV-D show that between 1964 and 1980 the proportion of three- to five-year-olds attending nursery school and kindergarten rose from 25.5 percent to 52.5 percent. As one would expect, enrollments for five-year-olds have always been higher than enrollments for three- and four-year-olds. Yet because the kindergartens that most of the older children attend are included in national statistics on primary education, we shall focus

[10] Costs per child in Head Start are calculated on the basis of both part-day and full-day programs. The full-day programs, however, seldom run for longer than six hours, and, along with part-day programs, run for only nine to eleven months a year. See our section on "Early Childhood Education: Formal Schooling in the Prekindergarten Years," pp. 42-46 and Note 16.

[11] Reuben Gronau makes this point in an unpublished manuscript on "Home Production—A Partial Survey," September 1983.

TABLE IV-D

POPULATION AND PREPRIMARY SCHOOL ENROLLMENT OF THREE-
TO FIVE-YEAR-OLDS, BY AGE GROUP, 1964-1980
(thousands)

Year	Total population	Total enrollment	3-year-olds enrollment	4-year-olds enrollment	5-year-olds enrollment
1964	12,496	3,187	181	617	2,389
1965	12,549	3,407	203	683	2,521
1966	12,486	3,674	248	785	2,641
1967	12,242	3,868	273	872	2,724
1968	11,905	3,928	317	911	2,701
1969	11,424	3,949	315	880	2,755
1970	10,949	4,104	454	1,007	2,643
1971	10,610	4,148	430	1,048	2,671
1972	10,166	4,231	535	1,121	2,575
1973	10,344	4,234	515	1,177	2,542
1974	10,393	4,699	685	1,322	2,693
1975	10,185	4,955	683	1,418	2,854
1976	9,727	4,790	602	1,346	2,839
1977	9,249	4,577	645	1,290	2,642
1978	9,111	4,584	759	1,313	2,512
1979	9,119	4,664	746	1,393	2,525
1980	9,284	4,878	857	1,423	2,598

SOURCE: NCES, *Digest of Education Statistics.*

this discussion of early childhood education on nursery school and other formal programs designed for youngsters before their kindergarten year.

ENROLLMENT IN NURSERY SCHOOL

The long history of day nurseries, day-care centers, and nursery schools in
this country is not reflected in historical statistics on education.[12] Since the
early nineteenth century, formal programs for the care and education of young
children were provided principally as private philanthropic, feminist, or avant-
garde concerns. Public authorities entered the field only for brief excursions
during times of national emergency when women were needed to labor in the
factories or when, as in the 1930s, the unemployed required jobs. It was only
in the early 1960s that political, economic, and pedagogical voices merged in
support of the educational benefits that formal schooling might provide to
young children themselves, and only in 1964 that the National Center for Education Statistics (NCES) first commissioned the Census Bureau to collect
data on education in the years before first grade.[13]

[12] A brief history of government involvement in formal child care programs can be found in
James D. Marver and Meredith A. Larson, "Public Policy Toward Child Care in America: A His-
torical Perspective," in Philip K. Robins and Samuel Weiner, eds. *Child Care and Public Policy*
(Lexington, Mass.: D.C. Heath and Company, 1978), pp. 17-42.

[13] NCES reports on preprimary education have been published under a variety of titles. The first

The reader should note that a distinction between "care," provided primarily as a service for parents, and "education," provided primarily as a service to the child, underlies the statistics that are available on prekindergarten education. The NCES restricts its coverage to children enrolled in schools that offer an "organized educational experience" and excludes "custodial care in private homes."[14] As we have shown in our discussion of education in the home, this definition excludes the arrangements made for the care of most children whose mothers are at work. To be sure, there probably is a wider range of quality among day-care homes and day-care centers than among nursery schools with professional teaching staffs. Yet Machlup's broad definition of education requires us to recognize that the daily routine imposed by even the least enlightened "custodian" is an "organized educational experience," and we have taken this into account in our discussion of replacement costs for education in the home. Here, we shall follow the NCES. Precisely because of its institutional bias, the annual statistics that it reports have been able to document the trend toward adding schooling to the educational experience of our young.

A great disparity between trends in population and trends in participation is evident in the statistics on nursery school enrollments presented in Table IV-E. The population of three- to five-year-olds actually declined by 26 percent between 1964 and 1980, whereas enrollment in nursery school for these same children rose from 471,000 to 1,982,000—an increase of 321 percent. Table IV-F shows that the proportion of students enrolled in full-day programs rose from 30 percent to 34 percent during the seven years between 1969 and 1975 and stood at 34 percent in 1980 when data were published again. The proportion of children enrolled in publicly controlled programs also rose, despite minor fluctuations, from 19 percent in 1964 to 32 percent in 1980. The higher proportions in recent years may reflect the entry of prekindergarten programs into public schools where enrollments in the primary grades have followed the general population decline.[15]

---

report in 1964 was *Enrollment of 3-, 4- and 5-Year-Olds in Nursery School and Kindergarten.* The 1965 and 1966 reports came out as *Nursery-Kindergarten Enrollment of Children Under Six;* in 1967 and 1968 the reports are on *Preprimary Enrollment of Children Under Six* whereas the title *Preprimary Enrollment* is found on the reports for 1969, 1970, 1971, 1972, 1974, 1975, and 1980 all published in Washington, D.C. by the Government Printing Office. Data for 1973 are reported in *Nursery School and Kindergarten Enrollment* in the Bureau of the Census Publication Series P-20, No. 268 (Washington, D.C.: Government Printing Office), whereas the only published data available for the years from 1976 to 1979 appear in the NCES annual *Digest of Education Statistics* (Washington, D.C.: Government Printing Office) and in a special section on "Preprimary Education" in NCES, *The Condition of Education,* 1980 ed. (Washington, D.C.: Government Printing Office, 1980).

[14] All of the NCES reports on preprimary education include appendices with definitions of terms. In NCES, *The Condition of Education,* 1980 ed., for example, the term "preprimary program" is defined as "a set of organized educational experiences for children attending prekindergarten and kindergarten classes including Head Start programs. . . . Custodial care in private homes is not included," (p. 312).

[15] In NCES reports, "public" and "private" refer to both control and finance. Thus, "a public

TABLE IV-E

POPULATION AND NURSERY SCHOOL ENROLLMENT OF THREE- TO
FIVE-YEAR-OLDS, BY AGE GROUP, 1964-1980
(thousands)

Year	Total population	Total enrollment	3-year-olds enrollment	4-year-olds enrollment	5-year-olds enrollment
1964	12,496	471	174	265	22
1965	12,549	520	194	281	45
1966	12,486	686	232	395	58
1967	12,242	712	245	420	46
1968	11,905	816	296	442	78
1969	11,424	857	293	485	79
1970	10,949	1,094	432	571	91
1971	10,610	1,062	381	611	69
1972	10,166	1,277	507	706	64
1973	10,344	1,318	489	753	76
1974	10,393	1,603	650	865	88
1975	10,185	1,745	653	976	115
1976	9,727	1,515	568	860	85
1977	9,249	1,612	615	892	105
1978	9,111	1,822	737	980	105
1979	9,119	1,862	725	1,023	114
1980	9,284	1,982	825	1,064	93

SOURCE: NCES, *Digest of Education Statistics.*

EXPENDITURES FOR NURSERY SCHOOL EDUCATION

The Head Start program initiated in 1965 has undoubtedly been the most widely publicized and influential development in early childhood education during the period following the publication of *The Production and Distribution of Knowledge in the United States.* It is important for us to outline some of the features of Head Start here, for although this "single" program accounts for less than 10 percent of the enrollments in preprimary education during most of the period under study, it is the only program for which systematic data on expenditures are available.[16] As we propose to use Head Start costs per child to estimate all expenditures for prekindergarten schooling, we must note some of the possibilities for bias that this procedure entails.

Head Start was not designed as an ordinary preschool program, but as a "new front" in the "war against poverty" waged under the leadership of President

school is defined as any educational institution operated by publicly elected or appointed school officials and supported by public funds. Nonpublic schools include educational institutions established and operated by religious groups, as well as those under other private control," *Preprimary Enrollment*, 1980, p. 19.

[16] The proportion of students in Head Start in the total population of children enrolled in nursery school cannot be ascertained from the published figures because NCES counts children enrolled in Head Start programs "under nursery school or kindergarten as appropriate," NCES, *Preprimary Enrollment*, 1980, p. 18.

TABLE IV-F

NURSERY SCHOOL ENROLLMENT OF THREE- TO FIVE-YEAR-OLDS,
BY CONTROL OF PROGRAM AND BY FULL-DAY AND PART-DAY
ATTENDANCE, 1964-1980
(thousands)

Year	Enrollment	Public	Private	Full-day	Part-day
1964	471	91	380		
1965	520	127	393		
1966	686	213	473		
1967	712	229	484		
1968	816	262	554		
1969	857	242	615	256	601
1970	1,094	331	762	291	803
1971	1,062	315	748	294	768
1972	1,277	396	881	404	873
1973	1,318	394	924	385	933
1974	1,603	422	1,182	532	1,071
1975	1,745	570	1,174	591	1,154
1976	1,515				
1977	1,612	557	1,054		
1978	1,822	584	1,237		
1979	1,862	633	1,229		
1980	1,982	628	1,353	681	1,301

SOURCES: Columns (1), (2), and (3): NCES, *Digest of Education Statistics*. Columns (4) and (5): NCES, *Preprimary Enrollment* (Washington, D.C.: Government Printing Office).

Lyndon B. Johnson. Although the inflated rhetoric with which the program was initiated has largely disappeared, Head Start has always aimed for more than the development of the intellectual, emotional, and social skills that provide the agenda for most educators in the field. Nutritional and medical services, for example, have remained important components in the plan for Head Start, as has its mission to involve local communities in its programs and to improve the parental and teaching skills of adults. Required to serve poor, handicapped, and otherwise disadvantaged youngsters, these broad goals are surely reflected in the program's costs. Although some centrally provided services like research and evaluation are excluded from the calculations, the average cost per child reported by Head Start is "equivalent to the total amount of funds available for the operation of local Head Start projects, divided by the number of children to be served.[17]

[17] U.S., Congress, Senate, Committee on Appropriations, *Departments of Labor, Health and Human Services, Education, and Related Agencies Appropriations for Fiscal Year 1981.* 96th Cong., 2nd sess., 1980, pt. 2, p. 731. The annual hearings on appropriations provide a wealth of information about Head Start programs over the years. For a general coverage of the history, philosophy, curricula, medical and social services, administration, and evaluation of Head Start, the uninitiated might consult *Project Head Start: A Legacy of the War on Poverty*, ed. Edward Zigler and Jeanette Valentine (New York: The Free Press, 1979).

The variety of programs through which local Head Start projects serve their clientele should also be mentioned. Whereas the summer programs with which Head Start began and which have declined precipitously over the years (see Table IV-G) are not included in the costs-per-child that we shall use, the full-year (nine to eleven month) programs for which the costs are calculated appear to include special and experimental programs alongside the regular programs and both "full-day" and "part-day" sessions. One might argue that the diversity within Head Start should enhance the applicability of its cost figures to nursery school education as a whole. For example, in 1971, 1972, and 1973—the only years for which data from both Head Start and NCES are available—the proportion of Head Start children in full-day programs was only slightly higher than the proportion for all children enrolled in nursery school.[18]

TABLE IV-G

APPROPRIATIONS, ENROLLMENTS, AND COSTS PER FULL-YEAR CHILD IN HEAD START
AND EXPENDITURES PER PUPIL IN PUBLIC PRIMARY AND SECONDARY SCHOOLS, 1965-1980

Year	Head Start appropriations (millions of dollars)	Head Start enrollments		Expenditures per pupil*	
		Summer	Full year	Head Start	Public schools
		(thousands)		(dollars)	
	(1)	(2)	(3)	(4)	(5)
1965	96.4	561			
1966	198.9	573	160	599	537
1967	349.2	466	215	825	
1968	316.2	477	217	983	658
1969	333.9	447	217	1,064	
1970	325.7	209	263	1,056	816
1971	360.0	118	276	1,109	
1972	376.0	86	270	1,118	990
1973	400.7	69	287	1,180	
1974	403.0	46	288	1,203	1,207
1975	403.0	46	303	1,293	
1976	441.0	26	323	1,346	1,504
1977	475.0	26	307	1,526	
1978	625.0	18	373	1,664	1,823
1979	680.0	18	369	1,864	
1980	735.0	4	362	2,110	

SOURCES: Columns (1), (2), and (3): NCES, *The Condition of Education: Statistical Report* (Washington, D.C.: Government Printing Office, 1980). Column (4): (1969-1974) U.S. Department of Health, Education, and Welfare, *Project Head Start Statistical Fact Sheet*; (1979-1980) U.S. Department of Health and Human Services, *Project Head Start Statistical Fact Sheet*; (1975-1978) estimated. Column (5): NCES, *Digest of Education Statistics*, 1981.

* Includes day school expenditures only for public schools, calculated on a pupil in average daily attendance basis. The Head Start figures for the full-year program are calculated per enrollee.

[18] From Table IV-F we can calculate that the proportion of nursery-school children attending full-day programs in 1971, 1972, and 1973 was 28 percent, 32 percent, and 29 percent, respec-

On the other hand, NCES counts as a full-day program any school that has both morning and afternoon sessions, even though it may meet only two days a week. Full-day programs in Head Start, however, have generally met for at least six hours for five days a week.[19]

Comparisons of the costs per child in Head Start with other programs for the occasional years in which such figures are available, indicate that Head Start costs are more akin to costs in full-time day-care centers and in public primary and secondary schools than to costs in more conventional nursery school programs with narrower goals and fewer hours of operation. Indeed, for October 1978, the NCES reports a mean annual tuition of only $540 per student in nonpublic nursery schools—about one-third the cost per child in Head Start of $1664 reported in Table IV-G. Of course, tuition in private nursery schools sponsored by nonprofit organizations may not cover the full costs, if one considers the value of donated services, supplies, and space, but there is no doubt that the costs of Head Start compare more favorably to the costs of other, more ambitious, educational programs. For example, expenditures for a full-time equivalent child in a sample of day-care centers was reported to have been $1,630 in 1977, whereas Table IV-G shows that the expenditures per student in average daily attendance in public schools was $1,823 in 1978.[20]

---

tively. The proportion of children in Head Start's full-year program who were attending full-day sessions was, for those same years, 29 percent, 34 percent, and 34 percent. See U.S., Congress, Senate, Committee on Appropriations, *Departments of Labor and Health, Education and Welfare and Related Agencies Appropriations for Fiscal Year 1973*, Hearings . . . on H.R. 15417, 92nd Cong., 2nd sess., 1972, pt. 4, p. 3663; *for Fiscal Year 1974*, Hearings . . . on H.R. 8877, 93rd Cong., 1st sess., 1973, pt. 3, p. 3338; *for Fiscal Year 1975*, Hearings . . . on H.R. 15580, 93rd Cong., 2nd sess., 1974, pt. 5, p. 3421.

[19] The NCES states that "A nursery school enrollee may attend only 1 or 2 days per week. A 'part-day' enrollee attends nursery school either in the morning or in the afternoon, but not in both. A 'full-day' enrollee usually attends nursery school in both the morning and the afternoon," *Preprimary Enrollment*, 1980, p. 18. In contrast, "Full-year, full-day Head Start programs operate up to 8 hours per day on an average of 11 months per year. Full year, part-day programs operate on an average of 4 hours per day for approximately 9 months per year," U.S., Congress, Senate, Committee on Appropriations, *Departments of Labor and Health, Education, and Welfare and Related Agencies Appropriations for Fiscal Year 1974*, Hearings . . . on H.R. 8877, 93rd Cong., 1st sess., 1973, pt. 3, p. 3340. According to a more recent evaluation, inflation has forced "many so-called full-day Head Start programs . . . to reduce the six hours they were previously in operation"; see U.S. Department of Health and Human Services, *Head Start in the 1980s: Review and Recommendations* (Washington, D.C.: Government Printing Office, September 1980), p. 29.

[20] The NCES figures on annual tuition and fees for nonpublic preprimary schools in October, 1978 are reported in *The Condition of Education*, 1980 ed., p. 222. This same publication (p. 224) summarizes the findings of the study on expenditures in day-care centers by Craig Coelen, Frederic Glantz, and Daniel Calore, *Day-Care Centers in the U.S.: A National Profile 1976-1977* (Cambridge, Mass.: Abt Books, 1979). These kinds of comparisons should be undertaken with extreme caution because of differences in methods of estimation. The Head Start costs per child would be higher if calculated on the basis of average expenditure for a full-time equivalent child (as in the day-care center study), but would be lower if calculated on the basis of average daily attendance (as in the case of the public schools).

Although the use of costs per child from Head Start to calculate national expenditures for prekindergarten education will cause us to miss a portion of the federal monies appropriated to Head Start (and used for central functions), it is clear that the danger of overestimation far outweighs the danger of underestimation in our procedure. In lieu of better figures to cover the time period with which we are concerned, we have simply had no choice but to use the Head Start costs per child, unqualified, for the final calculations presented in Table IV-H. Multiplying the total number of children aged three to five enrolled in nursery school by the costs per child in Head Start, we estimate that national expenditures for this type of early childhood education have risen from $410.9 million in 1966 (the first year for which data on costs are available) to $4,182.0 million in 1980.

ELEMENTARY AND SECONDARY EDUCATION[21]

Our first task in this section will be to update the statistics introduced by Machlup in his discussion of the history of enrollments and expenditures for elementary and secondary education. Our second task will be to introduce some

TABLE IV-H

EXPENDITURES FOR NURSERY SCHOOL EDUCATION, 1965-1980

Year	Enrollments (thousands) (1)	Head Start costs per child (dollars) (2)	Total (millions of dollars) (3)
1965	520		
1966	686	599	410.9
1967	712	825	587.4
1968	816	983	802.1
1969	857	1,064	911.8
1970	1,094	1,056	1,155.3
1971	1,062	1,109	1,177.8
1972	1,277	1,118	1,427.7
1973	1,318	1,180	1,555.2
1974	1,603	1,203	1,928.4
1975	1,745	1,293	2,256.3
1976	1,515	1,346	2,039.2
1977	1,612	1,526	2,459.9
1978	1,822	1,664	3,031.8
1979	1,862	1,864	3,470.7
1980	1,982	2,110	4,182.0

SOURCES: Column (1): NCES, *Digest of Education Statistics*. Column (2): From Table IV-G, Column 4. Column (3): Obtained by multiplying Column 1 by Column 2.

[21] Machlup, *Production and Distribution of Knowledge*, pp. 70-77.

new statistics in order to clarify some of the changes that have occurred in expenditures for these levels of schooling over the past twenty years. It should not surprise the reader to learn that the statistics for the period from 1960 to 1980 tell a somewhat different story than the statistics from the preceding seventy years.

All of the data that we present are from standard sources. Table IV-3 provides the necessary figures on population and enrollments; Table IV-4 provides figures on the gross national product and school expenditures, calculated as before on the assumption that costs per student in private schools are the same as in public school. Table IV-I, which is new, shows pupil-teacher ratios for selected years, and Table IV-J, also new, shows expenditures for elementary and secondary education by source of funds.

ENROLLMENTS AND EXPENDITURES FOR ELEMENTARY AND SECONDARY SCHOOLS

The period from 1890 to 1960 witnessed tremendous increases in school enrollments due in part to increases in the population of school-age youngsters and in part to changes in the educational system itself (see Machlup's discussion, *Production and Distribution of Knowledge*, pp. 74-76). Only two notable changes in the age-composition of elementary and secondary school students occurred for the period from 1960 to 1980. The continued expansion of kindergarten programs is reflected in the fact that the proportion of five- and six-year-olds enrolled in schools increased from 80.7 percent in 1960 to 95.7 percent in 1980. A significant change also occurred at the higher end of the school-age range, as the proportion of sixteen- and seventeen-year-olds enrolled in school rose from 82.6 percent in 1960 to 89.0 percent in 1980. For other age groups, levels of enrollment remained nearly constant. Youngsters from seven to thirteen years of age represented over 99 percent of their age group throughout the twenty years in question, whereas the proportion of fourteen- and fifteen-year-olds enrolled in school rose just slightly, from 97.8 percent in 1960 to 98.2 percent in 1980.[22]

As the reader can see from Table IV-3, however, the school-age population itself began to decrease in 1971, even as the proportion of youngsters in school continued to rise. The much publicized decline in school enrollments also began in 1971, although it was evident in elementary schools somewhat earlier and in high schools only after 1976.[23] Thus, while enrollments had increased at an annual rate of 1.6 percent between 1890 and 1960, almost tripling the

[22] The figures on rates of enrollment by age group for 1960 and 1980 are from U.S. Bureau of the Census, *The Statistical Abstract of the United States: 1982-83* (Washington, D.C.: Government Printing Office, 1982-1983), p. 140, table 221.

[23] NCES statistics show that total enrollment in grades K-8 peaked at 36,797,000 in 1969 and that total enrollment in grades 9-12 peaked at 15,710,000 in 1976 (NCES, *The Condition of Education*, 1980, table 2.1, p. 56).

TABLE IV-3

ENROLLMENT IN ELEMENTARY AND SECONDARY SCHOOLS
COMPARED WITH POPULATION, 1870-1980

	POPULATION (RESIDENT)			ENROLLMENT IN ELEMENTARY AND SECONDARY SCHOOLS					
	Total	Age 5-17		Total		Public schools		Non-public schools	
Year	(thousands)	(thousands)	% of (1)	(thousands)	% of (2)	(thousands)	% of (2)	(thousands)	% of (2)
	(1)	(2)	(3)	(4)	(5)	(6)	(7)	(8)	(9)
1870	39,905	12,055	30.2			6,872	57.0		
1880	50,262	15,065	29.9			9,868	65.5		
1890	63,056	18,546	29.4	14,479	78.1	12,723	68.6	1,757	9.4
1900	76,094	21,413	28.1	16,855	78.7	15,503	72.3	1,352	6.3
1910	92,407	24,237	26.2	19,372	79.9	17,814	73.4	1,558	6.4
1920	106,466	27,736	26.1	23,278	83.9	21,578	77.7	1,699	6.1
1930	123,077	31,584	25.6	28,329	89.6	25,678	81.3	2,651	8.3
1940	131,954	29,817	22.5	28,045	94.1	25,434	85.3	2,611	8.7
1950	151,234	30,774	20.3	28,492	92.5	25,111	81.5	3,380	10.9
1958	174,149	41,933	24.1	39,659	94.5	33,854	80.7	5,805	13.8
1959	177,135	43,456	24.5	41,029	94.4	34,929	80.3	6,100	14.0
1960	180,000	45,064	25.0	42,690	94.7	36,720	81.4	5,970	13.2
1961	183,000	46,314	25.3	43,964	94.9	37,964	81.9	6,000	12.9
1962	185,900	46,674	25.1	44,493	95.3	38,493	82.4	6,000	12.8
1963	188,500	48,039	25.5	46,854	97.5	40,217	83.7	6,637	13.8
1964	191,100	49,183	25.7	48,116	97.8	41,416	84.2	6,700	13.6
1965	193,500	49,904	25.8	49,000	98.1	42,400	84.9	6,600	13.2
1966	195,600	50,689	25.9	49,900	98.4	43,200	85.2	6,700	13.2
1967	197,500	51,462	26.1	50,100	97.3	44,100	85.6	6,000	11.6
1968	199,500	52,288	26.2	50,690	96.9	44,960	85.9	5,730	10.9
1969	201,400	52,541	26.1	50,990	97.1	45,360	86.3	5,630	10.7
1970	203,800	52,706	25.8	51,500	97.7	45,900	87.0	5,600	10.6
1971	206,200	52,545	25.4	51,281	97.5	46,081	87.6	5,200	9.8
1972	208,200	51,389	24.6	50,754	98.7	45,754	89.0	5,000	9.7
1973	209,900	50,760	24.1	50,209	98.9	45,409	89.4	4,800	9.4
1974	211,400	50,539	23.9	49,756	98.4	45,056	89.1	4,700	9.2
1975	213,100	50,012	23.4	49,938	99.8	44,838	89.6	5,100	10.1
1976	214,700	49,381	23.1	49,335	99.9	44,335	89.7	5,000	10.1
1977	216,400	48,796	22.5	48,731	99.8	43,731	89.6	5,000	10.2
1978	218,100	47,690	21.8	47,611	99.8	42,611	89.3	5,000	10.4
1979	220,099	46,693	21.2	46,660	99.9	41,560	89.0	5,100	10.9
1980	226,505			46,079		40,949		5,130	

SOURCES: Columns (1) and (2): U.S. Bureau of the Census, *Current Population Reports: Population Estimates*, Series P-25. (Washington, D.C.: Government Printing Office). Columns (4), (6), and (8): NCES, *Digest of Education Statistics*.

number of youngsters in school during the period discussed by Machlup, enrollments increased at an annual rate of only 0.4 percent in the following twenty years, leaving the number of children in school at the end of the period only slightly higher (7.9 percent) than it had been in 1960, at the start.

Although increasing expenditures for elementary and secondary schools can be expected to accompany increasing enrollments, a glance at Table IV-4 will show that in both the periods from 1890 to 1960 and from 1960 to 1980, ex-

TABLE IV-4

Expenditures for Elementary and Secondary Schools
Compared with National Aggregates, 1870-1980
(current expenditures plus capital outlays)

Year	GROSS NATIONAL PRODUCT billion dollars (10)	EXPENDITURES FOR ELEMENTARY AND SECONDARY SCHOOLS							
		Total		Public schools		Non-public schools		Per student	Per capita
		million dollars (11)	% of (10) (12)	million dollars (13)	% of (10) (14)	million dollars (15)	% of (10) (16)	(13)÷(6) dollars (17)	(11)÷(1) (18)
1870	6.7			63	0.94			9.17	
1880	9.2			78	0.85			7.90	
1890	13.5	160	1.19	141	1.04	19	0.14	11.08	2.54
1900	17.3	234	1.35	215	1.24	19	0.11	13.87	3.08
1910	31.6	436	1.47	426	1.35	37	0.12	23.91	5.01
1920	88.9	1,117	1.26	1,036	1.17	81	0.09	48.01	10.49
1930	91.1	2,556	2.81	2,317	2.54	239	0.26	90.23	20.77
1940	100.6	2,585	2.57	2,344	2.33	241	0.24	92.16	19.59
1950	284.6	6,624	2.33	5,838	2.05	786	0.28	232.48	43.80
1952	347.0	8,397	2.42	7,344	2.12	1,053	0.30	276.48	53.91
1954	363.1	10,460	2.88	9,092	2.50	1,368	0.38	315.30	64,89
1956	419.2	12,611	3.01	10,955	2.61	1,656	0.40	351.54	75.40
1958	442.2	15,648	3.54	13,569	3.07	2,079	0.47	401.45	90.31
1960	503.7	18,024	3.58	15,613	3.10	2,411	0.48	430.33	100.15
1962	560.3	20,795	3.71	18,338	3.28	2,457	0.43	473.25	111.96
1964	632.4	24,482	3.87	21,482	3.40	3,000	0.47	518.69	128.12
1966	749.9	29,923	3.99	26,248	3.50	3,675	0.49	609.87	153.06
1968	864.2	37,008	4.28	32,984	3.82	4,025	0.47	733.87	185.68
1970	944.1	45,300	4.80	40,800	4.32	4,500	0.48	889.49	222.35
1971	1,063.4	50,100	4.71	44,600	4.19	5,500	0.52	967.86	242.97
1972	1,171.1	54,000	4.61	48,300	4.12	5,700	0.49	1,055.65	259.37
1973	1,306.6	58,300	4.46	52,100	4.00	6,200	0.47	1,147.35	277.75
1974	1,412.9	63,700	4.51	57,200	4.05	6,500	0.46	1,269.53	301.33
1975	1,528.8	72,200	4.72	65,000	4.25	7,200	0.47	1,449.66	338.81
1976	1,702.2	79,100	4.65	71,100	4.18	8,000	0.47	1,603.70	368.42
1977	1,899.5	85,500	4.50	76,800	4.04	8,700	0.46	1,756.19	395.10
1978	2,127.6	90,900	4.27	81,200	3.82	9,600	0.45	1,905.61	416.78
1979	2,368.8	97,000*	4.09	87,000*	3.67	10,000*	0.42	2,093.36	440.71
1980	2,626.5	107,100*	4.08	95,400*	3.63	11,700*	0.45	2,338.63	482.87

Source: NCES, *Digest of Education Statistics.*

* Estimate

penditures grew at a far higher rate than might be expected from enrollment figures alone. In the years from 1890 to 1960, when enrollment grew at an annual rate of 1.6 percent, total expenditures increased by 7.0 percent each year. The disparity becomes even greater later on. From 1960 to 1970 enrollments rose at an annual rate of 1.9 percent per year, while expenditures rose at a rate of 9.7 percent per year; and from 1970 to 1980, when enrollments declined at a rate of 1.1 percent each year, the annual rate of growth for expenditures was only slightly modified—to 9.0 percent per year.

The relatively small role that changes of enrollment have played in determining changes in the level of total expenditures for elementary and secondary schools can be seen if we hold enrollment constant and examine the rates of increase in expenditures per student instead. From Table IV-4, column 17, we can calculate that expenditures per student rose at an annual rate of 5.4 percent between 1890 and 1960, whereas between 1960 and 1980, expenditures per student rose at a rate of 8.8 percent per year. Clearly, factors other than enrollment must be considered if we are to understand the high rate of growth in expenditures for elementary and secondary schools.

TEACHERS' SALARIES, STUDENT-TEACHER RATIOS, AND
OTHER EXPENDITURES

One of the reasons why expenditures for elementary and secondary schools rise so much faster than enrollments is that teachers' salaries must be increased as incomes rise in other sectors of the economy. Over the period from 1890 to 1960, for example, the average salary for teachers increased at a rate of 4.3 percent per annum (from $256 to $4,995), a rate somewhat higher than the rate of growth in GNP per head of 3.7 percent per year (from $214 to $2,798). From 1960 to 1980, however, teachers did less well in comparison to this national average. GNP per head rose at an annual rate of 7.4 percent from 1960 to 1980 (from $2,798 to $11,596), but the average salary for teachers rose at an annual rate of only 6.0 percent (from $4,995 to $16,001) during the same twenty years. These figures suggest that even as expenditures for education continued to rise, teaching as an occupation has been losing ground in the job market for able college graduates, especially as job opportunities for women broadened.[24]

Another reason for increasing expenditures for elementary and secondary education is that education, like many "personal services," has been resistant to changes in technology that would increase teachers' productivity.[25] Indeed, as Baumol and Oates have observed, declines in student-teacher ratios are widely taken to be improvements in the quality of education, rather than the

[24] The figures on teachers' salaries for 1960 and 1980 are from NCES, *The Digest of Education Statistics*, 1981, table 5.1, p. 69. A review of some of the issues involved in the controversy over the quality of college students entering the teaching profession is provided by Donna H. Kerr, "Teaching Competence and Teacher Education in the United States," *Teachers College Record*, Vol. 84, No. 3 (Spring 1983), pp. 525-592.

[25] W. J. Baumol and W. E. Oates, "The Cost Disease of the Personal Services and the Quality of Life," *Skandinaviska Enskilda Banken Quarterly Review*, No. 2 (1972), pp. 43-54. See also William J. Baumol and Wallace E. Oates, *Economics, Environmental Policy, and the Quality of Life* (Englewood Cliffs, N.J.: Prentice-Hall, Inc., 1979), especially Chapter 10, "The Provision of Urban Services," pp. 147-156.

reverse.[26] By this criterion, the experience of the 1960s and 1970s has been favorable: The decline in school enrollments after 1971 was not accompanied by a decline in the number of classroom teachers until 1978, with the result that student-teacher ratios were far lower at the end of the period than at its start.[27] Table IV-I shows that whereas the number of students in 1980 was only slightly higher than the number of students in 1960, the number of teachers had risen from 1,600,000 to 2,439,000 and that the number of students per teacher fell dramatically in both public and private schools. From the same table we can also see that elementary school students were the major beneficiaries of these declines. In public elementary schools the pupil-teacher ratio fell from 28.4 to 20.7 during the period from 1960 to 1980, whereas in private elementary schools, the decline in the pupil-teacher ratio was even steeper, from 36.1 to 19.8.

Finally, we should note the increasing role played by expenditures for items other than teacher salaries in total school expenditures. If we multiply the number of teachers in 1960 and in 1980 (Table IV-I) by the average teachers' salary for those years (see above) and divide the total salary bill by total school expenditures (Table IV-4), we find that the proportion of expenditures paid for classroom teachers declined from 44 percent in 1960 to 36 percent in 1980. Even though teachers' salaries and the number of teachers rose during the period under consideration, increases in the cost and amount of other items (buildings, operations, administration, supplies, transportation) may be playing an increasingly important role in raising the level of total expenditures for education in the schools.

TABLE IV-I

STUDENTS, TEACHERS, AND STUDENT-TEACHER RATIOS IN
ELEMENTARY AND SECONDARY SCHOOLS, 1960-1980

| | | | STUDENT-TEACHER RATIOS | | | |
| | ENROLLMENT* | TEACHERS | Public | | Private | |
Year	(thousands)	(thousands)	Elementary	Secondary	Elementary	Secondary
1960	42,181	1,600	28.4	21.7	36.1	18.6
1965	48,473	1,933	27.6	20.8	33.3	18.4
1970	51,272	2,288	24.4	19.9	26.5	16.4
1975	49,791	2,451	21.7	18.8	21.5	15.7
1980	46,095	2,439	20.7	16.9	19.8	15.7

SOURCE: U.S. Bureau of the Census, *Statistical Abstract of the U.S.: 1982-83* (Washington, D.C.: Government Printing Office, 1982-1983).

* These enrollment figures from the *Statistical Abstract of the U.S.* differ slightly from those reported in Table IV-1 from the *Digest of Education Statistics.*

[26] Baumol and Oates, "Personal Services," p. 46.
[27] NCES, *The Condition of Education*, 1980, p. 47.

CHANGES IN FINANCING ELEMENTARY AND
SECONDARY EDUCATION

Another change related to the rise in expenditures for education during the period from 1960 to 1980 has been the growing role of the federal government in providing funds for particular groups of students, such as compensatory education for the poor and aid to school districts for the education of handicapped children. In addition, concern for equitable spending levels among wealthier and poorer school districts has also led to an increased role in the funding of education by state governments and a decreasing role for local authorities. Table IV-J provides a picture of these changes over the twenty years from 1960 to 1980. We can see that while private expenditures for elementary and secondary education remained relatively constant as a proportion of the total, local government expenditures fell from 52.8 percent in 1960 to 38.2 percent in 1980. State governments' share in the total amount expended for elementary and secondary education rose during this period from 31.1 percent to 41.5 percent, while the role of the federal government increased from 3.9 percent to 8.7 percent during the same twenty years.

TABLE IV-J

EXPENDITURES FOR ELEMENTARY AND SECONDARY SCHOOLS,
BY SOURCE OF FUNDS, 1960-1980
(percent of total)

Year	Private	Local	State	Federal	Other
1960	11.7	52.8	31.1	3.9	0.6
1966	11.7	46.9	32.0	7.0	0.3
1970	10.3	47.5	34.6	7.4	0.2
1975	10.0	48.8	37.7	8.3	0.1
1980	11.2	38.2	41.5	8.7	0.3

SOURCE: U.S. Bureau of the Census, *Statistical Abstract of the U.S.*, 1982-1983.

HIGHER EDUCATION[28]

Machlup began his discussion of higher education in *The Production and Distribution of Knowledge in the United States* by asking "Higher than what is 'higher' education?" In the years between 1962 and 1980 Machlup wrote several essays elaborating on this query.[29] Although we cannot address directly the

[28] Machlup, *Production and Distribution of Knowledge*, pp. 77-91.

[29] See, for example, the following works by Fritz Machlup: *Die Hochschulausbildung im volkswirtschaftlichen Kalkül*, Veröffentlichungen der Schleswig-Holsteinischen Universitätsgesellschaft, Neue Folge, No. 38 (Kiel: Ferdinand Hirt, 1965); *Education and Economic Growth* (Lincoln: University of Nebraska Press, 1970); "Longer Education: Thinner, Broader, or Higher," in *Proceedings of the 1970 Invitational Conference on Testing Problems* (Princeton, N.J.: Educational Testing Service, 1971), pp. 3-13; "Matters of Measure," in Logan Wilson, ed., *Universal Higher*

question of quality that dominated Machlup's concern, the issue will of necessity be raised in our discussion of the numbers, just as it was in the original text. Indeed, what Machlup referred to as the "education experts' threat" (*Production and Distribution of Knowledge*, p. 91) has become fact. In 1966 enrollment in institutions of "higher" education exceeded 50 percent of the college-age population for the first time in the history of American education and rose to nearly 70 percent by 1979. Although many observers would interpret this figure as the fulfillment of a promise rather than a threat, recent discourse on such topics as the decline in scores on the Scholastic Aptitude Test and on the value of "basics" in college curricula underline Machlup's concern that the costs of universal higher education may have to be calculated in terms other than dollars alone.

The tables in this section reproduce and update those of the original text and use data from standard reference works. Some of these tables have become quite cumbersome because of our desire to give comprehensive coverage to the years between 1960 and 1980. We have tried to ease the reader's task by pointing to some of the most obvious trends in the following discussion. Nonetheless, these tables offer many opportunities for inquiry that we have had neither the time nor the space to explore.

ENROLLMENTS AND EXPENDITURES

Tables IV-5 and IV-6 indicate that in the twenty-odd years since Machlup's study, expenditures for higher education increased from $6,966.9 million in 1960 to $62,848.5 million in 1980, or 9.0 times, whereas the country's total population during the same period increased only 1.3 times. The Gross National Product in 1980 was 5.2 times that of 1960, so that as a percentage of GNP, expenditures for higher education increased—from 1.36 percent in 1960 to 2.39 percent in 1980.

Changes in enrollment explain some of the increase in expenditures. We may note from Table IV-5 that although enrollment increased 2.4 times between 1940 and 1960, enrollment rose 3.4 times between 1960 and 1980, a record exceeded in this century only in the two decades from 1950 to 1970 when enrollment rose 3.7 times. Indeed, between 1960 and 1979 enrollment in institutions of higher education rose from 38.4 to 68.1 percent of the pop-

---

Education: Costs, Benefits, Options (Washington, D.C.: American Council on Education, 1972), pp. 78-84; "Universal Higher Education: Promise or Illusion?" *The Humanist*, Vol. 32, No. 3 (May/June 1972), pp. 17-23; *Hochschulbildung für jedermann: Eine Auseinandersetzung mit einem Gleichheitsideal* (Zürich: Schulthess Polygraphischer Verlag, 1973); "Perspectives on the Benefits of Postsecondary Education," in Lewis C. Solmon and Paul J. Taubman, eds., *Does College Matter?* (New York: Academic Press, 1973), pp. 353-363; and "The Illusion of Universal Higher Education" and "A Reply to My Critics," in Sydney Hook, Paul Kurtz, and Miro Todorovich, eds., *The Idea of a Modern University* (Buffalo, N.Y.: Prometheus Books, 1974), pp. 3-19, and 53-57.

TABLE IV-5

Enrollment in Institutions of Higher Education,
Compared with Population, 1870-1980

Year	POPULATION (RESIDENT)			ENROLLMENT IN INSTITUTIONS OF HIGHER EDUCATION					
	Total (thousands)	Age 18-21 (thousands)	% of (1)	Total (thousands)	% of (2)	Public schools (thousands)	% of (2)	Non-public schools (thousands)	% of (2)
	(1)	(2)	(3)	(4)	(5)	(6)	(7)	(8)	(9)
1870	39,905	3,116	7.8	52	1.6				
1880	50,262	4,253	8.4	116	2.7				
1890	63,056	5,160	8.1	157	3.0				
1900	76,094	6,131	8.0	238	3.8	91	1.4	147	2.3
1910	92,407	7,254	7.8	355	4.8	167	2.3	189	2.6
1920	106,466	7,869	7.3	598	7.5	315	4.0	282	3.5
1930	123,077	9,369	7.6	1,101	11.7	533	5.6	568	6.0
1940	131,954	9,845	7.4	1,494	15.1	797	8.0	698	7.0
1950	151,234	8,439	5.5	2,297	27.2	1,154	13.6	1,142	13.5
1960	180,000	9,329	5.1	3,583	38.4	2,116	22.6	1,467	15.7
1961	183,000	10,046	5.4	3,861	38.4	2,329	23.1	1,532	15.2
1962	185,900	10,560	5.6	4,174	39.5	2,574	24.3	1,601	15.1
1963	188,500	10,928	5.7	4,766	43.6	3,066	28.0	1,700	15.5
1964	191,100	11,114	5.8	5,280	47.5	3,468	31.2	1,812	16.3
1965	193,500	11,953	6.1	5,921	49.5	3,970	33.2	1,951	16.3
1966	195,600	12,600	6.4	6,390	50.7	4,349	34.5	2,041	16.1
1967	197,500	13,217	6.6	6,912	52.2	4,816	36.4	2,096	15.8
1968	199,500	13,960	7.0	7,513	53.8	5,431	38.9	2,082	14.9
1969	201,400	13,906	6.9	8,005	57.5	5,897	42.4	2,108	15.1
1970	203,800	14,245	6.9	8,581	60.2	6,428	45.1	2,153	15.1
1971	206,200	14,704	7.1	8,949	60.8	6,804	46.2	2,144	14.5
1972	208,200	15,222	7.3	9,215	60.5	7,071	46.4	2,144	14.0
1973	209,900	15,588	7.4	9,602	61.5	7,420	47.6	2,183	14.0
1974	211,400	15,938	7.5	10,224	64.1	7,989	50.1	2,235	14.0
1975	213,100	16,317	7.6	11,185	68.5	8,834	54.1	2,350	14.4
1976	214,700	16,617	7.7	11,012	66.2	8,653	52.0	2,359	14.1
1977	216,400	16,801	7.7	11,286	67.1	8,847	52.6	2,439	14.5
1978	218,100	16,925	7.7	11,260	66.5	8,786	51.9	2,474	14.6
1979	220,099	16,991	7.7	11,570	68.1	9,037	53.2	2,533	15.0
1980	226,505			12,235		9,518		2,717	

Sources: Columns (1) and (2): U.S. Bureau of the Census, *Current Population Reports: Population Estimates*. Columns (4), (6), and (8): NCES, *Fall Enrollment in Higher Education* (Washington, D.C.: Government Printing Office).

ulation aged 18 to 21 years old, although these are somewhat misleading figures because they mask the trend toward "longer" education, in which growing numbers of older persons continue with, return to, or begin college studies. [30]

Accompanying the broader age range of students enrolled in institutions of

[30] "According to a sample survey conducted by the Bureau of the Census in October 1978, 2.5 percent of the students were under 18; 46.6 percent, 18 to 21; 16.1 percent, 22 to 24; and 34.8 percent, 25 or over," NCES, *Digest of Education Statistics*, 1980, note to table 78, "Total Enrollment in Institutions of Higher Education Compared with Population aged 18-24," p. 87.

TABLE IV-6

EXPENDITURES FOR INSTITUTIONS OF HIGHER EDUCATION, COMPARED
WITH NATIONAL AGGREGATES, 1930-1980
(current expenditures plus capital outlays)

Year	GROSS NATIONAL PRODUCT billion dollars (10)	EXPENDITURES FOR INSTITUTIONS OF HIGHER EDUCATION							
		Total million dollars (11)	% of (10) (12)	Public Schools million dollars (13)	% of (10) (14)	Non-public schools million dollars (15)	% of (10) (16)	Per student (11)÷(4) dollars (17)	Per capita (11)÷(1) dollars (18)
1930	91.1	631.2	.69	288.9	.32	343.3	.37	573	5.13
1940	100.6	758.5	.75	391.7	.39	366.8	.36	508	5.75
1950	284.6	2,662.5	.94	1,429.6	.50	1,232.0	.43	1,159	17.61
1952	347.0	2,874.3	.83	1,565.4	.45	1,308.9	.38	1,338	18.45
1954	363.1	3,435.6	.95	1,932.3	.53	1,503.3	.41	1,374	21.31
1956	419.2	4,210.3	1.00	2,376.0	.57	1,834.3	.44	1,429	25.17
1958	442.2	5,665.2	1.28	3,276.9	.74	2,388.3	.54	1,738	32.70
1960	503.7	6,966.9	1.38	3,944.4	.78	3,022.8	.60	1,944	38.70
1962	560.3	8,904.1	1.59	4,977.8	.89	3,926.4	.70	2,133	47.89
1964	632.4	11,691.0	1.85	6,632.5	1.05	5,058.5	.80	2,214	61.18
1966	749.9	15,822.9	2.11	9,178.7	1.22	6,644.3	.89	2,476	80.89
1968	864.2	20,750.7	2.40	12,834.9	1.49	7,916.2	.92	2,762	104.01
1970	984.1	25,493.6	2.59	16,416.4	1.69	9,078.0	.92	2,971	125.09
1971	1,063.4	27,859.2	2.62	18,259.3	1.72	9,600.0	.90	3,113	135.11
1972	1,171.1	30,054.5	2.57	19,764.1	1.69	10,290.0	.88	3,261	144.35
1973	1,306.6	32,234.4	2.47	21,393.4	1.64	10,840.6	.83	3,357	153.57
1974	1,412.9	35,356.6	2.50	23,772.3	1.68	11,586.2	.82	3,458	167.25
1975	1,528.8	40,099.1	2.62	27,157.6	1.78	12,941.4	.85	3,585	188.17
1976	1,702.2	43,960.0	2.58	29,979.5	1.76	13,980.4	.82	3,992	204.75
1977	1,899.5	47,693.4	2.51	32,333.2	1.70	15,361.2	.81	4,226	220.39
1978	2,127.6	50,909.0	2.39	34,361.9	1.62	16,547.6	.78	4,521	233.42
1979	2,368.8	55,649.3	2.35	37,353.3	1.58	18,295.6	.77	4,810	252.84
1980	2,626.5	62,848.5	2.39	41,695.7	1.59	21,153.2	.81	5,137	277.47

SOURCES: (1930-1966): U.S. Office of Education, *Biennial Survey of Education in the United States* (Washington, D.C.: Government Printing Office). (1968-1980): NCES, *Financial Statistics of Institutions of Higher Education* (Washington, D.C.: Government Printing Office).

NOTE: Statistics are for the various states plus the District of Columbia and the territories.

higher education have been an increase in the proportion of graduate to undergraduate enrollments and an increase in the proportion of students enrolled at two-year as opposed to four-year institutions. In 1960 graduate students accounted for only 10.6 percent of total enrollments, while in 1970 and in 1980 they accounted for 14.0 percent and 13.4 percent respectively. The statistical success of two-year institutions is a principal feature distinguishing the period from 1960 to 1980 from earlier years. Enrollment in junior colleges accounted for only 12.6 percent of total enrollments in 1960, 25.9 percent of enrollments in 1970, and 37.4 percent in 1980. Whereas in 1960, 87.4 percent of all students were enrolled in colleges or universities offering a four-year undergraduate program, that figure had declined to 62.6 percent in 1980.[31]

Quite aside from the increase in the absolute number of students enrolled at institutions of higher education, these changes in the composition of the student body have also affected expenditures. As Machlup argued earlier, graduate education is more costly than undergraduate education because of the more extensive laboratory and research facilities that graduate education requires and the higher salaries commanded by graduate faculty (Machlup, *Production and Distribution of Knowledge*, p. 78). The effect of expansion in two-year colleges is more ambiguous. Although the costs per student in these institutions may be lower than in four-year institutions, the initial costs for developing these facilities have largely been incurred in the period under consideration.

Unfortunately, the statistics available will not allow us to make easy or consistent distinctions between levels of education or between types of institution in the following discussions of expenditure and finance. For the most part, then, we shall be dealing with comprehensive statistics that cover the whole field. As Table IV-6 shows, overall expenditures per student—undergraduate and graduate, at two-year and at four-year institutions—increased from $1,944 in 1960 to $5,137 in 1980, or 2.6 times. We shall follow Machlup's analytical strategy henceforth and examine faculty salaries and student-faculty ratios before turning to other factors that have contributed to this increase—i.e., expenditures for functions other than teaching itself.

FACULTY SALARIES AND STUDENT-FACULTY RATIOS

The average salary for faculty members, all ranks combined, rose from $6,711 in 1960 to $11,745 in 1970, and to $17,846 in 1978 (Table IV-7). The Consumer Price Index of 1978 was approximately 120 percent over that of 1960 and about 68 percent over that of 1970. Hence, in order to maintain the purchasing power of the 1960 salary, the 1978 salary would have had to be $14,764; and to maintain the purchasing power of the 1970 salary, the 1978 salary would have had to be $19,732. As the actual salary of 1978 was $17,846, college faculty enjoyed a raise of 21 percent in real income over the 1960 level, but suffered a decrease of 10 percent from their real income of 1970. If the same calculations are done with the figures shown in Table IV-7 for per capita GNP, we find that the 1978 figure of $9,733 represents a gain of 59 percent in real income over the figure for 1960 and of 21 percent over the 1970 figure for per capital GNP.

It is interesting to note that although the average annual income of physi-

[31] See, for example, NCES, *The Condition of Education*, 1975 ed., table 67, p. 190 and *The Condition of Education*, 1983 ed., table 2.1, p. 80. The figures on graduate enrollment and on enrollment in junior colleges for 1960 are from U.S. Bureau of the Census, *Historical Statistics of the United States: Colonial Times to 1970*, part 1, table H 700-715, p. 383 (Washington D.C.).

TABLE IV-7

AVERAGE ANNUAL INCOME OF VARIOUS PROFESSIONS, IN CURRENT DOLLARS, 1930-1979

Year	College Teachers (1)	Non-salaried Lawyers (2)	Non-salaried Physicians (3)	Non-salaried Dentists (4)	GNP per capita (5)
1930	3,065	5,194	4,870	4,020	740
1940	2,906	4,507	4,441	3,314	761
1950	4,354	8,349	12,324	7,436	1,876
1960	6,711		22,100	13,400	2,788
1961		11,604			2,820
1962	7,486	11,844			2,974
1963		12,300			3,117
1964	8,163	12,816			3,288
1965		13,644	28,960	12,700	3,525
1966	9,081	14,052			3,796
1967		14,419			3,966
1968	10,235	15,283	37,620		4,306
1969		19,163	40,550		4,590
1970	11,745	20,304	41,550	28,100	4,769
1971		22,178	42,700		5,098
1972	12,932	23,448	40,700	32,500	5,531
1973		24,693	42,100		6,210
1974	14,373	25,956	44,600	30,200	6,666
1975		28,159	47,500		7,159
1976	16,313	29,828	52,400	40,000	7,901
1977		30,973	52,600		8,702
1978	17,846	33,547	54,700		9,733
1979		37,807			10,745

SOURCES: Column (1): NCES, *Digest of Education Statistics*. Column (2): U.S. Bureau of Labor Statistics, *Handbook of Labor Statistics* (Washington, D.C.: Government Printing Office). Columns (3), (4), and (5): U.S. Bureau of the Census, *Statistical Abstract of the U.S.*.

cians has been much higher than that of college teachers, physicians' income in 1978 had fallen even further in purchasing power from their real income in 1970—i.e., by 22 percent. Nonetheless, as Table IV-7 shows, the average (salary) income of college teachers remained quite low compared to the income of other professionals. In 1960, college teachers' average salary was only 30 percent that of physicians' income and by 1978 had increased only slightly in proportion, to 33 percent. In comparison to changes in lawyers' incomes, college faculty's salaries did even worse, dropping from 63 percent in 1962 to 53 percent in 1978. Clearly college teaching has become less, rather than more attractive in terms of salary than these other professional careers.

We may note that while the overall increase in faculty salaries from 1960 to 1978 of 2.7 times slightly exceeded the rise in expenditures per student of 2.3 times, neither one kept up with growth in GNP per head. From Table IV-7 we can see that GNP per head rose 3.5 times, from $2,788 in 1960 to $9,733 in

1978. The difference may in part be due to the fact that the student-faculty ratio actually increased over the same period of time (see Table IV-8).

OTHER EXPENDITURES

Although "resident instruction" forms the major item for expenditures by institutions of higher education, it comprised only 25.9 percent of total expenditures in 1960, and 29.7 percent and 29.6 percent of total expenditures in

TABLE IV-8

NUMBERS OF FACULTY AND STUDENTS IN INSTITUTIONS
OF HIGHER EDUCATION, 1870-1980

Year	Faculty members	Enrollment	Students per faculty members
1870	5,553	52,286	9.4
1880	11,522	115,817	10.1
1890	15,809	156,756	9.9
1900	23,868	237,592	10.0
1910	36,480	355,213	9.7
1920	48,615	597,880	12.3
1930	82,386	1,100,737	13.4
1940	146,929	1,494,203	10.2
1950	246,722	2,659,021	10.8
1960	380,544	3,215,544	8.4
1970	825,000	7,136,075	8.6
1980	1,097,000*	12,234,644	11.2

SOURCE: NCES, *Digest of Education Statistics.*

* 1979 Data.

1970 and 1980, respectively. Even though the costs of resident instruction rose 10.3 times between 1960 and 1980, the increase in total costs of 9.0 times, from $6,966.9 million in 1960 to $62,848.5 million in 1980, must be explained by increases in expenditures for other activities as well. Table IV-9 provides the data available for our discussion. Because so many years are reported in this table, our discussion will be much simplified if we restrict ourselves to the data presented in Table IV-9A. As these data show, the costs of resident instruction rose 6.6 times over the years from 1964 to 1980, while total expenditures rose 5.4 times.

It is easy to see from Table IV-9A that expenditures for several other items rose at a greater rate than both resident instruction and total expenditures. Leading the field were expenditures for administrative and general purposes (increasing 7.4 times between 1964 and 1980), student aid (increasing 7.3 times), libraries and plant operation and management (each increasing 6.9 times). Rising less than expenditures for resident instruction but more than total expenditures were expenditures for public service (rising 6.1 times). Auxiliary enterprises (including dormitories, dining halls, etc.) increased 4.5 times, while capital costs for plant expansion rose only 2.3 times during the period under question. Research expenditures are more difficult to gauge and will be discussed below.

The most striking change in the composition of the columns in Table IV-9 is the decreasing importance of capital outlays as a proportion of total expenditures. Indeed, plant expansion rose steadily from 19.2 percent of the total in 1960 to a high of 21.1 percent in 1964, but then dropped just as consistently to a low of 8.3 percent in 1979, rising somewhat to account for 8.9 percent of total expenditures in 1980. Clearly, resident instruction and administration were major "beneficiaries" of this change, rising in their share of total expenditures while capital outlays decreased. It is more difficult to generalize about expenditures for research because of changes in reporting conventions between 1968 and 1969 (see Table IV-9). If we combine expenditures for hospitals and centers for research and development with expenditures for organized research in the later years, however, we see that expenditures for "research" dropped from 17.0 percent of the total in 1964 to 14.1 percent in 1970 and then increased to 17.5 percent in 1980—mostly because of the rising costs of hospital operation.

The reader will recall that for accounting purposes, Machlup "disallowed" various categories in Table IV-9 as expenditures for higher education. The troublesome research expenditures are deducted from the total as belonging properly to "research and development." We shall also exclude hospitals although, as an integral part of medical education, this may be a debatable decision. Other exclusions include student aid—actually a "transfer payment" within the institutions themselves, public service programs, and auxiliary enterprises. The last two rows of Table IV-9 give the total and current allowed expenditures that we will report in our summary tables on national expenditures for education.

FINANCING HIGHER EDUCATION

Table IV-10, showing the sources of income for institutions of higher education and their relative contributions to "allowed current expenditures," requires less exegesis than most of the other tables in this section. As no serious problems of interpretation arise from the categories used to classify these sources of income, we can confine our discussion to the findings themselves and in particular to rows 15-20, which show changes in the pattern of finance by percent.

State and local governments have clearly maintained their role as the principal source of revenue for institutions of higher education. Indeed the contributions of state and local governments show a marked upward trend, rising as a proportion of allowed current expenditures from around 44 percent in the early 1960s to over 56 percent from 1975 to 1980. As these funds were rising

TABLE IV-9

EXPENDITURES OF INSTITUTIONS OF HIGHER EDUCATION, 1960-1980
(millions of dollars)

	1960	1962	1964	1966	1968	1969	1970
(1) Administrative and general	890.7	1,111.4	1,437.5	2,377.7	2,792.7	2,972.3	3,430.0
(2) Resident instruction	1,802.9	2,216.0	2,820.6	3,780.7	5,807.6	6,509.1	7,571.0
(3) Organized research	1,024.4	1,481.4	1,982.9	2,453.0	2,709.9	2,046.0	2,155.0
(4) Libraries	135.9	178.1	237.9	347.6	505.7	574.5	656.4
(5) Plant operation and maintenance	473.7	566.0	689.3	847.8	1,132.1	1,343.4	1,549.2
(6) Public service programs	208.4	245.2	298.2	442.7	602.5	541.6	602.7
(7) Hospitals						526.9	671.2
(8) Auxiliary enterprises	917.9	1,160.7	1,455.2	1,891.1	2,306.5	2,544.2	2,775.1
(9) Student aid	174.0	231.3	303.4	429.2	718.7	823.2	993.6
(10) R & D centers						697.3	757.4
(11) Total current expenditures	5,627.9	7,190.1	9,225.0	12,569.9	16,575.7	18,578.8	21,161.6
(12) Capital outlays	1,339.0	1,714.0	2,466.0	3,253.0	4,175.0	4,057.0	4,332.0
(13) Total expenditures	6,966.9	8,904.1	11,691.0	15,882.9	20,750.7	22,635.8	25,493.6
(14) Not allowed as cost of education [(3) and (6) through (10)]	2,324.7	3,118.6	4,039.7	5,216.0	6,337.6	7,179.2	7,955.0
(15) Total allowed expenditures for education [(13) minus (14)]	4,642.2	5,785.5	7,651.3	10,606.9	14,413.1	15,456.6	17,538.6
(16) Allowed current expenditures [(11) minus (14)]	3,303.2	4,071.5	5,185.3	7,353.9	10,238.1	11,399.6	13,206.6

	1971	1972	1973	1974	1975	1976	1977	1978	1979	1980
(1) Administrative and general	3,911.2	4,452.3	5,053.9	5,218.8	6,344.6	7,107.4	7,802.1	8,688.2	9,680.6	10,700.3
(2) Resident instruction	8,549.3	9,276.3	10,097.8	11,512.5	11,877.8	13,175.1	14,131.7	15,450.2	16,784.2	18,624.6
(3) Organized research	2,222.9	2,278.3	2,407.4	2,503.6	3,161.5	3,310.9	3,615.7	3,936.1	4,465.7	5,120.4
(4) Libraries	720.8	769.4	847.2	946.1	1,010.1	1,232.7	1,259.5	1,358.6	1,436.9	1,635.7
(5) Plant operation and maintenance	1,739.9	1,937.7	2,155.4	2,512.7	2,806.3	3,105.3	3,460.6	3,822.6	4,206.1	4,736.7
(6) Public service programs	594.7	623.7	677.9	741.7	1,109.1	1,250.7	1,353.5	1,435.7	1,604.6	1,830.3
(7) Hospitals	842.6	998.6	1,183.7	1,431.7	2,350.8	2,695.6	3,155.1	3,597.7	4,131.7	4,763.4
(8) Auxiliary enterprises	2,994.1	3,185.1	3,344.3	3,620.2	4,081.5	4,484.4	4,868.1	5,271.5	5,761.2	6,497.6
(9) Student aid	1,110.1	1,256.3	1,340.9	1,414.2	1,473.7	1,656.8	1,793.4	1,866.3	1,974.2	2,228.2
(10) R & D centers	829.6	940.8	1,033.8	1,015.1	1,085.7	1,132.1	1,434.7	855.1	1,007.1	1,127.8
(11) Total current expenditures	23,515.2	25,718.5	28,142.4	30,916.6	35,301.1	39,151.0	42,874.4	46,282.0	51,052.3	57,264.9
(12) Capital outlays	4,344.0	4,336.0	4,092.0	4,440.0	4,798.0	4,809.0	4,819.0	4,627.0	4,597.0	5,583.6
(13) Total expenditures	27,859.2	30,054.5	32,234.4	35,356.6	40,099.1	43,960.0	47,693.4	50,909.0	55,649.3	62,848.5
(14) Not allowed as cost of education [(3) and (6) through (10)]	8,594.0	9,282.8	9,988.0	10,726.5	13,262.3	14,530.5	16,220.5	16,962.4	18,944.5	21,567.7
(15) Total allowed expenditures for education [(13) minus (14)]	19,265.2	20,771.7	22,246.4	24,630.1	26,836.8	29,429.5	31,472.9	33,946.6	36,704.8	41,280.8
(16) Allowed current expenditures [(11) minus (14)]	14,921.2	16,435.7	18,154.4	20,190.1	22,038.8	24,620.5	26,653.9	29,319.6	32,107.8	35,697.2

SOURCES: (1960-1966): U.S. Office of Education, *Biennial Survey of Education*, and NCES, *Digest of Education Statistics*. (1968-1980): NCES, *Financial Statistics of Institutions of Higher Education*.

NOTE: Statistics are for the various states plus the District of Columbia and the territories. Tables may not add due to the rounding off of numbers. Where possible, changes in categories for expenditures have been treated to allow comparisons for different years.

TABLE IV-9A

SUMMARY OF EXPENDITURES OF INSTITUTIONS OF HIGHER EDUCATION FOR 1964, 1970, AND 1980
(millions of dollars and as percent of total expenditures)

	1964		1970		1980		absolute increase
(1) Administration and general	1,437.5	(12.3)	3,430.0	(13.5)	10,700.3	(17.0)	7.4 times
(2) Resident instruction	2,820.6	(24.1)	7,571.0	(29.7)	18,624.6	(29.6)	6.6 times
(3) Organized research	1,982.9	(17.0)	2,155.0	(8.5)	5,120.4	(8.1)	***
(4) Libraries	237.9	(2.0)	656.4	(2.6)	1,635.7	(2.6)	6.9 times
(5) Plant operation and management	689.3	(5.9)	1,549.2	(6.1)	4,736.7	(7.5)	6.9 times
(6) Public service programs	298.2	(2.6)	602.7	(2.4)	1,830.3	(2.9)	6.1 times
(7) Hospitals			671.2	(2.6)	4,763.4	(7.6)	***
(8) Auxiliary enterprises	1,455.2	(12.4)	2,755.1	(10.9)	6,497.6	(10.3)	4.5 times
(9) Student aid	303.4	(2.6)	993.6	(3.9)	2,228.2	(3.5)	7.3 times
(10) R & D centers			757.4	(3.0)	1,127.8	(1.8)	***
(11) Total current expenditures	9,225.0	(78.9)	21,161.6	(83.0)	57,264.9	(91.1)	6.2 times
(12) Capital outlays	2,466.0	(21.1)	4,332.0	(17.0)	5,583.6	(8.9)	2.3 times
(13) Total expenditures	11,691.0		25,493.6		62,848.5		5.4 times

SOURCE: Table IV-9 in this book.

*** Absolute increase not shown because of change in categories between 1968 and 1969.

in importance during the latter decade of our study, federal funding suffered a relative decline. The contribution of federal funds never fell below 28 percent of current expenditures (rising as high as 41.8 percent in 1964) between 1960 and 1970, but then declined in relation to other sources of finance to between 19.9 percent and 22.8 percent in the decade ending in 1980. One must recall, too, that much of this funding was actually received for research and may thus have contributed only indirectly to the needs of colleges and universities for revenue to cover actual educational expenses. Loans to students, another source of federal support to higher education during the years under study, are, of course, excluded from these figures on institutional receipts.

Net student payments (tuition and fees, less student aid) have amounted to between 25.4 percent (1974) and 30.8 percent (1964) of current educational expenditures in the years from 1960 to 1980, fluctuating less widely than in the preceding twenty years. Both endowment earnings and private gifts and grants, however, failed to keep up in proportion to the general rise in expenditures. Endowment earnings dipped from nearly 6 percent of allowed current expenditures in 1960 to around 3 percent in the last few years of our study. Private gifts and grants also dropped, from a high of nearly 11 percent of allowed current expenditures in 1960 to around 8 percent from 1973 through 1980.[32]

PUBLIC AND PRIVATE INSTITUTIONS

In Table III-4 we have followed Machlup's procedures to tabulate expenditures for knowledge production by source of funds. Tables IV-IIA and IV-11B separate the expenditures of public and private institutions of higher education—a step that was required for this exercise. We may note from these tables that of the total allowed expenditures for all institutions of higher education (Row 15, Table IV-9), public institutions were responsible for 55 percent in 1960, 67 percent in 1970, and 69 percent in 1980.

It is not surprising to find that during this same period when public institutions were spending an increasing share of total allowable expenditures for higher education, public institutions were also enjoying an increasing share of total college and university enrollments. Table IV-12 shows that whereas predominance shifted back and forth between public and private institutions from 1910 to 1950, the proportion of enrollments at public institutions climbed steadily thereafter, rising from 59 percent in 1960 to 78 percent in 1974, where it remained through 1980.

Accompanying the rise in the proportion of total enrollments at public institutions has been a rise in the proportion of public institutions within the total number of American colleges and universities. As Machlup pointed out earlier (*Production and Distribution of Knowledge*, p. 88), the number of private institutions was almost twice (1.9 times) as high as public ones in 1960. By 1970 the lead of private institutions had narrowed to 1.4 times, and by 1980 to only 1.1 times the number of public colleges and universities. Table IV-13 presents a statistical picture of institutional growth by level (in terms of highest degree offered) and type of control. It is interesting to note that whereas the total number of institutions grew from 2,011 to 3,152, or 1.6 times, from 1960 to 1980, the number of public institutions rose from 698 to 1,475 or 2.1 times, whereas the number of private institutions grew from 1,313 to 1,677—only 1.3 times.

As Table IV-14 shows, our large number of colleges and universities, and our high level of college enrollment continue to give a distinctive cast to higher education in the United States. Using data available in standard guides to education in different nations, however, we can see that between 1957 and 1975 several other countries experienced expansion in the field of higher education that compares with our own. For example, these data indicate that whereas the number of American institutions of higher education increased 1.8 times between 1957 and 1975, the increases in Poland (4.6 times), France (3.4 times),

---

[32] This discussion is clearly limited by its concern with presenting the overall picture of finance for all institutions of higher education combined. The annual reports of the National Center for Education Statistics on *The Condition of Education* usually contain both a narrative summary and tables that shed some light on the different patterns of finance that characterize different kinds of institution.

TABLE IV-10

INCOME OF INSTITUTIONS OF HIGHER EDUCATION, 1930-1980

(millions of dollars)

	1930	1940	1950	1960	1962	1964	1966	1968	1969	1970
(1) Student fees	144.1	200.9	394.6	1,161.8	1,505.3	1,899.5	2,679.6	3,393.6	3,829.8	4,438.5
(2) Endowment earnings	68.6	71.3	96.3	206.7	232.3	266.2	316.3	364.1	474.1	516.1
(3) Federal government	20.7	38.9	524.3	1,040.7	1,542.0	2,170.6	2,633.9	3,363.1	3,531.8	3,813.2
(4) State governments	150.8	151.2	492.0	1,389.3	1,689.1	2,133.7	3,012.0	4,219.7	4,936.7	5,938.0
(5) Local governments	26.2	24.4	61.4	151.7	191.2	240.4	318.0	503.7	616.5	785.4
(6) Private gifts and grants		40.4	118.6	383.2	450.8	551.5	642.7	553.4	1,055.7	1,161.8
(7) Organized activities relating to instruction	72.7	32.8	112.0	244.9	304.1	363.6		692.5	421.4	485.1
(8) Miscellaneous		11.4	34.6	134.1	157.3	204.4	707.6	829.8	838.5	892.5
(9) Auxiliary enterprises and activities	60.4	143.9	511.3	1,005.9	1,274.1	1,610.4	2,142.6	2,486.8	2,695.8	2,906.3
(10) Other noneducational income	11.0		29.5	94.2	120.2	150.9	313.4	503.9	573.9	702.2
(11) Total current income	554.5	715.2	2,374.6	5,782.5	7,466.4	9,591.2	12,796.1	16,910.6	18,974.3	21,638.6
(12) Student aid (Table IV-9, item 9)	15.1	14.3	36.3	174.0	231.3	303.4	429.2	718.7	823.2	993.6
(13) Net student payments [(1) minus (12)]	129.0	186.6	358.3	987.8	1,274.0	1,596.1	2,250.4	2,674.9	3,006.6	3,444.9
(14) Allowed current expenditures (Table IV-9, item 16)	470.9	509.0	1,507.7	3,511.6	4,316.7	5,185.3	7,353.9	10,228.1	11,399.6	13,206.6
		Percent of line 14						Percent of line 14		
(15) Net student payments	27.4	36.7	23.8	28.1	29.5	30.8	30.6	26.2	26.4	26.1
(16) State and local governments	32.0	34.5	36.7	43.9	43.6	45.8	45.3	46.2	48.7	50.9
(17) Endowment earnings	14.6	14.0	6.4	5.9	5.4	5.1	4.3	3.6	4.2	3.9
(18) Private gifts and grants	5.6	7.9	7.9	10.9	10.4	10.6	8.7	5.4	9.3	8.8
(19) Sum of (15), (16), (17) and (18)	79.6	93.1	74.8	88.8	88.9	92.3	88.9	81.3	88.6	89.7
(20) Federal government	4.4	7.6	34.8	29.6	35.7	41.8	35.8	32.9	31.0	28.9

	1971	1972	1973	1974	1975	1976	1977	1978	1979	1980
(1) Student fees	5,043.0	5,624.2	6,047.6	6,543.3	7,284.6	8,236.8	9,101.0	9,948.2	10,807.2	12,045.3
(2) Endowment earnings	540.9	561.0	601.7	668.1	718.5	688.0	765.2	832.9	986.1	1,177.3
(3) Federal government	3,256.9	3,534.7	3,831.5	4,025.9	5,029.9	5,448.5	5,769.4	6,154.9	6,889.2	7,812.2
(4) State governments	6,671.3	7,322.6	8,155.8	9,448.2	10,990.7	12,395.0	13,426.0	14,891.0	16,530.7	18,559.2
(5) Local governments	919.8	1,006.4	1,160.6	1,281.6	1,430.2	1,621.7	1,631.3	1,751.2	1,579.3	1,594.9
(6) Private gifts and grants	1,262.4	1,392.6	1,491.9	1,623.4	1,747.5	1,919.3	2,107.2	2,322.7	2,491.2	2,810.1
(7) Organized activities relating to instruction	524.8	590.5	610.3	611.8						
(8) Miscellaneous	1,055.1	1,119.9	1,247.6	1,549.1	556.2	646.5	907.5	885.2	1,338.9	1,242.0
(9) Auxiliary enterprises and activities	3,130.8	3,315.2	3,473.1	3,741.0	4,087.8	4,556.3	4,928.8	5,337.4	5,751.4	6,492.9
(10) Other noneducational income	1,616.0	1,934.0	2,181.6	2,434.8	4,089.2	4,446.4	5,079.0	5,214.7	5,810.8	7,157.5
(11) Total current income	24,019.0	26,400.9	28,801.9	31,927.2	35,934.6	39,958.8	43,715.4	47,338.3	52,184.8	58,891.5
(12) Student aid (Table IV-9, item 9)	1,110.1	1,256.3	1,340.9	1,414.2	1,473.7	1,656.8	1,793.4	1,866.3	1,974.2	2,228.2
(13) Net student payments [(1) minus (12)]	3,932.9	4,367.9	4,706.7	5,129.1	5,810.9	6,580.0	7,307.6	8,081.9	8,833.0	9,817.1
(14) Allowed current expenditures (Table IV-9, item 16)	14,921.2	16,435.7	18,154.4	20,190.0	22,038.8	24,620.5	26,653.9	29,319.6	32,107.8	35,697.2
			Percent of line 14							
(15) Net student payments	26.4	26.6	26.0	25.4	26.4	26.7	27.4	27.3	27.3	27.5
(16) State and local governments	50.9	50.7	51.3	53.1	56.4	56.9	56.5	56.8	56.4	56.5
(17) Endowment earnings	3.6	3.4	3.3	3.3	3.3	2.8	2.9	2.8	3.1	3.3
(18) Private gifts and grants	8.5	8.5	8.2	8.0	7.9	7.8	7.9	7.9	7.8	7.9
(19) Sum of (15), (16), (17) and (18)	89.4	89.2	88.8	89.8	94.0	94.2	94.7	94.8	94.8	95.2
(20) Federal government	21.8	21.5	21.1	19.9	22.8	22.1	21.6	21.0	21.5	21.9

SOURCES: (1930–1966): U.S. Office of Education, Biennial Survey of Education, and NCES, Digest of Education Statistics. (1968–1980): NCES, Financial Statistics of Institutions of Higher Education.

NOTE: Statistics are for the various states plus the District of Columbia and the territories. Tables may not add due to the rounding of numbers. Where possible, changes in categories for expenditures have been treated to allow comparisons for different years.

TABLE IV-11A

PUBLIC INSTITUTIONS OF HIGHER EDUCATION: EXPENDITURES, 1960-1980

(millions of dollars)

	1960	1962	1964	1966	1968	1969	1970	1971	1972	1973
(1) Administrative and general	458.1	563.3	1,025.4	1,298.4	1,633.6	1,772.5	2,094.9	2,420.6	2,816.4	3,205.8
(2) Resident instruction	1,075.0	1,315.9	1,713.4	2,376.5	3,878.1	4,373.5	5,177.8	5,934.4	6,485.6	7,154.8
(3) Organized research	524.6	733.7	935.9	1,149.6	1,416.5	1,210.4	1,281.9	1,334.3	1,353.6	1,524.0
(4) Libraries	74.5	97.3	133.0	201.3	307.6	360.6	417.9	467.1	502.3	564.0
(5) Plant operation and maintenance	272.5	322.3	392.1	491.9	702.3	846.6	1,005.8	1,144.4	1,291.9	1,458.1
(6) Public service programs	195.7	224.7		396.5	492.6	481.1	543.8	548.9	567.3	613.9
(7) Hospitals						342.5	415.1	549.3	626.9	702.5
(8) Auxiliary enterprises	492.5	630.0	804.2	1,044.1	1,340.1	1,463.7	1,628.3	1,785.2	1,916.2	2,025.5
(9) Student aid	61.5	80.6	110.5	156.4	332.1	374.3	464.5	536.5	630.7	667.4
(10) R & D Centers						287.4	320.4	391.6	417.2	432.4
(11) Total current expenditures	3,154.4	3,967.8	5,114.5	7,114.7	10,102.9	11,512.8	13,350.4	15,112.3	16,608.1	18,348.4
(12) Capital outlays	790.0	1,010.0	1,518.0	2,064.0	2,732.0	2,978.0	3,066.0	3,147.0	3,156.0	3,045.0
(13) Total expenditures	3,944.4	4,977.8	6,632.5	9,178.7	12,834.9	14,490.8	16,416.4	18,259.3	19,764.1	21,393.4
(14) Not allowed as cost of education [(3) and (6) through (10)]	1,274.3	1,669.0	1,850.6	2,746.6	3,581.3	4,159.4	4,654.0	5,145.8	5,511.9	5,965.7
(15) Total allowed expenditures for education [(13) minus (14)]	2,670.1	3,308.8	4,781.9	6,432.1	9,253.6	10,331.4	11,762.4	13,113.5	14,252.2	15,427.7
(16) Allowed current expenditures [(11) minus (14)]	1,880.1	2,298.8	3,263.9	4,368.1	6,521.6	7,353.4	8,696.4	9,966.5	11,096.2	12,382.7

	1974	1975	1976	1977	1978	1979	1980
(1) Administrative and general	3,221.7	4,265.3	4,843.4	5,277.7	5,885.5	6,488.0	7,093.9
(2) Resident instruction	8,350.7	8,634.6	9,575.3	10,273.8	11,226.1	12,146.6	13,403.2
(3) Organized research	1,604.1	2,071.3	2,177.9	2,366.3	2,599.6	2,961.3	3,429.7
(4) Libraries	639.3	685.5	830.3	849.4	907.5	959.6	1,122.0
(5) Plant operation and maintenance	1,729.0	1,949.6	2,174.5	2,425.9	2,683.3	2,933.3	3,291.7
(6) Public service programs	673.4	935.2	1,046.5	1,121.8	1,201.5	1,345.5	1,526.6
(7) Hospitals	878.5	1,369.1	1,609.7	1,925.1	2,187.3	2,523.1	2,953.9
(8) Auxiliary enterprises	2,212.5	2,541.5	2,833.9	3,093.1	3,349.4	3,664.4	4,139.1
(9) Student aid	717.3	739.6	812.9	872.8	854.9	877.1	986.9
(10) R & D Centers	469.8	491.9	463.1	625.3	44.8	62.4	60.7
(11) Total current expenditures	20,496.3	23,683.6	26,367.5	28,831.2	30,939.0	33,961.3	38,007.7
(12) Capital outlays	3,276.0	3,474.0	3,612.0	3,502.0	3,422.0	3,392.0	3,688.0
(13) Total expenditures	23,772.3	27,157.6	29,979.5	32,333.2	34,361.9	37,353.3	41,695.7
(14) Not allowed as cost of education [(3) and (6) through (10)]	6,555.6	8,148.6	8,944.0	10,004.4	10,237.5	11,433.8	13,096.9
(15) Total allowed expenditures for education [(13) minus (14)]	17,216.7	19,009.0	21,035.5	22,328.8	24,124.4	25,919.5	28,598.8
(16) Allowed current expenditures [(11) minus (14)]	13,940.7	15,535.0	17,423.5	18,826.8	20,702.4	22,527.5	24,910.8

SOURCES: (1960-1966): U.S. Office of Education, *Biennial Survey of Education*. (1968-1980): NCES, *Financial Statistics of Institutions of Higher Education*.

NOTE: Statistics are for the various states plus the District of Columbia and the territories. Where possible, changes in categories for expenditures have been treated to allow comparisons for different years.

TABLE IV-11B

Private Institutions of Higher Education: Expenditures, 1960-1980

(millions of dollars)

	1960	1962	1964	1966	1968	1969	1970	1971	1972	1973
(1) Administrative and general	432.7	548.1	710.3	1,079.3	1,159.2	1,199.7	1,336.1	1,490.6	1,635.8	1,847.9
(2) Resident instruction	727.8	900.1	1,107.2	1,404.2	1,929.6	2,135.7	2,393.1	2,615.9	2,790.6	2,942.9
(3) Organized research	499.9	747.7	1,047.0	1,303.3	1,293.5	835.6	872.9	888.5	924.7	883.4
(4) Libraries	61.2	80.9	104.9	146.4	198.1	213.9	238.5	253.6	267.1	283.4
(5) Plant operation and maintenance	201.4	243.7	297.2	356.0	429.9	496.8	543.4	595.5	645.8	697.3
(6) Public service programs	12.8	20.5		46.3	109.8	60.4	58.9	45.8	56.3	63.9
(7) Hospitals						184.5	256.2	293.2	371.7	481.2
(8) Auxiliary enterprises	425.5	530.7	651.0	847.0	966.5	1,080.5	1,146.8	1,208.9	1,269.0	1,318.8
(9) Student aid	112.5	150.7	192.9	272.8	386.6	448.9	529.1	573.6	625.4	673.6
(10) R & D Centers						409.9	437.0	437.9	523.6	601.4
(11) Total current expenditures	2,473.8	3,222.4	4,110.5	5,455.3	6,473.2	7,065.9	7,812.0	8,403.5	9,110.0	9,793.6
(12) Capital outlays	549.0	704.0	948.0	1,189.0	1,443.0	1,079.0	1,266.0	1,197.0	1,180.0	1,047.0
(13) Total expenditures	3,022.8	3,926.4	5,058.5	6,644.3	7,916.2	8,144.9	9,078.0	9,600.0	10,290.0	10,840.6
(14) Not allowed as cost of education [(3) and (6) through (10)]	1,050.7	1,449.6	1,890.9	2,469.4	2,756.4	3,019.8	3,300.9	3,447.9	3,770.7	4,402.3
(15) Total allowed expenditures for education [(13) minus (14)]	1,972.1	2,476.8	3,167.6	4,174.9	5,159.8	5,125.1	5,777.1	6,152.1	6,519.3	6,818.3
(16) Allowed current expenditures [(11) minus (14)]	1,423.1	1,772.8	2,219.6	2,985.9	3,716.8	4,046.1	4,511.1	4,955.6	5,339.3	5,771.3

	1974	1975	1976	1977	1978	1979	1980
(1) Administrative and general	1,997.1	2,079.2	2,263.9	2,524.2	2,802.8	3,192.6	3,606.4
(2) Resident instruction	3,161.8	3,243.2	3,599.7	3,857.9	4,224.1	4,637.6	5,221.4
(3) Organized research	899.5	1,090.2	1,133.1	1,249.4	1,336.5	1,504.4	1,690.7
(4) Libraries	306.8	324.6	402.4	410.1	451.1	477.3	513.8
(5) Plant operation and maintenance	783.7	856.7	930.9	1,034.7	1,139.2	1,272.8	1,445.0
(6) Public service programs	68.3	173.8	204.2	231.7	234.9	259.1	303.7
(7) Hospitals	555.1	981.8	1,085.9	1,230.1	1,410.3	1,608.6	1,809.5
(8) Auxiliary enterprises	1,407.7	1,540.1	1,650.5	1,775.0	1,922.1	2,096.8	2,358.5
(9) Student aid	696.9	734.1	843.9	920.6	1,011.4	1,097.0	1,241.2
(10) R & D Centers	545.3	593.7	668.9	809.5	810.2	944.7	1,067.0
(11) Total current expenditures	10,422.2	11,617.4	12,783.4	14,043.2	15,342.6	17,090.6	19,257.2
(12) Capital outlays	1,164.0	1,324.0	1,197.0	1,318.0	1,205.0	1,205.0	1,896.0
(13) Total expenditures	11,586.2	12,941.4	13,980.4	15,361.2	16,547.6	18,295.6	21,153.2
(14) Not allowed as cost of education [(3) and (6) through (10)]	4,172.8	5,113.7	5,586.5	6,216.3	6,725.4	7,510.6	8,470.6
(15) Total allowed expenditures for education [(13) minus (14)]	7,413.4	7,827.7	8,393.9	9,144.9	9,822.2	10,785.0	12,682.6
(16) Allowed current expenditures [(11) minus (14)]	6,249.4	6,503.7	7,196.9	7,826.9	8,617.2	9,580.0	10,786.6

SOURCES: (1960-1966): U.S. Office of Education, *Biennial Survey of Education*. (1968-1980): NCES, *Financial Statistics of Institutions of Higher Education*.

NOTE: Statistics are for the various states plus the District of Columbia and the territories. Where possible, changes in categories for expenditures have been treated to allow comparisons for different years.

TABLE IV-12

ENROLLMENT IN INSTITUTIONS OF HIGHER EDUCATION,
PUBLIC AND PRIVATE, 1870-1980

Year	Total thousands	Public		Private	
		thousands	% of (1)	thousands	% of (1)
	(1)	(2)	(3)	(4)	(5)
1870	52				
1880	116				
1890	157				
1900	238	91	38	147	61
1910	355	167	47	189	53
1920	598	315	52	282	47
1930	1,101	533	48	568	51
1940	1,494	797	53	698	46
1950	2,297	1,154	50	1,142	49
1960	3,583	2,116	59	1,467	40
1961	3,861	2,329	60	1,532	39
1962	4,174	2,574	61	1,601	38
1963	4,766	3,066	64	1,700	35
1964	5,280	3,468	65	1,812	34
1965	5,921	3,970	67	1,951	32
1966	6,390	4,349	68	2,041	31
1967	6,912	4,816	69	2,096	30
1968	7,513	5,431	72	2,082	27
1969	8,005	5,897	73	2,108	26
1970	8,581	6,428	74	2,153	25
1971	8,949	6,804	76	2,144	23
1972	9,215	7,071	76	2,144	23
1973	9,602	7,420	77	2,183	22
1974	10,224	7,989	78	2,235	21
1975	11,185	8,834	78	2,350	21
1976	11,012	8,653	78	2,359	21
1977	11,286	8,847	78	2,439	21
1978	11,260	8,786	78	2,474	21
1979	11,570	9,037	78	2,533	21
1980	12,235	9,518	78	2,717	22

SOURCE: NCES, *Fall Enrollment in Higher Education*.

NOTE: Data are for total enrollment, including both degree credit and other; coverage includes the various states, District of Columbia, and the territories.

West Germany (2.8 times), the Netherlands (2.3 times), and Sweden (2.3 times) were higher than in the United States, albeit with far lower absolute numbers of institutions involved. The findings on levels of enrollment are even more striking. Although enrollments in the United States continued to lead the field as a percentage of the population from 20 to 24 years of age, the 129 percent rise in this proportion from 1957 to 1975 was exceeded by all the other countries mentioned in Table IV-14. The rise in the proportion enrolled

TABLE IV-13

NUMBER OF INSTITUTIONS OF HIGHER EDUCATION,
BY LEVEL OF HIGHEST DEGREE OFFERED AND BY
TYPE OF CONTROL, 1958-1980

Highest Degree Offered	Total Number	Public						Private		
		Total	Federal	State	Local	State and local	State re-lated	Total	Nonde-nomina-tional	De-nomina-tional
1958-1959										
Ph.D. or equivalent	197	86	1	82	3			111	67	44
Master's and/or second professional	449	164	1	151	12			285	136	149
Bachelor's and/or first professional	720	112	5	103	4			608	181	427
No degree 2 to 4 years beyond 12th grade	557	309	1	36	272			248	108	140
Other	34	6	4	2				28	17	11
Total	1,957	677	12	374	291			1,280	509	771
1959-1960										
Ph.D. or equivalent	205	90	1	86	3			115	70	45
Master's and/or second professional	462	170	1	158	11			292	138	154
Bachelor's and/or first professional	718	101	5	91	5			617	179	438
No degree 2 to 4 years beyond 12th grade	585	330	1	38	291			255	111	144
Other	41	7	4	2	1			34	22	12
Total	2,011	698	12	375	311			1,313	520	793
1960-1961										
Ph.D. or equivalent	210	94	1	89	4			116	70	46
Master's and/or second professional	455	171	1	159	11			284	131	153
Bachelor's and/or first professional	739	97	5	88	4			642	189	453
No degree 2 to 4 years beyond 12th grade	593	334	1	39	294			259	114	145
Other	31	7	4	2	1			24	16	8
Total	2,028	703	12	377	314			1,325	520	805
1961-1962										
Ph.D. or equivalent	219	99	1	92	6			120	71	49
Master's and/or second professional	455	171	1	161	9			284	124	160
Bachelor's and/or first professional	741	98	5	89	4			643	183	460

TABLE IV-13
NUMBER OF INSTITUTIONS OF HIGHER EDUCATION,
BY LEVEL OF HIGHEST DEGREE OFFERED AND BY
TYPE OF CONTROL, 1958-1980

Highest Degree Offered	Total Number	Public						Private		
		Total	Federal	State	Local	State and local	State re-lated	Total	Nonde-nomina-tional	De-nomina-tional
No degree										
2 to 4 years										
beyond 12th grade	593	346	1	37	308			247	115	132
Other	32	7	4	2	1			25	19	6
Total	2,040	721	12	381	328			1,319	512	807
1962-1963										
Ph.D. or equivalent	223	104	1	96	7			119	70	49
Master's and/or										
second professional	458	171	1	162	8			287	123	164
Bachelor's and/or										
first professional	766	98	5	89	4			668	186	482
No degree										
2 to 4 years										
beyond 12th grade	628	366	1	39	326			262	117	145
Other	25	4	4					21	19	2
Total	2,100	743	12	386	345			1,357	515	842
1963-1964										
Ph.D. or equivalent	223	106	1	99	6			117	68	49
Master's and/or										
second professional	455	175	1	164	10			280	117	163
Bachelor's and/or										
first professional	792	96	5	87	4			696	192	504
No degree										
2 to 4 years										
beyond 12th grade	644	381	1	43	337			263	113	150
Other	25	4	4					21	17	4
Total	2,139	762	12	393	357			1,377	507	870
1964-1965										
Ph.D. or equivalent	224	107	1	101	5			117	68	49
Master's and/or										
second professional	464	177	1	167	9			287	121	166
Bachelor's and/or										
first professional	801	99	5	90	4			702	194	508
No degree										
2 to 4 years										
beyond 12th grade	656	397	1	55	341			259	110	149
Other	23	4	4					19	14	5
Total	2,168	784	12	413	359			1,384	507	877

TABLE IV-13
NUMBER OF INSTITUTIONS OF HIGHER EDUCATION,
BY LEVEL OF HIGHEST DEGREE OFFERED AND BY
TYPE OF CONTROL, 1958-1980

Highest Degree Offered	Total Number	Public						Private		
		Total	Federal	State	Local	State and local	State re-lated	Total	Nonde-nomina-tional	De-nomina-tional
1965-1966										
Ph.D. or equivalent	227	107	1	101	5			120	70	50
Master's and/or second professional	472	183	1	175	7			289	120	169
Bachelor's and/or first professional	823	99	5	91	3			724	207	517
No degree 2 to 4 years beyond 12th grade	664	397	1	57	339			267	114	153
Other	21	4	4					17	13	4
Total	2,207	790	12	424	354			1,417	524	893
1966-1967										
Ph.D. or equivalent	235	112	1	106	5			123	74	49
Master's and/or second professional	483	188	1	180	7			295	116	179
Bachelor's and/or first professional	828	95	5	87	3			733	215	518
No degree 2 to 4 years beyond 12th grade	685	408	1	61	346			277	117	160
Other	21	3	3					18	14	4
Total	2,252	806	11	434	361			1,446	536	910
1967-1968										
Ph.D. or equivalent	263	123	2	113	8			140	81	59
Master's and/or second professional	511	199		193	6			312	127	185
Bachelor's and/or first professional	828	94	5	81	8			734	230	504
No degree 2 to 4 years beyond 12th grade	866	583	1	149	433			283	123	160
Other	21	1	1					20	15	5
Total	2,489	1,000	9	536	455			1,489	576	913
1968-1969*										
1969-1970										
Ph.D. or equivalent	296	140	2	130	8			156	91	65
Master's and/or second professional	517	200		194	6			317	137	180

TABLE IV-13
NUMBER OF INSTITUTIONS OF HIGHER EDUCATION,
BY LEVEL OF HIGHEST DEGREE OFFERED AND BY
TYPE OF CONTROL, 1958-1980

Highest Degree Offered	Total Number	Public						Private		
		Total	Federal	State	Local	State and local	State re-lated	Total	Nonde-nomina-tional	De-nomina-tional
Bachelor's and/or first professional	835	89	5	79	5			746	289	457
No degree 2 to 4 years beyond 12th grade Other	903	650	1	304	345			253	120	133
Total	2,551	1,079	8	707	364			1,472	637	835
1970-1971										
Ph.D. or equivalent	298	143	2	134	7			155	91	64
Master's and/or second professional	528	202		196	6			326	147	179
Bachelor's and/or first professional	850	93	6	83	4			757	304	453
No degree 2 to 4 years beyond 12th grade Other	897	532		205	327			365	244	121
Total	2,573	970	8	618	344			1,603	786	817
1971-1972										
Ph.D. or equivalent	312	147	2	137	6	2		165	101	64
Master's and/or second professional	543	209		203	6			334	154	180
Bachelor's and/or first professional	828	91	6	77	6	2		737	293	444
No degree 2 to 4 years beyond 12th grade Other	943	705		236	318	151		238	123	115
Total	2,626	1,152	8	653	336	155		1,474	671	803
1972-1973										
Ph.D. or equivalent	327	152	2	143	5	2		175	107	68
Master's and/or second professional	546	213		206	6	1		333	169	164
Bachelor's and/or first professional	843	91	6	77	6	2		752	298	454
No degree 2 to 4 years beyond 12th grade Other	970	737	1	248	318	170		233	122	111
Total	2,686	1,193	9	674	335	175		1,493	696	797

TABLE IV-13
NUMBER OF INSTITUTIONS OF HIGHER EDUCATION,
BY LEVEL OF HIGHEST DEGREE OFFERED AND BY
TYPE OF CONTROL, 1958-1980

Highest Degree Offered	Total Number	Public						Private		
		Total	Federal	State	Local	State and local	State re-lated	Total	Nonde-nomina-tional	De-nomina-tional
1973-1974										
Ph.D. or equivalent	336	152	2	143	5	2		184	112	72
Master's and/or second professional	547	213		206	6	1		334	176	158
Bachelor's and/or first professional	847	81	6	68	5	2		766	319	447
No degree 2 to 4 years beyond 12th grade	1,008	764	1	260	299	204		244	139	105
Other										
Total	2,738	1,210	9	677	315	209		1,528	746	782
1974-1975*										
1975-1976										
Ph.D. or equivalent	401	195	2	181	5	2	5	206	126	80
Master's and/or second professional	597	247		237	6	1	3	350	189	161
Bachelor's and/or first professional	851	103	5	88	6	2	2	748	318	430
No degree 2 to 4 years beyond 12th grade	1,128	897	2	330	216	329	20	231	136	95
Other Undergraduate non-degree grant	15							15	13	2
Graduate non-degree grant	34							34	20	14
Total	3,026	1,442	9	836	233	334	30	1,584	802	782
1976-1977*										
1977-1978										
Ph.D. or equivalent	419	196	2	183		6	5	223	132	91
Master's and/or second professional	617	250	1	238	2	6	3	367	205	162
Bachelor's and/or first professional	849	106	5	90	3	6	2	743	319	424
No degree 2 to 4 years beyond 12th grade	1,155	921	4	343	201	352	21	234	146	88

TABLE IV-13
NUMBER OF INSTITUTIONS OF HIGHER EDUCATION,
BY LEVEL OF HIGHEST DEGREE OFFERED AND BY
TYPE OF CONTROL, 1958-1980

Highest Degree Offered	Total Number	Public						Private		
		Total	Federal	State	Local	State and local	State re-lated	Total	Nonde-nomina-tional	De-nomina-tional
Other										
Undergraduate non-degree grant	18							18	15	3
Graduate non-degree grant	37							37	25	12
Total	3,095	1,473	12	854	206	370	31	1,622	842	780
1978-1979										
Ph.D. or equivalent	427	198	2	186		5	5	229	134	95
Master's and/or second professional	624	254	1	241	3	5	4	370	208	162
Bachelor's and/or first professional	847	98	5	87	1	4	1	749	328	421
No degree 2 to 4 years beyond 12th grade	1,193	924	3	342	199	360	20	269	185	84
Other										
Total	3,091	1,474	11	856	203	374	30	1,617	855	762
1979-1980										
Ph.D. or equivalent	436	203	3	190	0	5	5	233	134	99
Master's and/or second professional	641	253	1	241	2	5	4	388	216	172
Bachelor's and/or first professional	827	94	5	83	0	4	2	733	324	409
No degree 2 to 4 years beyond 12th grade	1,190	925	3	348	195	359	20	265	185	80
Other	58							58	42	16
Total	3,152	1,475	12	862	197	373	31	1,677	901	776

SOURCES: (1958-1974): U.S. Office of Education, *Educational Directory* (Washington, D.C.: Government Printing Office), and NCES, *Education Directory: Higher Education* (Washington, D.C.: Government Printing Office). (1975-1979): NCES, *Digest of Education Statistics*. (1979-1980): NCES, *Education Directory: Colleges and Universities* (Washington, D.C.: Government Printing Office).

* Data were not published for 1968-1969, 1974-1975, and 1976-1977.

TABLE IV-14

HIGHER EDUCATION IN VARIOUS COUNTRIES (NOT INCLUDING TEACHER TRAINING), 1957, 1968, AND 1975

Country	Number of institutions	Enrollment (number of students)	Population ages 20-24 (thousands)	Enrollment as % of age group 20-24
1957				
United States	1,681	2,742,250	11,162[a]	24.6
Canada	33	84,498	1,198[a]	7.1
Belgium	19	37,890	590	6.4
France	22	175,500	3,025[b]	5.8
Western Germany	26	153,923	3,835	4.0
Netherlands	11	32,385	785[b]	4.1
Poland	17	124,094	2,342	5.3
Sweden	15	25,900	432	6.0
Switzerland	9	17,625	360	4.9
United Kingdom	26	97,137	3,310[b]	2.9
1968				
United States	2,483	7,513,091	15,788	47.6
Canada	45	270,093	1,659	16.3
Belgium	22	64,779	682	9.5
France	28	551,940	3,786	14.6
Western Germany	35	430,904	3,524	12.2
Netherlands	19	77,896	1,114	7.0
Poland	25	305,561	2,401	12.7
Sweden	23	115,610	665	17.4
Switzerland	10	38,197	567	6.7
United Kingdom	47	217,625	2,225	9.8
1975				
United States	3,055	11,184,859	19,882.0[c]	56.3
Canada	45	818,153	2,121.4	38.6
Belgium	24	159,660	748.5	21.3
France	75	1,038,576	4,393.8[d]	23.6
Western Germany	73	836,002	4,239.9	19.7
Netherlands	25	288,026	1,130.7	25.5
Poland	78	575,499	3,423.6	16.8
Sweden	34	162,640	564.9	28.8
Switzerland	10	64,720	478.4	13.5
United Kingdom	47	703,645[e]	3,376.6	20.8

SOURCES: The Association of Universities of the British Commonwealth, *Commonwealth Universities Yearbook* (London, 1960, 1971, and 1981 ed.); The International Association of Universities, *International Handbook of Universities and Other Institutions of Higher Education* (London, 1959, 1968, and 1981 ed.); United Nations, Department of International Economic and Social Affairs, Statistical Office, *Statistical Yearbook* (New York, 1959, 1970, and 1971 eds.); United Nations, Department of International Economic and Social Affairs, Statistical Office, *Demographic Yearbook* (New York, 1959 and 1970 ed.); NCES, *Digest of Education Statistics*, 1969; United Nations Educational Scientific and Cultural Organization (UNESCO), *Statistical Yearbook* (Paris, 1981); Marquis Academic Media, *Yearbook of Higher Education* (Chicago: Marquis Who's Who Inc., 1981).

[a] Data for the year 1959.
[b] Data for the year 1958.
[c] Data for the year 1977.
[d] Data for the year 1972.
[e] Data for the year 1974.

in the United Kingdom was 617 percent; in the Netherlands, 522 percent; in Canada, 444 percent; in West Germany, 393 percent; in Sweden, 380 percent; in France, 307 percent; in Belguium, 233 percent; in Poland, 217 percent; and in Switzerland, 176 percent.

Whether this expansion has been accompanied by a decrease in the higher quality of higher education traditionally assumed to exist in these countries is not a matter that we can discuss here. The United States still boasts the most diversified institutional structure for the delivery of higher education, and the problem of identifying appropriate and illuminating points for comparison has not lessened over the past twenty years.

ACADEMIC DEGREES

Machlup clearly feared that the rising percentage of college-age people going on to study at institutions of higher education had already been accompanied by falling standards in comparison to European institutions. His comments on academic degrees awarded in the United States, however, expressed a cautious optimism about our capacity to maintain the academic value of the doctor's degree (see *Production and Distribution of Knowledge*, pp. 90-91). Unfortunately, if numbers are our only guide, this optimism may have been unfounded. Table IV-13 shows that the number of Ph.D. granting institutions more than doubled in the years between 1960 and 1980, a rate of growth that exceeded that of all other types of institutions of higher education.[33] Although Machlup hoped that the rising popularity of undergraduate study would not be accompanied by a rising ratio of doctorate to bachelor's degrees, Table IV-15 shows that in fact it has. Doctorate degrees as a percent of bachelor's degrees rose from 2.50 percent in 1960 to a high of 3.66 percent in 1971, although they then dropped to 3.20 percent and 3.22 percent in 1979 and in 1980, respectively.

NEGLECTED COST ITEMS[34]

This section considers several costs of education that are not included in official published cost data. These opportunity costs include students' foregone earnings and implicit rents and tax exemptions for school buildings and property. In addition, an estimate is made of students' costs for transportation, books, and clothing.

---

[33] Table IV-13 shows that the number of Ph.D. granting institutions rose from 205 in 1959/60 to 436 in 1979/80, or 2.1 times. The number of institutions granting the Master's and/or second professional degree grew from 462 to 641, or 1.4 times; the number of institutions granting the Bachelor's and/or first professional degree grew from 718 to 827, only 1.2 times; and those offering two to four years of education beyond the 12th grade for only a lower degree, or none, rose from 585 to 1,190—2.0 times, but still less than the growth in the number of institutions granting the Ph.D. or equivalent degree.

[34] Machlup, *Production and Distribution of Knowledge*, pp. 92-103.

TABLE IV-15

EARNED DEGREES CONFERRED, BY LEVEL OF DEGREE, 1870-1980

Year	Bachelor's or first professional	Master's or second professional	Doctor's or equivalent	Master's as percent of bachelor's	Doctor's as percent of master's	Doctor's as percent of bachelor's
1870	9,371		1			0.01
1880	12,896	879	54	6.8	6.1	0.42
1890	15,539	1,015	149	6.5	14.7	0.96
1900	27,410	1,583	382	5.8	24.1	1.39
1910	37,199	2,113	443	5.7	21.0	1.19
1920	48,622	4,279	615	8.8	14.4	1.26
1930	122,484	14,969	2,299	12.2	15.4	1.88
1940	186,500	26,731	3,290	14.3	12.3	1.76
1950	432,058	58,183	6,633	13.5	11.4	1.54
1960	392,440	74,435	9,829	19.0	13.2	2.50
1961	401,784	78,269	10,575	19.5	13.5	2.63
1962	417,846	84,855	11,622	20.3	13.7	2.78
1963	447,622	91,366	12,822	20.4	14.0	2.86
1964	498,654	101,050	14,490	20.3	14.3	2.91
1965	535,031	112,124	16,467	21.0	14.7	3.08
1966	551,040	140,555	18,237	25.5	13.0	3.30
1967	583,100	147,300	19,800	25.3	13.4	3.39
1968	666,710	176,749	23,089	26.5	13.1	3.46
1969	764,185	193,756	26,188	25.4	13.5	3.43
1970	827,234	208,291	29,866	25.2	14.3	3.61
1971	877,676	230,509	32,107	26.3	13.9	3.66
1972	930,684	251,633	33,363	27.0	13.3	3.58
1973	972,380	263,371	34,777	27.1	13.2	3.58
1974	999,592	277,033	33,816	27.7	12.2	3.38
1975	978,849	292,450	34,083	29.9	11.7	3.48
1976	988,395	311,771	34,064	31.5	10.9	3.45
1977	983,908	317,164	33,232	32.2	10.5	3.38
1978	987,785	311,620	32,131	31.5	10.3	3.25
1979*	1,001,230	314,250	32,000	31.4	10.2	3.20
1980*	1,017,250	315,090	32,750	31.0	10.4	3.22

SOURCE: NCES, *Digest of Education Statistics.*

* Projected figures.

TABLE IV-16

PROPORTION OF WORKERS IN THE POPULATION
OF FIFTEEN- TO NINETEEN-YEAR-OLDS

Country	Year	Male	Female
United Kingdom	1971	61.1%	55.2%
West Germany	1970	66.7	64.3
Switzerland	1970	62.8	58.7
France	1968	42.5	31.4
United States	1970	40.7	29.3

SOURCE: U.N., *Demographic Yearbook*, 1972, 1979.

EARNINGS FOREGONE

The cost to society, in terms of potential product remaining unproduced, is reflected in the statistics of the different proportions of young workers in various countries who are working. Table IV-16 shows that around 1970, a lower proportion of 15- to 19-year-olds was working in the United States than in several Western European countries. This pattern also holds true for the 20- to 24-year-old age group. Referring to Table IV-14, we see that while 56.3 percent of that age group was enrolled in colleges and universities in the United States in 1975, less than half that proportion was enrolled in various European countries. This pattern of higher school attendance in the United States compared to that in European countries points out both the loss of production felt by the U.S. economy and also the loss of income of the students involved.

Table IV-17 presents estimates of this loss of income for students attending high school, college, and universities. The table summarizes material that was prepared for Machlup by Stephen Kagann. Kagann's methods are described in his article "The Foregone Earnings of High School, College and University Students."[35] Foregone annual earnings per high school student have increased from $1,705 in 1958 to $5,221 in 1980, whereas earnings foregone per college or university student have risen from $1,933 to $7,918 over the same period.

Economy-wide, all students sacrificed earnings totalling $21,552 million in

TABLE IV-17

ANNUAL EARNINGS FOREGONE BY STUDENTS ATTENDING
HIGH SCHOOL, COLLEGE, OR UNIVERSITY: 1958,
1963, 1967, 1972, 1977, AND 1980

Year	Number of full-time students attending		Annual earnings foregone per student attending		Earnings foregone by students attending		
	High school	College or university	High school	College or university	High school	College or university	Total
	(millions)		(dollars)		(millions of dollars)		
1958	8.9	3.3	1,705	1,933	15,172	6,380	21,552
1963	11.5	4.2	2,071	2,395	23,813	10,060	33,873
1967	13.4	5.9	2,435	2,818	32,623	16,624	49,247
1972	15.2	5.7	2,917	4,794	46,962	27,849	74,811
1977	15.8	6.7	4,151	6,259	65,578	41,939	107,517
1980*	15.3	6.6	5,221	7,918	79,886	52,260	132,146

SOURCE: This table summarizes research that was completed by Stephen Kagann. The results for 1972 were published in his article "The Foregone Earnings of High School, College and University Students," *Eastern Economic Journal*, Vol. 2 (October 1975), pp. 331–341. The remaining years were prepared for Machlup by Kagann and have not been published elsewhere.

* 1979 figures.

[35] See the *Eastern Economic Journal*, Vol. 2 (October 1975), pp. 331-341.

1958 and $132,146 million in 1980 in order to attend school. These are, of course, estimates only of wages that were never paid and do not represent actual transactions.

IMPLICIT RENTS OF SCHOOL BUILDINGS AND GROUNDS AND THE COST OF TAX EXEMPTIONS OF SCHOOLS

These elements of our statistical puzzle perhaps present greater difficulties than do any other. The calculation of implicit rents of schools, for example, requires an estimate of the book value of the real property of both public and private elementary and secondary schools and also of both public and private colleges and universities. The computation of the cost of tax exemptions for these institutions requires estimates of the replacement value of their properties and also of the effective property tax rates for various years.

ELEMENTARY AND SECONDARY SCHOOLS

The valuation of the real property of both public and private elementary and secondary schools is our first hurdle. The only available data, from the National Center for Education Statistics (NCES), present neither the book nor the replacement value of this real property. "Value" instead is not precisely defined, but depending upon the state reporting might mean book, replacement, or insurance value. The data are further limited since only public institutions are reported. The authors have been unable to find any reliable measurement of the value of private elementary and secondary schools' real property. If these problems are not sufficient, the final straw on the camel's back might be that the data are also incomplete, representing for any one year only those states that filed voluntary reports. At its low point in 1976, only 29 of the 50 states filed such reports.

The approach we have chosen under these difficult circumstances is to use the NCES information in both the calculation of the implicit rent and tax exemptions of public elementary and secondary schools. We must recognize that the result will be a substantial understatment of these costs since we are working with incomplete data. Further, the definitional problem of the use of "value" as defined by NCES will have opposite effects upon our calculation of implicit rents on the one hand and the cost of tax exemptions on the other. In the computation of implicit rents there will be some tendency to overstate costs since we are unable to use book value, but are instead forced to use a hybrid of book value and replacement costs. In the environment of continued inflation that we saw over these two decades, the replacement cost, and hence the NCES value, of a building or piece of land would almost invariably have been higher than its book value. Conversely, the computation of the cost of tax exemptions will be understated, since the NCES hybrid value would be lower than replacement costs. On balance, there would seem to be a strong downward bias overall.

Table IV-K presents our calculations for the costs of implicit rents and tax exemptions for public and private elementary and secondary schools. In 1980 the implicit rents of public schools are estimated at $5,840 million and of private schools at $716 million. The cost of tax exemptions is estimated at $1,314 million for public schools and $161 million for private schools in 1980.

HIGHER EDUCATION

We are fortunate that the calculation of the costs of implicit rents and tax exemptions for institutions of higher education present far fewer difficulties than those we experienced for elementary and secondary schools. The book value of public and private institutions has been reported at regular intervals for many years by NCES and its predecessors. In addition, the replacement value has been reported annually since 1975. We introduce some downward

TABLE IV-K

IMPLICIT RENT AND COST OF TAX EXEMPTIONS OF ELEMENTARY AND
SECONDARY SCHOOLS: 1958, 1963, 1967, 1972, 1977, AND 1980
(millions of dollars)

Year	Book or other value* (1)	Implicit Rent (.08 × (1)) (2)	Effective property tax rate (3)	Cost of tax exemption (1) × (3) (4)
		Public institutions		
1958	20,641	1,651	.015	310
1963	29,495	2,360	.014	413
1967	31,681	2,534	.018	570
1972	39,494	3,160	.021	829
1977	57,647	4,612	.018	1,038
1980	73,000	5,840	.018	1,314
		Private institutions		
1958	2,726	218	.015	41
1963	3,896	312	.014	55
1967	4,184	335	.018	75
1972	4,700	376	.021	99
1977	6,815	545	.018	123
1980	8,953	716	.018	161

SOURCES: Column (1): Public Institutions: U.S. Office of Education, *Biennial Survey of Education*, and NCES, *Statistics of State School Systems* (Washington, D.C.: Government Printing Office); Private Institutions: Estimated, using the ratio of expenditures by public to private elementary and secondary institutions. Column (3): U.S. Bureau of the Census, *Census of Governments* (Washington, D.C.: Government Printing Office).

NOTE: Data for public institutions are incomplete, representing only those states reporting to a particular survey.

* Whereas the principal basis for determining "value" is original cost plus cost of all additions and alterations, other bases used probably include insurance and replacement costs.

bias into our estimates on the cost of tax exemptions for the years before replacement value is available by making our calculations from book value.
Otherwise, our calculations are straightforward.

Table IV-L presents our calculations for the costs of implicit rents and tax
exemptions for public and private institutions of higher education. In 1980 the
implicit rents of public institutions are estimated at $4,579 million and of pri-
vate institutions at $2,147 million. The cost of tax exemptions is estimated at
$1,560 million for public institutions and $795 million for private institutions
in 1980.

TRANSPORTATION, BOOKS, AND CLOTHING

We follow Machlup's approach in this section of attributing 3 percent of
earnings foregone by high school students and 6 percent of earnings foregone
by college students to the costs of their expenditures for transportation, supplies, and clothing. Working from the estimates of earnings foregone presented

TABLE IV-L

IMPLICIT RENT AND COST OF TAX EXEMPTIONS OF INSTITUTIONS OF
HIGHER EDUCATION: 1958, 1963, 1967, 1972, 1977, AND 1980
(millions of dollars)

Year	Book value (1)	Replacement value (2)	Implicit rent (.08 × (1)) (3)	Effective property tax rate (4)	Cost of tax exemption (1) or (2) × (4) (5)
			Public institutions		
1958	6,462		516	.015	97
1963*	12,500		999	.014	175
1967	18,231		1,458	.018	328
1972	32,562		2,604	.021	684
1977	48,147	63,539	3,851	.018	1,144
1980	57,238	86,668	4,579	.018	1,560
			Private institutions		
1958	4,718		377	.015	71
1963*	8,836		706	.014	124
1967	12,150		971	.018	219
1972	17,757		1,420	.021	373
1977	22,860	32,668	1,828	.018	588
1980	26,838	44,159	2,147	.018	795

SOURCES: Columns (1), (2), and (3): NCES, *Financial Statistics of Institutions of Higher Education*. Column
(4): U.S. Bureau of the Census, *Census of Governments*. The 1980 rate is assumed to be the same as for 1977.

NOTE: For years prior to 1977, where replacement values were not reported, the cost of tax exemption has
been calculated using the book value.

in Table IV-17, we calculate that for all high school students, the results are—in millions of dollars—$455, $714, $979, $1,409, $1,967, and $2,397 respectively for each of the years of our study from 1958 to 1980. The results for all college students are—in millions of dollars—$383, $604, $997, $1,671, $2,516, and $3,136 over the same period.

EDUCATION IN THE CHURCH[36]

Machlup conceived education in the church to include a wide range of local congregational activities, excepting only benevolences and the support of such schools, colleges, and seminaries as are included in national statistics on primary, secondary, and tertiary education. We have little to add to Machlup's historical, theoretical, and practical arguments for considering congregational outlays for local church expenses to be expenditures for education. We have, however, found it necessary to revise Machlup's methods for estimation in order to bring the figures up to date. Our results, presented in Table IV-O, suggest a higher figure than Machlup had proposed in the original text and show that expenditures for education in the church have risen from $3,320 million in 1958 to $17,720 million in 1980.

ESTIMATING THE FUNDS AVAILABLE FOR
CONGREGATIONAL EXPENSES

It is no easier now than it was in 1962 to estimate the expenditures of congregations in the United States. Statistics on church finance are simply not published on a wide enough base. The most detailed source of data remains an annual survey of contributions reported to the National Council of the Churches of Christ (NCC) by some three to five dozen Protestant denominations.[37] As Table IV-M indicates, however, the churches participating in the NCC studies have generally accounted for only one-third of the members of all American churches. Although there are many Protestant bodies that do not report financial data to the NCC, and which, like the Mormons may be expected to have different habits of giving, the most serious problem is that comparable sources on church finance are not available for Roman Catholic and Jewish congregations. From 1958 to 1980 NCC figures show that Roman

---

[36] Machlup, *Production and Distribution of Knowledge*, pp. 64-68.

[37] National Council of the Churches of Christ in the U.S.A., *Yearbook of American Churches* (New York: National Council of the Churches of Christ in the U.S.A.), through the edition for 1971. Beginning with the edition for 1972, the *Yearbook* has been published in Nashville by Abingdon Press and begining with the 1973 edition, the title has been *Yearbook of American and Canadian Churches*. It should be noted that the participant churches have varied from year to year, and thus the results of any one year cannot be compared directly with those of the preceding or following years. The NCC figures represent a composite of donations and expenditures, made necessary by the vicissitudes of accounting practice among reporting religious bodies.

TABLE IV-M

Membership of Religious Bodies in the
United States, 1958-1980

Year	Total number of religious bodies	Total membership (millions)	Number of bodies in NCC sample	Membership in sample (millions)	Membership in sample as percent of total
1958	251	109.6	49	37.8	34
1959	254	112.2	49	34.8	31
1960	259	114.4	47	37.9	33
1961	258	116.1	47	39.3	34
1962	252	117.9	42	40.7	35
1963	253	121.0	41	40.9	34
1964	250	123.3	41	41.3	33
1965	251	124.7			
1966	241	125.8	60		
1967	238	126.4	59	45.1	36
1968	226	128.5	52	43.4	34
1969	230	128.5	48	35.6	28
1970	236	131.0	45	42.9	33
1971	223	131.4	42	47.0	36
1972	223	131.4	39	46.5	35
1973	221	131.2	40	45.5	35
1974	223	132.3	44	45.2	34
1975	223	131.0	43	44.9	34
1976	223	131.9	43	45.2	34
1977	222	132.8	45	46.9	35
1978	222	133.4	42	46.0	34
1979	219	133.5	44	44.6	33
1980	218	134.8	40	44.7	33

Sources: National Council of the Churches of Christ in the U.S.A., *Yearbook of American Churches* (New York, annual ed. through the edition for 1971); National Council of the Churches of Christ in the U.S.A., *Yearbook of American Churches, 1972* (Nashville, Tenn.: Abingdon); National Council of the Churches of Christ in the U.S.A., *Yearbook of American and Canadian Churches* (Nashville, Tenn.: Abingdon, for the editions of 1973 and after). Data for any one year generally appear in the edition published two years later.

Catholics alone comprised between 36 percent and 38 percent of the total membership reported by all religious bodies in the United States.[38]

[38] The NCC warns its readers that criteria of membership differ between denominations. "The Roman Catholics count all baptized persons, including infants. The Jews regard as members all Jews in communities having congregations. The Eastern Orthodox Churches include all persons in their nationality or cultural groups. Most Protestant bodies count only the persons who have attained full membership, and previous estimates have indicated that all but a small minority of these are over 13 years of age. However, many Lutheran bodies and the Protestant Episcopal Church now report all baptized persons, and not only those confirmed." *The Yearbook of American Churches* for 1960, p. 253, and repeated in most subsequent editions. This problem alone would vitiate any naive attempt to generalize *per capita* figures for giving from the NCC studies to other denominations. An *Interfaith Research Study* that projected income for Catholic, Jewish, and Protestant congregations in 1972 is summarized in *The Yearbook of American and Canadian Churches* for 1976, pp. 258-259.

Machlup's strategy for avoiding an impasse was first to construct a set of limiting figures for the relevant years, with minima based on data for Protestant churches from the NCC and maxima based on published estimates of expenditures for all "religious and private welfare organizations." Fortunately, the American Association of Fund-Raising Counsel (AAFRC) now provides estimates of giving to "religion" separately, and we shall use these figures as a more fitting series of maxima for our estimates of total congregational receipts.[39] From Table IV-N we can see that for 1980 the NCC reported that its sample

TABLE IV-N

MINIMUM AND MAXIMUM ESTIMATES OF EXPENDITURES
FOR EDUCATION IN THE CHURCH

Year	Minimum: NCC sample (millions)	Maximum: AAFRC total (millions)	NCC membership as percent of national total	Sample expenditures as percent of AAFRC total
1958	2,352.2	4,150	34	57
1959	2,407.5	4,560	31	53
1960	2,533.1	4,790	33	53
1961	2,708.7	5,010	34	54
1962	2,799.7	5,250	35	53
1963	2,858.6	5,580	34	51
1964	2,973.3	5,910	33	50
1965		6,510		
1966	3,226.5	7,060		46
1967	3,612.7	7,400	36	49
1968	3,580.2	8,220	34	44
1969	3,099.6	8,850	28	35
1970	3,826.9	9,300	33	41
1971	4,386.7	9,980	36	44
1972	4,615.6	10,020	35	46
1973	4,840.3	10,520	35	46
1974	5,278.5	11,940	34	44
1975	5,694.5	12,910	34	44
1976	6,207.2	14,220	34	44
1977	6,765.6	16,930	35	40
1978	7,454.3	18,450	34	40
1979	8,082.8	20,140	33	40
1980	8,781.9	22,150	33	44

SOURCES: Column (1): NCC, *Yearbook of American Churches*, through the 1972 edition; NCC, *Yearbook of American and Canadian Churches*, beginning with the 1973 edition and annually thereafter. Column (2): NCC, *Yearbook of American and Canadian Churches*, 1982. Column (3): From Table IV-M. Column (4): Column 1 as percent of Column 2.

[39] The American Association of Fund-Raising Counsel's estimates are reported in the *Yearbook of American and Canadian Churches*, 1982, p. 253. Estimates by the AAFRC are derived from the figures reported by the NCC and other less systematic, but presumably suggestive, sources on other denominations.

of religious bodies received contributions of $8,782 million, whereas the AAFRC reported total contributions to "religion" of $22,150 million.

It is interesting to note that although the churches reporting to the NCC have accounted for only one-third of church members in the United States, the AAFRC figures (themselves partly based on NCC data) indicate that contributions to these same churches comprised well over half of the total contributions to religious organizations in 1958, and still comprised 44 percent of the total in 1980. These results suggest that extreme caution should be used in generalizing from the patterns reported by the NCC to other denominational groups, especially in the earlier years of our series. Nonetheless, if we are to locate an estimate for congregational expenditures between the minima and the maxima reported in Table IV-N, we must—after warning the reader—do just that.

The only source available for estimating the proportion of contributions made by congregations to their local churches for benevolences, as opposed to congregational expenses, is the annual survey by the NCC. Although churchmen and churchwomen may argue that contributions to benevolence funds are an integral part of spiritual formation to the donors, Machlup preferred to consider benevolences as receipts for the recipients and to exclude contributions to charitable causes from his estimates for education in the church. In lieu of separate data for Catholic and Jewish congregations, we shall simply assume that contributions to all churches in the United States are divided between operating expenses and benevolences in roughly the same proportion as reported by Protestant churches to the NCC. Table IV-O presents our adjustments to the aggregate estimates of contributions to religion provided by the AAFRC. In 1980 benevolences comprised 20 percent of total contributions to the NCC sample of churches; if the same proportion is deducted from the total reported by the AAFRC, our final estimate for funds available to local congregations in 1980 is $17,720 million.

CURRENT EXPENDITURES AND FUTURE INVESTMENT

Given the limitations of the data, our estimates for funds available for local congregational expenses cannot be broken down in much detail. An annual series by the Department of Commerce on the cost of new religious construction based on a nationwide, interdenominational sample can provide estimates for at least one type of expenditure. Table IV-P indicates that only 10 percent of the funds donated for congregational expenses in 1980 were spent on new construction—a notable decline from 26 percent in 1958. As Machlup noted in 1962, these expenditures for new buildings and construction are investments for the future of education in the church, whereas the remainder (spent on salaries, supplies, utilities, etc.) may be considered current congregational expense.

TABLE IV-O

EXPENDITURES FOR EDUCATION IN THE CHURCH

Year	Benevolences as percent of donations for NCC sample (1)	Total donations AAFRC (millions) (2)	Total donations for congregational expenses (millions) (3)
1958	20	4,150	3,320
1959	18	4,560	3,769
1960	18	4,790	3,928
1961	19	5,010	4,058
1962	18	5,250	4,305
1963	19	5,580	4,520
1964	19	5,910	4,787
1965		6,510	
1966		7,060	
1967	19	7,400	5,994
1968	20	8,220	6,576
1969	21	8,850	6,991
1970	20	9,300	7,440
1971	19	9,980	8,084
1972	20	10,020	8,016
1973	20	10,520	8,416
1974	20	11,940	9,522
1975	22	12,910	10,070
1976	21	14,220	11,234
1977	20	16,930	13,544
1978	20	18,450	14,760
1979	20	20,140	16,112
1980	20	22,150	17,720

SOURCES: Column (1): NCC, *Yearbook of American Churches*, through the 1972 edition; NCC, *Yearbook of American and Canadian Churches*, beginning with the 1973 edition, and annually thereafter. Column (2): NCC, *Yearbook of American and Canadian Churches*, 1982. Column (3): Obtained by decreasing the figures in Column 2 by the proportion indicated in Column 1.

EDUCATION IN THE ARMED FORCES[40]

The opportunities for learning skills in the armed services have been so much publicized by recruiters for the volunteer force that there should be few readers left who doubt that at least some of the training offered to members of the Army, Navy, Air Force, and Marines should be considered under the rubric of "education." One may suspect that the promises made by recruiters are sometimes exaggerated, but one should not doubt that exposure to such training is an important feature of military life. For enlisted personnel as well as for officers, for men and women in the reserve as well as for members of the active

[40] Machlup, *Production and Distribution of Knowledge*, pp. 68-70.

TABLE IV-P

EXPENDITURES BY RELIGIOUS BODIES FOR NEW CONSTRUCTION
AND FOR OTHER CONGREGATIONAL EXPENSES
(millions of dollars)

Year	Total donations for congregational expenses (1)	Expenditures for new construction (2)	Funds available for other expenses (3)
1958	3,320	863	2,457
1959	3,769	947	2,792
1960	3,928	1,013	2,915
1961	4,058	1,003	3,055
1962	4,305	1,033	3,272
1963	4,520	1,001	3,519
1964	4,787	992	3,795
1965			
1966			
1967	5,994		
1968	6,576	1,079	5,497
1969	6,991	989	6,002
1970	7,440	929	6,511
1971	8,084	813	7,271
1972	8,016	845	7,171
1973	8,416	814	7,602
1974	9,522	918	8,604
1975	10,070	867	9,203
1976	11,234	956	10,278
1977	13,544	1,046	12,498
1978	14,760	1,248	13,512
1979	16,112	1,548	14,564
1980	17,720	1,637	16,083

SOURCES: Column (1): From Table IV-O, Column 3. Column (2): U.S. Bureau of the Census, *Construction Reports* (Washington, D.C.: Government Printing Office). Column (3): Obtained by subtracting Column 2 from Column 1.

force, careers begin and are punctuated throughout with periods of formal instruction for subsequent assignments.[41]

[41] Harold Clark and Harold Sloan observed in 1964 that "literature is replete with stories of runaway boys who have joined the Army or the Navy to seek adventure and escape school. Whatever may be the opportunities for adventure today, the chances of escaping school are dim"; see *Classrooms in the Military: An Account of Education in the Armed Forces of the United States* (New York: Institute for Instructional Improvement), p. 42. It should not be necessary to point out that the technical and bureaucratic demands of the military place a premium upon the prior preparation of its recruits as well as on their capacity and willingness to learn from the instruction that they receive on a military base. For one account of the barriers encountered in the Navy by servicemen with inadequate literacy skills, see Thomas G. Sticht, "Developing Literacy and Learning Strategies in Organizational Settings," in H. F. O'Neil and C. D. Spielberger, eds., *Cognitive and Affective Learning Strategies* (New York: Academic Press, 1979), pp. 275-307.

TABLE IV-Q

EXPENDITURES OF THE ARMED SERVICES FOR EDUCATION, 1962-1980
(millions of dollars)

Year	Total	Recruit training	Special skill training	Flight training	Officer acquisition training	Professional development education
1962	2296	492	908	554	156	186
1963	2322	518	875	576	167	186
1964	2411	522	947	572	169	201
1965	2593	592	905	664	205	227
1966	3386	902	1277	696	245	266
1967	3822	983	1419	896	232	292
1968	4157	1130	1451	951	295	330
1969	4335	1168	1590	929	301	347
1970	4572	1112	1678	1091	302	389
1971	4533	1009	1654	1097	323	450
1972	4446	1025	1630	964	333	494
1973	4667	1071	1820	838	374	564
1974						
1975	6511	978	3420	1169	352	592
1976	6873	1290	3552	1154	358	519
1977	5978	982	3231	996	370	399
1978	6134	998	3387	939	379	431
1979	5932	1024	2982	1092	424	410
1980	7617	1725	3392	1528	469	503

SOURCES: (1962-1973): Office of the Assistant Secretary of Defense for Manpower, Reserve Affairs, and Logistics, unpublished data. (1975-1980): U.S. Department of Defense, *Military Manpower Training Report* (Washington, D.C.: Government Printing Office).

NOTE: Pay and allowances for the students undergoing training are included in these statistics. For 1980 overhead costs have been distributed on a pro rata basis among the various training categories.

Formal education does not, of course, cover the whole range of learning and training for members of the armed forces. Yet learning gained from experience, though often deemed a valuable outcome of a person's military service, will not be considered here, nor will we consider the training of individuals actually on the job. We omit the former because learning from experience is not to be treated as "education," and we omit the latter because virtually all military units are continually in training to maintain readiness for the missions to which they are assigned. The restriction of our discussion to training conducted outside the context of normal work routines has the advantage of preserving comparability with Machlup's earlier treatment of education in the armed forces, and it conforms to the conventions developed for official reports on the training of military manpower.[42]

[42] See Fritz Machlup's discussion of learning from experience on p. 57 of *Production and Distribution of Knowledge*. The Military Manpower Training Reports actually distinguish between two kinds of training on the job, but exclude both from consideration. First, they restrict them-

We need no longer rely upon isolated estimates of the costs of this training. Since 1962 the Department of Defense has reported annually on the funding required for its education programs. Table IV-Q presents the figures from these reports in millions of dollars. Expenditures for education in the armed forces, including the pay and allowances for students in training, rose by 232 percent, from $2,296 million in 1962, to $7,617 million in 1980.

TYPES OF MILITARY TRAINING

Machlup's division of education in the armed forces into "basic" and "special" training would seem to exhaust the logical possibilities of the field. As Table IV-Q indicates, however, publications of the Department of Defense distinguish five major types of military training in place of Machlup's two:

(1) *Recruit Training*, given to all enlisted entrants to the Services who have not had previous military service;
(2) *Specialized Skill Training*, needed to perform specific jobs in the Military Service;
(3) *Flight Training*, primarily for prospective pilots and navigators before they receive an initial operational assignment;
(4) *Officer Acquisition Training*, which leads to a commission in one of the Services;
(5) *Professional Development Education*, relating to the professional duties of senior military personnel or in advanced academic disciplines to meet service requirements.[43]

We shall follow Machlup's practice and discuss "basic" (recruit) training and "special" (specialized skill and flight) training as the principal forms of education in the armed forces: together these have accounted for at least 80 percent of the military's training budget since 1962. Officer acquisition training and

---

selves to "individual training and education" as opposed to the "training of operational mission units or crews," and then they restrict themselves to formal education as opposed to the training received by individuals new to a job. The latter is sometimes referred to as a substitute for, and sometimes as a supplement to, formal course training, but it is not considered in official estimates for "training loads" and costs. See, for example, U.S. Department of Defense, *Military Manpower Training Report for FY 1982* (Washington, D.C.: Government Printing Office, 1981), pp. 2 and I-1.

[43] These definitions are given each year in the *Military Manpower Training Report*. From 1962 to 1973, the categories were somewhat different: Recruit Training, Specialized Training, Professional Training, Flight Training, Service Academies, Reserve Officer Training Corps (ROTC), and Education Programs (Other). The two series, from 1962-1973, and from 1975-1980 are therefore not entirely consistent. We have added the figures for the service academies and for ROTC to arrive at the figures listed under Officer Acquisition Training for the earlier period. We have not attempted to correct for the few changes in the classification of specific programs. Officer training schools, for example, used to be treated as "Specialized Training" but were later switched to "Officer Acquisition Training."

professional development education present some special statistical problems
that will be discussed separately below.

BASIC AND SPECIAL TRAINING PROGRAMS

Basic training still appears to have the same emphasis on "physical exercise,
marching drills, promptness, superficial neatness, and potato peeling" sus-
pected by Machlup in 1962. We may add form filling and test taking to the list,
as well as instruction in the use and care of weapons and other military equipment. The purpose of basic training is to bridge the gap between civilian and
military life as quickly and thoroughly as possible, but each service has its own
ideas about how this is best done. Recruit training varies in time from six weeks
in the Air Force to over ten weeks in the Marines. This discrepancy is explained by noting that the Air Force does not believe that its entrants need
many skills in common, whereas the Marine Corps wants all of its recruits to
be proficient in ground combat techniques regardless of their later occupation.[44]

Virtually all entrants to the services are assigned to special skill or flight training courses after the completion of basic training, and those who stay past an
initial tour of duty are likely to return for more advanced instruction in their
particular fields of expertise. Officers also receive special skill and flight training at "initial" and "progressive" levels. Each service recognizes a large number of occupational specialties required for its operations, and although some
courses are now provided jointly (for example, in weather forecasting, music,
computer programming, foreign languages, etc.), most training is conducted
separately by the different branches of service.

The most heavily enrolled courses for initial skill training reflect similarities
as well as differences in the services' occupational needs. In 1981-1982,
administration (clerking) was among the top five or six courses for the Army,
the Marines, and the Air Force. Supply and inventory management appeared
in lists for both the Army and the Air Force, and basic electronics was a common specialty for the Navy and the Marines. Other heavily enrolled courses,
unique to the different services, included basic medical specialist, food service
specialist, and motor transport officer in the Army; apprentice training as sea-
man, fireman, airman, or constructionman in the Navy; rifleman, field radio
operator, and mortarman in the Marines; security specialist and aircraft main-

---

[44] See the section on "Course Length and Course Content" in the chapter on recruit training in
any of the Military Manpower Training Reports. The "emphases" in basic training that are mentioned in Machlup's text may be compared with the following statement from the 1977 report:
"Recruit Training in each of the Services covers four areas: (1) some processing and testing; (2)
introduction into Service life; (3) instruction in military courtesy, discipline, and hygiene; and (4)
fundamental military-related training involving physical fitness, military drill, and self-defense"
(U.S. Department of Defense, *Military Manpower Training Report*, p. III-9).

tenance specialist in the Air Force. Flight training is provided by all the services, but is understandably undertaken on the largest scale by the Air Force.

We can see from Table IV-Q that expenditures for basic and special training
appear to be complementary: when one has fallen in proportion to the total
training budget, the other has risen. During the height of the war in Viet Nam
in 1968 and 1969, basic training accounted for 27 percent of the expenditures
for education in the armed forces, while flight training and special skill training
together accounted for 58 percent of the training budget. By contrast, from
1975 to 1979 basic training accounted for 15 to 19 percent of training expenditures, and the share allocated for special training was at its height, from 69 to
71 percent.

OFFICER ACQUISITION TRAINING AND PROFESSIONAL
DEVELOPMENT EDUCATION

Although basic and special training programs are conducted almost entirely
on military bases and are not usually considered in accounts for education in
the United States, many of the programs that comprise officer acquisition
training and professional development education raise problems concerning
double counting. The military academies, for example, are included in the figures reported for officer acquisition training in Table IV-Q, but they are also
considered institutions of higher education by the National Center of Education Statistics and are included in their figures for colleges and universities as
well. The military's expenditures for the Reserve Officer Training Corps (reported by the Department of Defense as part of military manpower training
from 1962-1973), include scholarship funds paid directly to the colleges and
universities from which student participants are drawn, and several programs
for professional development education provide scholarships for persons already in active military status to study at civilian institutions.[45]

We can deduct the expenses of the military academies from the total figures
presented in Table IV-Q, but we shall have to tolerate double counting in the
case of the scholarship funds. The figures that are available for officer acquisition training and for professional development education do not allow us to
separate direct payments to civilian institutions from other expenses incurred
by the military when its members are in school (for example, the salaries of
those undergoing training). Nor, for that matter, can we separate scholarship
programs from others that are run entirely on military installations. Commis-
sioning programs that are run off-campus during the summers, for example,
are not reported elsewhere, nor are expenditures for the officer training schools

[45] After 1973 only programs for personnel in an active military status were included in the financial statistics reported in the military manpower training reports. Thus the Reserve Officer
Training Corps, which actually supplies more officers to the armed services than do the service
academies, is excluded from the figures for 1975-1980.

that enable enlisted men to qualify for commission. Professional Development Education includes, besides opportunities for graduate and undergraduate study, a ranked series of service schools and war colleges where selected officers take courses en route to assignments of greater responsibility and/or prestige.

Table IV-R presents the figures for the military academics separately, and Table IV-S presents the figures that result from deducting expenditures for the academies from the total for education in the armed forces as reported in Table IV-Q. When we summarize our findings on nationwide expenditures for education, these adjusted figures will be used for our entries on training in the military. The figure that we will report for 1980 is $7299 million.

Commercial Vocational Schools[46]

Commercial vocational schools receive special notice in *The Production and Distribution of Knowledge in the United States* as the only "entry according to market value" in the summary table on the total costs of education. Most ed-

TABLE IV-R

Expenditures of the Service Academies, 1962-1980
(millions of dollars)

Year	Army	Air Force	Navy	Total
1962	21.4	31.6	36.1	89.1
1963	27.3	28.7	40.2	96.2
1964	30.2	29.7	33.3	93.2
1965	50.5	42.4	33.1	126.0
1966	59.0	50.6	50.0	159.6
1967	36.5	50.3	38.3	125.1
1968	56.5	47.2	42.2	145.9
1969	57.9	47.5	44.2	149.6
1970	65.9	55.4	62.7	184.0
1971	70.9	57.4	66.1	194.4
1972	68.1	55.6	65.6	189.3
1973	80.9	62.8	69.9	213.6
1974	91.9	82.5	67.9	242.3
1975	100.1	89.4	68.7	258.2
1976	104.4	98.5	74.3	277.2
1977	112.2	103.9	77.8	293.9
1978	121.2	108.8	47.2	277.2
1979	125.1	112.9	65.2	303.2
1980	140.9	121.1	55.8	317.8

Sources: U.S. Department of Defense, unpublished data.

Note: Data for 1978 to 1980 for the Naval Academy do not include cadet pay or allowances.

[46] Machlup, *Production and Distribution of Knowledge*, p. 105.

TABLE IV-S

ADJUSTED TOTAL FOR EDUCATION IN THE ARMED FORCES
(millions of dollars)

Year	Total in Table IV-Q (1)	Total academies (2)	Adjusted total (1)-(2)
1962	2296	89	2207
1963	2322	96	2226
1964	2411	93	2318
1965	2593	126	2467
1966	3386	160	3226
1967	3822	125	3697
1968	4157	146	4011
1969	4335	150	4185
1970	4572	184	4388
1971	4533	194	4339
1972	4446	189	4257
1973	4667	214	4453
1974		242	
1975	6511	258	6253
1976	6873	277	6596
1977	5978	294	5684
1978	6134	277	5857
1979	5932	303	5629
1980	7617	318	7299

SOURCES: Column (1). From Table IV-Q, Column 1. Column (2): From Table IV-R, Column 4.

ucational institutions in the United States do not "sell" their services at cost-covering prices. Day-care homes and for-profit day-care centers and nursery schools may be one exception to this general rule. Postsecondary, noncollegiate vocational education, however, remains the only field in which private, for-profit enterprise ranks as the principal provider.

Although Machlup recorded that commercial vocational schools enjoyed gross receipts of $196 million in 1955-1956, and $223 million in 1957-1958, he did not note the source for these figures. Fortunately, two new sources for the construction of our statistical series have since become available. In 1963 the "Statistics of Income" series published by the Internal Revenue Service began to report separately the receipts of businesses engaged in providing educational services and then, in 1974, the National Center for Education Statistics initiated its series on "Enrollments and Programs in Noncollegiate Post-Secondary Schools." Whereas the IRS figures enable us to present estimates of sales from 1963 through 1980, the NCES series will make it possible to provide a statistical portrait of the place of for-profit schools in the general field of postsecondary noncollegiate education during the later years of our study.

REVENUES OF COMMERCIAL VOCATIONAL SCHOOLS

Table IV-T presents data on the numbers and revenues of businesses providing educational services as reported by the IRS for the Standard Industrial Classification's "Major Group 82." These figures require some comment because
this grouping actually appears to include establishments that we have already
discussed. In addition to commercial vocational schools, "Major Group 82"
includes elementary and secondary schools; colleges and universities, and
professional schools; junior colleges and technical institutes; and libraries and
information centers. The reader should recall, however, that so far we have
dealt only with nonprofit organizations, whereas the IRS materials deal only
with for-profit businesses. These figures thus represent real additions to the
costs of education that we have reported so far. It should also be pointed out
that as few elementary and secondary schools, colleges and universities, and
libraries or information centers are operated on a for-profit basis, most of the
institutions and revenues reported in Table IV-T are, in fact, for commercial
vocational education.

TABLE IV-T

NUMBER AND REVENUES OF BUSINESSES PROVIDING
EDUCATIONAL SERVICES, 1963-1980

Year	Number of businesses			Business receipts (thousands)			
	Proprietorships	Partnerships	Corporations	Proprietorships	Partnerships	Corporations	Total
1963	86,633	1,498	2,976	$302,846	$30,532	$336,078	$669,456
1964	92,044	1,517	3,290	308,477	37,763	388,957	735,197
1965	90,748	2,487	3,383	359,262	72,683	353,792	785,737
1966	94,585	1,520	3,600	365,609	24,173	457,465	847,247
1967	97,686	1,129	4,633	443,252	38,309	606,365	1,087,926
1968	94,852	2,483	6,122	403,356	55,467	881,695	1,340,518
1969	102,403	1,893	6,204	470,566	61,732	979,753	1,512,051
1970	107,059	2,467	7,687	542,095	47,216	828,888	1,418,199
1971	101,203	2,922	6,749	443,563	68,043	921,491	1,433,097
1972	118,701	2,654	7,878	643,242	72,341	987,651	1,703,234
1973	93,488	1,987	9,049	470,802	89,964	1,497,842	2,058,608
1974	89,773	1,963	7,819	440,390	89,471	1,328,439	1,858,300
1975	115,193	1,696	8,610	652,353	72,739	1,540,540	2,265,632
1976	113,632	1,832	9,525	723,017	97,413	1,910,414	2,730,844
1977	127,470	2,780	14,358	754,576	107,170	2,125,713	2,987,459
1978	134,450	2,955	11,700	856,729	104,848	2,423,237	3,384,814
1979	150,237	2,894	12,376	1,318,587	116,337	2,756,983	4,191,907
1980	176,148	3,448	10,515	1,260,138	148,569	3,400,400	4,809,107

SOURCE: Internal Revenue Service, *Statistics of Income* (Washington, D.C.: Government Printing Office).

NOTE: For 1969-1972, dollar figures given for partnerships are total receipts because business receipts were not available. For
1973-1976, figures given for both proprietorships and partnerships pertain to those businesses that earned net income, whereas all
other figures pertain to all businesses (with and without net income).

Commercial vocational schools are, of course, a most diverse group and include (1) correspondence schools, (2) data-processing schools, (3) business and secretarial schools; (4) schools specializing in trade and commercial courses such as aviation, banking, commercial art, practical nursing, etc.; and (5) other specialized schools for art, drama, language, music, public speaking, vocational counselling, etc. The only important skills frequently taught by for-profit institutions that are excluded from the IRS figures are beauty parlor operation and barbering. We will simply assume that the underreporting caused by the exclusion of these two groups of schools will be roughly matched by the overreporting caused by the inclusion of the few for-profit academic and professional institutions mentioned above. We shall retain Machlup's figures for 1958 in our summary tables, but shall take the IRS figures for 1963, 1967, 1973, 1977, and 1980 as the best available approximations for the income of businesses providing vocational education on a for-profit basis.

Two important features of this educational domain are displayed in the figures presented in Table IV-T: the great number of for-profit businesses providing educational services and their diversity in size, as measured by business receipts. The total number of businesses rose from 91,107 in 1963 to 190,111 in 1980, or 2.1 times, while total receipts rose from $669 million in 1963 to $4,809 million in 1980, or 7.2 times. Of course, these total figures obscure differences between proprietorships, partnerships, and corporations. From 1963 to 1980, we can calculate that the average receipts of proprietorships rose from $3,500 to $7,150, or 2.0 times; the average receipts of partnerships rose from $20,380 to $43,090, or 2.1 times; and the average receipts of corporations increased from $112,930 to $323,390, or 2.9 times. The rise in total receipts of 7.2 times is in part explained by the fact that the number of corporations—with their larger average receipts—rose at a greater rate (3.5 times) than the number of proprietorships (2.0 times) and partnerships (2.3 times) over the period under consideration.

In comparison with overall expenditures for education in the United States (see Summary Table IV), the receipts of commercial vocational schools are quite low. Machlup's figure for commercial vocational schools and special residential schools combined amounted to 0.4 percent of the total costs of education in 1958, although our figures show that commercial vocational schools accounted for an increasing percent of the total thereafter, rising from 0.7 percent in 1963 to 1.4 percent in 1980. Comparison with the monetary expenditures of colleges and universities may be more helpful. In 1958 the receipts of commercial vocational and special residential schools amounted to 6.3 percent of the expenditures of institutions of higher education, and thereafter rose to 8.4 percent in 1963, 7.5 percent in 1967, 8.2 percent in 1972, 9.5 percent in 1977, and 11.6 percent in 1980. It is interesting to note that in 1978, when the receipts of commercial vocational schools reported by the IRS were 10.0 percent of our total allowed expenditures for institutions of higher education,

NCES statistics showed enrollments to be in roughly the same proportion, i.e., the 1,193.4 thousand enrollments in commercial vocational schools reported by the NCES were 10.6 percent of the 11,260 thousand enrollments in institutions of higher education (see Table IV-U and IV-5).

ENROLLMENTS AND TYPES OF COMMERCIAL VOCATIONAL SCHOOLS

The information compiled by the National Center for Education Statistics on enrollments and programs in commercial vocational schools covers a somewhat different field than the information on business receipts published by the Internal Revenue Service. In 1978, for example, the NCES reported on 5,896 private for-profit schools—only 4 percent of the total number of such businesses reported by the IRS in the same year. There is no doubt, however, that the findings of the NCES pertain to a substantial portion of the field, as measured in monetary terms. The programs offered by these 5,896 for-profit schools accounted for receipts of $1,751.4 million in 1978—i.e., slightly over half (51.7 percent), of the amount reported by the IRS.

Table IV-U presents the latest NCES data that are available on for-profit schools as a separate category. We can see from this table that while the cosmetology/ barber schools that were omitted from the IRS figures form 37 percent of the schools surveyed by the NCES, they accounted for only 14 percent of the enrollments in 1978. The highest enrollments were enjoyed by schools specializing in business/office skills such as accounting, data processing, word processing, and secretarial training, including special-purpose instruction in court reporting, insurance, real estate and sales.[47] Data from a smaller sample

[47] The following definitions of terms are from the NCES publication, *Enrollments and Programs in Noncollegiate Postsecondary Schools* (Washington, D.C.: Government Printing Office, 1978), p. 63:

Vocational/technical school: A school offering a wide variety of occupational programs or clusters of programs. . . .

Technical institutes: An institution (usually 2-year) offering instruction in one or more of the technologies at a level above the skilled trades and below the professional level.

Business/commercial school: A school offering programs in business occupations such as accounting, data processing, word processing, and secretarial. Special-purpose schools that offer the following programs are included: Court reporting, finance, insurance, real estate, and sales.

Cosmetology/barber school: A school offering programs in hairstyling for men and women and in the care and beautification of hair, complexion, and hands.

Flight school: A school offering programs for training as aircraft mechanic, commercial pilot, or in other technical fields related to aviation.

Trade school: A school offering training in one trade or craft or a single cluster of trades or crafts, such as auto mechanics, baking, bartending, carpentry, commercial diving, cooking, dog grooming, drafting, fire protection, horseshoeing, locksmithing, meat processing, police training, truck driving, and welding.

Arts/design school: A school offering training in the performing arts, such as acting, dance, music, and singing; creative design, such as commercial art, fashion design, floristry, interior design, and photography; and radio/television broadcasting.

TABLE IV-U

NUMBER, ENROLLMENTS, AND AVERAGE CHARGE PER PROGRAM OF COMMERCIAL VOCATIONAL SCHOOLS, 1978

Type of School	Number	Percent	Enrollment (thousands)	Percent	Average charge	Total (millions)
Noncorrespondence						
Vocational/technical	76	1	66.0	7		
Technical institute	83	1	21.3	2		
Business/office	1,201	21	423.1	46		
Cosmetology/barber	2,162	37	132.4	14		
Flight	1,055	18	62.6	7		
Trade	616	11	116.1	13		
Arts/design	220	4	32.4	3		
Hospital	18		1.6			
Allied health	195	3	42.6	5		
Other	188	3	29.7	3		
Total	5,814	100	927.8	100	$1,616	$1,499.3
Correspondence	82		265.6		$949	$252.1
Total	5,896		1,193.4			$1,751.4

SOURCE: NCES, *Enrollments and Programs in Noncollegiate Postsecondary Schools* (Washington, D.C.: Government Printing Office, 1978).

NOTE: The average charge is computed for programs offered by all private noncollegiate postsecondary schools and thus includes charges for programs offered by 999 nonprofit institutions, 75 percent of which are hospitals.

of these schools indicate that the average charge for programs in the business/office field was $1821, while the average charges for programs in cosmetology and barbering were $842 and $1265 respectively.[48] If these charges are indeed representative, it is clear that the receipts of business/office schools account for more and the receipts of cosmetology/barber schools account for less of the total revenue of commercial vocational schools than even the enrollment figures suggest.

For our purposes, the most interesting findings of the NCES concern the place of for-profit schools in the field of noncollegiate postsecondary education as a whole. Table IV-V shows that while the proportion of noncorrespondence schools remained relatively constant between the public and private, and for-

---

Hospital school: A hospital offering programs in paraprofessional health or medical fields, such as nursing or radiologic technology.

Allied health school: A school (other than hospital school) offering programs in paraprofessional health or medical fields, such as dental assisting, medical assisting, practical nursing, and mortuary science.

Other: Schools or institutions not classified in any of the above groups include schools of modeling, brewing, maritime occupations, and horsemanship.

[48] NCES, *Enrollments and Programs in Noncollegiate Postsecondary Schools*, 1978, table A-11, pp. 44-45.

TABLE IV-V

NUMBER AND ENROLLMENTS IN NONCORRESPONDENCE SCHOOLS OFFERING NONCOLLEGIATE,
POSTSECONDARY PROGRAMS: 1974, 1976, AND 1978

	1974		1976		1978	
	Number of Schools					
Public	892	(10%)	990	(12%)	812	(11%)
Private	7,824		7,509		6,813	
For Profit	6,512	(75%)	6,435	(76%)	5,814	(76%)
Nonprofit	1,312	(15%)	1,074	(13%)	999	(13%)
Total	8,716	(100%)	8,499	(100%)	7,625	(100%)
	Enrollments (thousands)					
Public	453.7	(34%)	468.4	(33%)	451.8	(30%)
Private	887.4	(66%)	930.7		1,043.4	
For Profit			778.9	(56%)	927.8	(62%)
Nonprofit			151.8	(11%)	115.6	(8%)
Total	1,341.1	(100%)	1,399.1	(100%)	1,495.2	(100%)

SOURCE: NCES, *Enrollments and Programs in Noncollegiate Postsecondary Schools*, 1978.

profit and nonprofit sectors between 1974 and 1978, the proportion of enrollments in private schools grew from 66 percent to 70 percent over these four
years and that enrollments in schools run on a for-profit basis increased from
56 percent to 62 percent of total enrollments between 1976 and 1978. The relative popularity of commercial vocational schools appears to be related to the
length of their program: Even though the average charge is less at public
schools ($345 in 1978, as compared to $1,616 for private schools), the length
of public programs was longer (14 months as compared to 10 months in the
private sector). As the authors of the NCES report point out, this means that
private school students "can enter the labor market 4 months earlier, thus earn-
ing a salary or wage while their counterparts are still in public school."[49]

TRAINING ON THE JOB[50]

Some readers will be surprised to see that we have not included separate figures
for training on the job in our summary table on the total costs of education in
the United States. There are two reasons for this omission. First, although estimates of national expenditures for training on the job have been published
for one or another specific year, these vary so much in the care with which they

[49] NCES, *Enrollments and Programs in Noncollegiate Postsecondary Schools*, 1978, p. 11. A
suggestive comparison of curricula in secretarial studies at "proprietary business schools" and community colleges may be found in Elizabeth Swain Kasl, "Proprietary Occupational Schools," in
Richard E. Anderson and Elizabeth Swain Kasl, *The Costs and Financing of Adult Education
and Training* (Lexington, Mass.: D.C. Heath and Company), pp. 92-93.
[50] Machlup, *Production and Distribution of Knowledge*, pp. 57-64.

have been presented and in their definitions of "expenditures" and "training" that they simply cannot provide support for the series of estimates that we would have to make in order to update Machlup's figures from 1956 and 1958 to 1980. Second, and of even greater concern, is the fact that a relatively large—if not fully specifiable—proportion of the expenditures reported in recent studies are made for services and/or supplies registered elsewhere in our accounts. Employers not only pay members of their own staff to develop training programs and to instruct trainees, but they also provide tuition aid to employees who wish to attend college and university courses, and they purchase training supplies and services from other suppliers whose income is reported in this chapter (commercial vocational schools) and in the chapters on media of communication (book publishers, conventions), information services (management consultants), and information machines (i.e., corporate suppliers of computer equipment).

In view of the inadequate data at our disposal, and in view of the dangers of double counting involved in the use of such data, we have decided to limit our discussion to some of the most widely cited estimates for training on the job in recent years and not to add new estimates to a literature already overburdened with speculation. The reader should realize, however, that in so doing, we are omitting from our accounts a field that most students believe to be extremely large, and one that has grown at a rapid rate.

NATIONAL EXPENDITURES FOR FORMAL TRAINING PROGRAMS

Most national estimates of the resources committed to the training of employees are, curiously, for expenditures on formal training programs in which the trainees are in classrooms and not actually "on the job."[51] Although estimates of expenditures for these programs alone are sizeable, Machlup noted in *The Production and Distribution of Knowledge in the United States* that the cost of the informal training that takes place while employees are actually on their jobs is likely to be much higher and much more difficult to estimate, involving considerations of productivity, supervision, maintenance and depreciation, accident rates, and inspection. Higher still in dollar value and involving even more complex considerations are the investments made by employees in learning on the job. Fortunately, for our task of exposition, Machlup excluded such investments from his education accounts on the grounds that "this learning process is not paid for by an employer, nor guided by a supervisor, and not designed as training for the job assigned to a new employee." We may note here, however, that Machlup cited Jacob Mincer's estimate that employees' in-

---

[51] In a later discussion of issues in the theory of human capital, Machlup uses the term "in-service training" to encompass training that is "separate from actual work performance." See Fritz Machlup, *The Economics of Information and Human Capital*, vol. III of *Knowledge: Its Creation, Distribution, and Economic Significance* (Princeton, N.J.: Princeton University Press, 1984), p. 434.

vestments in learning on the job amounted to $12.5 billion in 1958.[52] Machlup himself estimated that employers spent $2 billion on informal training, and $1 billion on formal training programs in the same year. He warned, however, that the pattern of employers' expenditures on training would be likely to change in the future as the rate of labor turnover changed and in concert with changes in the ratio of skilled to unskilled work.

What, then, have employers spent on training in more recent years? Seymour Lusterman's estimate of $2 billion and Thomas Gilbert's estimate of $100 billion—both for 1975—are frequently cited to indicate the extremes within which the answer may lie. Although many writers use the immense gap between these figures to indicate the difficulties inherent in the exercise, a careful examination shows that Lusterman's and Gilbert's findings are not as wildly divergent as they appear. Gilbert's figure of $100 billion is an estimate of the costs of formal and informal training for the entire civilian labor force, including the salaries of trainees, while Lusterman's figure of $2 billion is an estimate of expenditures by large corporations for formal training programs only, and excludes the salaries of trainees. Expenditures for formal training programs excluding trainee compensation, comprise only 9 percent of Gilbert's estimate, or $9 billion. Although the remaining gap of $7 billion is still considerable, the two estimates could be brought even closer by extrapolating from Lusterman's large corporations to the economy as a whole. Yet even this exercise would be of little value. Lusterman's study was designed to map differences between expenditures for training among companies of different types and sizes, whereas Gilbert's article was a promotion piece, designed to boost the morale of specialists in the training and development field.[53]

One other national estimate, far exceeding those of Lusterman and Gilbert, has also received attention in the literature. This study, sponsored by the American Society for Training and Development (ASTD), proposes that public and private employers spent neither $2 billion nor $9 billion on formal training programs in 1980, but $30 billion instead. It is interesting to note that if one accepts Machlup's figure of $1 billion for such expenditures in 1958 and ASTD's estimate of $30 billion for 1980, one would have to conclude that expenditures for formal training programs for the employees of business and gov-

[52] Machlup's discussion of learning on the job was written before the publication of Mincer's study. See Jacob Mincer, "On-the-Job Training: Costs, Returns, and Some Implications," *Journal of Political Economy*, Vol. 70, Suppl. (October 1962), pp. 50-79.

[53] Seymour Lusterman, *Education In Industry* (New York: The Conference Board, 1977); Thomas Gilbert, "Training: The $100 Billion Opportunity," *Training and Development Journal*, Vol. 30, No. 11 (November 1976), pp. 3-8. Gilbert's total of $100 billion includes an estimate of $90 billion for "scheduled" training, and $10 billion for the costs of "OJT" (on-the-job, or informal, training). He estimated that "student costs" (wages, etc.) accounted for 90 percent of employers' expenditures for scheduled training (p. 3). Thus, his total estimate includes $9 billion for the costs of developing and delivering "scheduled training," and $81 billion for "student costs" in these formal training programs.

ernment in the United States grew 30 times in a period of twenty-two years. The total number of employed civilians, incidentally, grew only 1.6 times during these same years, from 64.0 million in 1958 to 99.3 million in 1980.[54]

Is such a growth in expenditures for formal training plausible? Table IV-W shows that total expenditures reported by the federal government for the training of civilian employees rose only 4.1 times from 1967 to 1980. Of course, private employers may have increased spending on formal training at a rate far higher than the federal government. Yet a growth in expenditures of 30 times is so far out of line with the growth that we have documented for any other area of educational expenditure from 1958 to 1980 that this alone should justify our decision to exclude these estimates for formal training programs from our summary table. No serious estimates for informal training are available, so we cannot even begin to address the interesting question of whether increases in ex-

TABLE IV-W

EXPENDITURES FOR EMPLOYEE TRAINING IN THE
FEDERAL SERVICE, 1967-1980

Year	Individuals trained (thousands)	Total costs (millions)	Salaries of training personnel (millions)	Other direct costs (millions)	Travel and per diem (millions)
1967	1,009	$ 80	$ 46	$ 23	$ 11
1968	1,035	84	63	20	11
1969					
1970					
1971	968	200	105	($95)	
1972	946	182	74	46	62
1973	958	174	74	48	52
1974		178	64	46	68
1975		199	70	53	76
1976		238	86	59	93
1977	556	257	97	63	97
1978	516	276	111	71	94
1979	504	288	112	80	96
1980	522	327	128	108	92

SOURCE: (1967-1977): U.S. Civil Service Commission, *Employee Training in the Federal Service* (Washington, D.C.: Government Printing Office). (1978-1980): U.S. Office of Personnel Management, *Employee Training in the Federal Service* (Washington, D.C.: Government Printing Office).

NOTE: The figures on total costs for 1967-1971 use a different method of computing the salaries of training personnel than the figures of later years.

[54] Some of the findings of the study sponsored by the American Society for Training and Development are discussed by Robert L. Craig and Christine J. Evers, "Employers as Educators: The 'Shadow Education System,' " in Gerard G. Gold, ed. *Business and Higher Education: Toward New Alliances* (San Francisco: Jossey Bass, 1981), pp. 29-44. The statistics on the labor force are from the 1960 and 1982-1983 editions of the U.S. Bureau of the Census, *Statistical Abstract of the United States*.

penditures for formal training programs have been accompanied by a decrease in the costs of informal training incurred while employees literally remain on the job.

THE DANGERS OF DOUBLE COUNTING

If the rate of growth of expenditures for formal training programs for employees cannot yet be ascertained, there is no doubt that a training industry has developed to sell training products and services to employers who wish to offer such programs to their employees. In their article "Employers as Educators: The 'Shadow Education System,' " Robert Craig and Christine Evers suggest as "one believable estimate" that "35 percent to 40 percent of employers' training expenditures were spent externally with the rapidly growing training industry."[55] Although we have found no evidence for or against this particular estimate it is clear from the more carefully documented studies available that the proportion of external expenditures may indeed be high.

The categories used to classify training programs in the literature on employer-provided training seldom make clear and consistent distinctions between internal and external expenditures. Seymour Lusterman's study of corporations employing over 500 people, for example, distinguishes (1) "company courses . . . in which all participants are employees of the firm providing them," (2) "tuition-aid program courses," and (3) "other outside courses . . . that are open to a wider public than employees of a particular company." Lusterman found that 20 percent of total expenditures on formal training were for the latter two types, which are—by definition—supplied by external agencies: colleges and universities; "corporate suppliers"; "such organizations as the American Management Association and The Conference Board"; "professional and trade groups"; and "proprietary organizations and consultants." Company courses, too, however, may "be designed and conducted by company personnel, by outside institutions and contractors, or by the two together."[56]

Lusterman suggests that 80 percent of total expenditures for formal training among large corporations are devoted to the provision of company, or "in-house" courses. But while his data show that larger firms (employing over 5000 people) spend a much greater share of their training dollars for company courses than smaller firms, he provides no figures that would enable us to estimate what proportion of these expenditures go to the "external" training industry for course materials and instructors. In his study of the costs of training in a small number of large firms, Lawrence Weinstein found that outside instructors were used exclusively in seven of the fifteen training programs that he examined and that four other programs used at least one instructor who

[55] Craig and Evers, "Employers as Educators," p. 32.
[56] Lusterman, *Education in Industry*, pp. 9-10.

was not a full-time employee of the firm providing the course. Weinstein suggests "that employers frequently reach outside their education staff personnel for instructor services," but argues that this may not be an "economical" practice when the outsiders are senior faculty or consultants commanding high hourly rates of pay. Other writers too have suggested that just as the largest firms find it cost-efficient to provide more in-house training than smaller firms, so these larger firms also find it more cost-efficient to develop their own course materials and employ their own instructors than to bring them in from the outside.[57]

The problem of establishing what proportion of expenditures for "in-house" training go to outside organizations or individuals is, of course, dependent on which items are included in one's estimate of total expenditures for such training. Lusterman asked his respondents to provide estimates of "direct costs": the salaries of training staff personnel, "travel and living expenses, payments to outside institutions or individual contractors, and costs of equipment and material purchased and rented." The federal government includes a similar catalog of items in its reports of expenditures on training. Weinstein, however, proposes that an adequate costing formula should include not only such direct, or "classroom" costs, but administrative expenses, including the costs of program development, and organization costs, including a portion of overhead for the use of central facilities (i.e., the services of the accounting personnel).[58]

The major issue is whether or not to include compensation for trainees who attend training programs during working hours. Weinstein suggests that "lost time" was valued at from 19 to 1,300 percent of classroom and administrative costs in eleven of the fifteen programs in his study, whereas Gilbert estimated trainee compensation to be 900 percent of direct costs (or $81 billion on a national level) in 1975.[59] Training professionals have noted that this issue alone has created intense pressure to develop time-efficient training methods.[60] The potentially high cost of trainee time also raises the issue of weighing the benefits and costs of formal training programs against the benefits and costs of informal training where employees remain on their jobs. Whether or not chang-

[57] Lusterman, *Education in Industry* tables 2.4 and 2.5, p. 14; Lawrence M. Weinstein, "Employers in the Private Sector," in Richard E. Anderson and Elizabeth Swain Kasl, *The Costs and Financing of Adult Education and Training* (Lexington, Mass.: D.C. Heath and Company, 1982), pp. 263-298, quotation from p. 288. "Other writers" include Lusterman, *Education in Industry*, p. 44, and Craig and Evers, "Employers as Educators," p. 41.

[58] Lusterman, *Education in Industry*, p. 12, n. 4; Weinstein, "Employers in the Private Sector," pp. 286-294.

[59] Weinstein, "Employers in the Private Sector," p. 291; Gilbert, "Training," pp. 3-4.

[60] See Lewis M. Branscomb and Paul C. Gilmore, "Education in Private Industry," *Daedalus*, Vol. 104, No. 1 (Winter 1975), pp. 222-233, especially pp. 229-230; and Ernest A. Lynton, "Colleges, Universities, and Corporate Training" in Gerard G. Gold, ed. *Business and Higher Education: Toward New Alliances* (San Francisco: Jossey Bass, 1981), pp. 65-71, especially pp. 66-67.

ing technologies will permit these types of training to remain real alternatives for many training purposes is, of course, another important question.

OTHER FEDERAL FUNDS FOR EDUCATION[61]

Our selection of programs to report under the heading of "other federal funds for education" has been made from categories reported in the *Digest of Education Statistics,* and published annually by the National Center for Education Statistics. We have omitted all categories of federal funds that we believe to contain substantial areas of double counting with expenditures made by recipient institutions (i.e., elementary and secondary schools, military academies), or for activities to be reported in later chapters (i.e., research and development, educational television). Remaining are only the few odd items listed in Table IV-X.

"International education" includes expenditures for education exchange

TABLE IV-X

OTHER FEDERAL FUNDS FOR EDUCATION
(millions of dollars)

Year	Total	International education	Agricultural extension service	Penal education	Surplus property transfers	Grants for training government personnel	Other
1960	483	84	54	1	310	22	12
1961							
1962	490	109	59	2	266	34	20
1963	480	116	63	3	245	33	20
1964	575	130	79	3	284	54	25
1965	674	179	85	4	295	82	29
1966	745	233	91	4	282	96	39
1967	835	327	93	6	232	123	54
1968	723	272	90	4	226	84	47
1969	783	278	97	4	237	113	54
1970	660	193	125	5	259	25	53
1971	728	181	155	6	281	34	71
1972	729	123	170	9	312	20	95
1973	708	78	186	9	302	17	116
1974	698	95	193	10	274	24	102
1975	722	93	219	11	253	47	99
1976	839	74	219	12	316	65	153
1977	864	105	239	7	291	51	171
1978	765	81	240	5	212	54	173
1979	805	120	239	6	222	52	166
1980	901	145	232	6	299	42	177

SOURCE: NCES, *Digest of Education Statistics,* 1972 and 1980 eds.

[61] Machlup, *Production and Distribution of Knowledge,* p. 105.

programs, projects supported by the Agency for International Development, the Peace Corps and its successor ACTION, as well as other ventures in international education and training. Programs conducted at home include the agricultural extension service, education in federal prisons, and the transfer of surplus property to educational institutions. Although we have attempted to avoid double counting by not reporting expenditures for on-the-job training in general, we have decided to include here the relatively small amounts of federal grants made for the training of state, local, and federal civilian personnel. The category "other" in the final column of Table IV-X includes the Education Division of the Office of Education, administrative expenditures of government offices concerned with education, and miscellaneous federal education programs not listed separately by the NCES.

PUBLIC LIBRARIES[62]

Public libraries should, perhaps, be included in the chapter on information services rather than in the chapter on education. Yet libraries, along with museums, zoos, aquaria, planetaria, and parks are important community resources for "self-education" that have explicit educational aims and that not infrequently sponsor formal instructional programs. Unfortunately, we shall have to limit our coverage here to public libraries, but we mention these other institutions as a reminder that the field of education may be construed even more broadly than we have defined it here.

LEVELS OF FUNDING AND CAPITAL EXPENDITURES

The figures presented in Table IV-Y on the funding provided by government bodies for public libraries are taken from annual publications of the Bureau of the Census and the National Center for Education Statistics (NCES). The figures on capital outlays from 1968-1980, from the *Bowker Annual of Library and Book Trade Information*, indicate a downward trend in the proportion of funds invested in new building, books, and equipment for public libraries. Indeed, the *Public Library Survey* conducted by the NCES in 1974 and 1977 shows that the number of library outlets actually declined from 89,142 in 1974 to 70,956 in 1977 although the loss was entirely of mobile unit stops and "other outlets." The number of central libraries increased by 2 percent, from 8,307 in 1974 to 8,456 in 1977, while the number of branch libraries grew by 12 percent, from 5,852 to 6,527 over the same years. Although direct circulation and the number of books held by public libraries increased by 11 percent and 13 percent respectively, the number of new books added to public library collections decreased 6 percent, from 27,578 in 1974 to 26,007 in 1977.[63]

[62] Machlup, *Production and Distribution of Knowledge*, p. 106.
[63] Results of the *Public Library Survey* for 1974 are summarized in the NCES, *Digest of Education Statistics*, 1980 ed., table 189, p. 219. The results of this survey for 1977 are summarized in the same publication, 1981 edition, in table 190, p. 212.

TABLE IV-Y

Expenditures for Public Libraries, 1958-1980
(millions of dollars)

Year	CAPITAL OUTLAY (1)	Total (3+4+5) (2)	GOVERNMENT EXPENDITURES		
			State and Local Government (3)	Federal Government	
				Transfers to states (4)	Federal libraries (5)
1958		224	224		
1959		243	243		
1960		299	278	6	15
1961		389	368	6	15
1962		362	340	7	15
1963		399	375	7	17
1964		427	401	8	18
1965		527	444	55	28
1966		572	486	55	31
1967		659	518	76	65
1968	91	709	573	62	74
1969	107	820	634	63	123
1970	98	873	700	53	120
1971	76	946	761	52	133
1972	94	977	814	54	109
1973	100	1044	877	46	121
1974	83	1176	968	44	164
1975	81	1347	1119	62	166
1976	125	1500	1249	58	193
1977	132	1471	1259	43	169
1978	91	1580	1362	42	176
1979	106	1760	1505	53	202
1980	108	1963	1694	56	213

Source: Column (1): *Bowker Annual of Library and Book Trade Information* (New York: R.R. Bowker Company). Column (2): Bureau of the Census, *Governmental Finances*, (Washington, D.C.: Government Printing Office). Columns (4) and (5): NCES, *Digest of Education Statistics*.

Note: Capital outlay is included in the total outlays reported in Column 2. It is only reported separately for the years shown and must be subtracted from the total in order to obtain separate figures for operating expenditures.

THE PATTERN OF OPERATING EXPENDITURES

Although the NCES surveys suggest a slightly higher level of capital expenditure for 1974 than the source that we have used for our table, they also indicate that the pattern of operating expenditures of public libraries remained fairly constant from the mid to the late 1970s. According to these NCES figures, operating expenditures accounted for about 90 percent of the total expenditures in both 1974 and 1977, with salaries for librarians and other staff accounting for slightly over half of total expenditures. Supplies and materials accounted for about 15 percent of the total, while operations and maintenance, and "other library expenditures" each comprised about 10 percent of total expenditures in the two survey years.

CHAPTER V   Research and Development

This chapter updates the four statistical elements of Chapter V of *The Production and Distribution of Knowledge in the United States*. Among the topics covered are: (1) expenditures for basic research in the economic census years from 1958 to 1980; (2) expenditures for applied research and development for the economic census years from 1958 to 1980; (3) a continuing relative decline in the number of patent applications filed, in proportion to the number of scientists, and in proportion to expenditures for research and development; and (4) the supply and demand of scientists and engineers for the competing needs of research and development, on the one hand, and the training of future researchers on the other.

Summary Table V presents information on research and development expenditures in the United States for each of the economic census years since 1958, plus 1980. The three major components of these expenditures are itemized separately: basic research, applied research, and development. Over the period of the study, total research and development expenditures increased from $10,711 million in 1958 to $62,222 million in 1980. Despite minor fluc-

SUMMARY TABLE V

RESEARCH AND DEVELOPMENT AND GNP
(millions of dollars)

	1958	1963	1967	1972	1977	1980
Basic research	877	1,965	3,056	3,829	5,550	8,071
Applied research	2,699	3,742	4,780	5,984	9,755	13,940
Development	7,135	11,352	15,310	18,664	27,677	40,211
Total	10,711	17,059	23,146	28,477	42,982	62,222
Percent of adjusted GNP	2.21	2.60	2.60	2.23	2.09	2.20
Paid for by						
Government expenditures	6,779	11,204	14,395	15,808	21,727	29,576
Industry expenditures	3,707	5,456	8,142	11,710	19,696	30,400
Personal consumption expenditures	225	399	609	959	1,559	2,246

SOURCES: Tables V-2 and V-3 in this book.

tuations in the course of the two decades, these expenditures consistently accounted for roughly 2.2 percent of GNP in the years of our study.

During the period of our study, the bulk of expenditures for research and development have been paid for by the federal government and by industry. Over the last two decades, industry's share of these expenditures has increased substantially so that in 1980 for the first time, industrial expenditures were larger than the contribution by the government.

The topics are treated in more detail in the following sections.

EXPENDITURES FOR RESEARCH AND DEVELOPMENT[1]

Expenditures for research and development can be thought of as being composed of three major elements. Basic research has been defined by Machlup as creating "basic knowledge on which practical, applicable knowledge may rest but which itself is too general, too broad or too deep, to have direct applications." In contrast, "applied research creates directly applicable knowledge."[2] Applied research crosses into development when the end result is to be a "final" product for use by some consumer.

This section examines several trends in expenditures for research and development. Who pays for research and development and who conducts it are two of the more interesting questions we will address here. Before examining each element of this activity in detail, however, we examine the mix of expenditures among these activities over time. The small share enjoyed by basic research in the nation's total budget for research and development was observed by Machlup. That share has increased by over 50 percent in the years of our study, rising from 8.2 percent in 1958 to 13.0 percent in 1980. This increase came at the expense of applied research and development. These trends are shown in more detail in Table V-1. Over the same period, expenditures for applied research have ranged between 20.7 percent and 25.2 percent of the total; expenditures for development between 64.4 percent and 66.6 percent of the total.

BASIC RESEARCH

Table V-2, originally Machlup's table V-1, presents a breakdown of all expenditures in the United States for basic research in each of the economic census years since 1958, plus 1980. The material in the table is derived from publications of the National Science Foundation, which is the same source used by Machlup. Who conducted the basic research is shown on the right side,

---

[1] See Fritz Machlup, *The Production and Distribution of Knowledge in the United States* (Princeton, N.J.: Princeton University Press, 1962), pp. 151-161.

[2] See *Production and Distribution of Knowledge*, pp. 146-148 for a fuller discussion of these matters.

TABLE V-1*

DISTRIBUTION OF EXPENDITURES AMONG RESEARCH LEVELS
(percent of total expenditures)

Year	Basic research	Applied research	Development	Total
1958	8.2	25.2	66.6	100.0
1963	11.5	22.0	66.5	100.0
1967	13.2	20.7	66.1	100.0
1972	13.5	21.0	65.5	100.0
1977	12.9	22.7	64.4	100.0
1980	13.0	22.4	64.6	100.0

SOURCE: Table V-4 in this book.

* This is a new table and has no counterpart in Machlup, *Production and Distribution of Knowledge*.

who paid for it is shown on the left side. The upper part of the table gives the amounts, in millions of dollars, the lower part in percentages of the total.

The increase in the proportional share of basic research in the total research and development budget noted earlier can be attributed largely to an increase in support for basic research by the federal government. That contribution in-

TABLE V-2*

EXPENDITURES FOR BASIC RESEARCH: 1958, 1963, 1967, 1972, 1977, AND 1980

Year	Sources of funds					Uses of funds			
	Federal govern-ment	Industry	Univer-sities	Other non-profit	Total	Federal govern-ment	Industry	Univer-sities	Other non-profit
	(millions of dollars)								
1958	478	292	50	57	877	126	295	359	97
1963	1,311	425	121	108	1,965	255	522	973	215
1967	2,201	492	223	140	3,056	435	629	1,707	285
1972	2,633	563	415	218	3,829	625	593	2,266	345
1977	3,836	850	526	338	5,550	925	911	3,204	510
1980	5,547	1,265	799	460	8,071	1,193	1,325	4,793	760
	(percent of total)								
1958	55	33	6	6	100	14	34	41	11
1963	67	22	6	5	100	13	27	50	10
1967	72	16	7	5	100	14	21	56	9
1972	69	15	11	5	100	16	16	59	9
1977	69	15	9	7	100	17	16	58	9
1980	69	16	10	5	100	15	16	59	10

SOURCE: National Science Foundation, *National Patterns of Science and Technology Resources* (Washington, D.C.: Government Printing Office, annual eds.).

* Formerly Table V-1 in Machlup, *Production and Distribution of Knowledge*.

creased substantially in the late 1950s and early 1960s, as the federal share rose from 55 percent to 67 percent of the total in the five-year period between 1958 and 1963. Federal contributions for basic research have since remained at about 70 percent of the national total. As we will see soon, this federal contribution has largely taken the form of transfer payments to universities.

The increased federal contributions for basic research have been accompanied by relative decreases in such expenditures by industry. As shown in Table V-2, industrial expenditures for basic research have been virtually identical historically with the amount of research conducted by industry. That is to say, little money has been transferred from industry to universities or to other organizations for the conduct of basic research. Rather, this research appears to have been conducted largely "in-house." In any event, this industrial research activity has become a steadily smaller piece of the nation's total budget for basic research, declining from 33 percent in 1958 to only 16 percent in 1980.

The focal point for the conduct of basic research in the United States has increasingly become the university. It is the recipient of the large transfer payments made by the federal government. Thus, although universities have historically funded only 6 percent to 10 percent of the nation's basic research, they have conducted a steadily increasing proportion of that research, rising from 41 percent to 59 percent of the total in the period of our study.

Expenditures for basic research in the United States came to $8,071 million in 1980.

APPLIED RESEARCH

The transfer payments between the federal government and universities that characterize basic research do not occur in the funding of applied research. They are replaced by transfers from the federal government to private industry. As shown in Table V-3, a modified version of Machlup's, the sources of contributions to funding for applied research have remained relatively stable over the years of our study. The federal contribution has ranged between 46 percent and 57 percent of the total, and the industry contribution between 40 percent and 50 percent.

The preponderance of applied research is conducted by industry, whose share of the total has varied from 58 percent to 71 percent in the years of our study. Whereas the federal share has remained constant at something between 18 to 20 percent, universities have enjoyed a slowly increasing share of the total, rising from 9 percent to 17 percent over the last two decades.

Total expenditures for applied research in the United States came to $13,940 million in 1980.

DEVELOPMENT

As we noted earlier in Table V-1, the lion's share of the nation's total budget for research and development, roughly two-thirds, is spent annually on devel-

TABLE V-3*

EXPENDITURES FOR APPLIED RESEARCH AND DEVELOPMENT: 1958, 1963, 1967, 1972, 1977, AND 1980

	Sources of funds					Uses of funds			
Year	Federal govern- ment	Industry	Univer- sities	Other non- profit	Total	Federal govern- ment	Industry	Univer- sities	Other non- profit
	(millions of dollars)								
Applied research									
1958	1,439	1,163	61	36	2,699	474	1,911	250	64
1963	2,125	1,483	72	62	3,742	715	2,457	397	173
1967	2,694	1,889	102	95	4,780	1,027	2,915	593	245
1972	3,104	2,615	140	125	5,984	1,360	3,514	745	365
1977	4,783	4,424	303	245	9,755	2,033	5,656	1,533	533
1980	6,453	6,725	424	338	13,940	2,473	8,360	2,387	720
Development									
1958	4,862	2,252	10	11	7,135	774	6,183	140	38
1963	7,768	3,548	14	22	11,352	1,309	9,651	241	151
1967	9,500	5,761	20	29	15,310	1,934	12,841	294	241
1972	10,071	8,532	19	42	18,664	2,605	15,445	372	242
1977	13,108	14,422	58	89	27,677	3,147	23,361	717	452
1980	17,576	22,410	90	135	40,211	4,263	34,194	1,104	650
	(percent of total)								
Applied research									
1958	53	43	2	1	100	18	71	9	2
1963	57	40	2	1	100	19	66	11	4
1967	56	50	2	2	100	21	61	12	6
1972	52	44	2	2	100	23	59	12	6
1977	49	45	3	3	100	21	58	16	5
1980	46	48	3	3	100	18	60	17	5
Development									
1958	68	32			100	11	87	2	
1963	68	31		1	100	12	85	2	1
1967	62	38			100	13	84	2	1
1972	54	46			100	14	83	2	1
1977	47	52		1	100	11	84	3	2
1980	44	56			100	11	85	3	1

SOURCE: National Science Foundation, *National Patterns of Science and Technology Resources*, annual eds.

NOTE: Components may not add to 100 percent because they have been rounded off.
* This is a new table and has no counterpart in Machlup, *Production and Distribution of Knowledge*.

opment. The bulk of that activity is conducted by industry, usually on the or-der of 85 percent of the total. The remainder is scattered among federal gov-ernment laboratories, universities, and other nonprofit activities. Funding for development has come almost exclusively from the federal government and in-dustry. The proportional share contributed by the federal government, how-ever, has declined steadily over the period of our study from 68 percent in 1958 to 44 percent in 1980.

Expenditures for developmental research activities in the United States came to $40,211 million in 1980. Table V-4 summarizes total expenditures for research and development in the United States for the years of our study. The changes in the funding patterns of various R & D activities that we have noted here aggregate to a substantial overall decline in federal funding for this activity, combined with a parallel increase in the contribution by industry. Thus, 1980 marked the first year in recent history in which industrial expenditures for R & D exceeded those of the federal government.

SCIENTISTS AND ENGINEERS IN RESEARCH AND DEVELOPMENT

A measure of the "absolute" growth of expenditures for research and development that is unaffected by inflation is the number of scientists and engineers employed in the activity, the "labor input." Table V-5 presents such data for each of the years of our study. It is interesting to note that whereas annual expenditures for research and development increased sixfold from 1958 to 1980, the number of scientists and engineers involved in research and development merely doubled over the same period.

The reader may recall our findings in Chapter III, which show that in constant dollars total expenditures for research and development increased somewhat more than twofold over the period of our study. Thus, our findings on the labor input to R & D are consistent with those earlier findings.

TABLE V-4

EXPENDITURES FOR RESEARCH AND DEVELOPMENT: 1958, 1963, 1967, 1972, 1977, AND 1980

	Sources of funds					Uses of funds			
Year	Federal govern- ment	Industry	Univer- sities	Other non- profit	Total	Federal govern- ment	Industry	Univer- sities	Other non- profit
	(millions of dollars)								
1958	6,779	3,707	121	104	10,711	1,374	8,389	749	199
1963	11,204	5,456	207	192	17,059	2,279	12,630	1,611	539
1967	14,395	8,142	345	264	23,146	3,396	16,385	2,594	771
1972	15,808	11,710	574	385	28,477	4,590	19,552	3,383	952
1977	21,727	19,696	887	672	42,982	6,105	29,928	5,454	1,495
1980	29,576	30,400	1,313	933	62,222	7,929	43,879	8,284	2,130
	(percent of total)								
1958	63	35	1	1	100	13	78	7	2
1963	66	32	1	1	100	13	74	9	4
1967	62	35	2	1	100	15	71	11	3
1972	56	41	2	1	100	16	69	12	3
1977	51	46	2	1	100	14	70	13	3
1980	48	49	2	1	100	13	71	13	3

SOURCES: Tables V-2 and V-3 in this book.

TABLE V-5

SCIENTISTS AND ENGINEERS IN RESEARCH AND DEVELOPMENT: 1958, 1963, 1967, 1972, 1977, AND 1980
(in thousands of workers)

Year	Total	Industry	Universities and colleges	Federal government	Federally funded R & D centers	Other nonprofits
1958	326.9	241.5	42.9	36.6		5.9
1963	471.5	343.2	59.3	56.4		12.6
1967	550.2	384.2	77.1	74.5		14.4
1972	518.5	353.3	66.5	65.2	11.7	21.8
1977	570.3	393.2	74.4	64.7	14.0	24.0
1980	647.2	458.4	79.1	67.0	15.2	27.5

SOURCES: (1958-1967): Bureau of Labor Statistics, *Employment of Scientists and Engineers 1950-1970* (Washington, D.C.: Government Printing Office, 1971); (1972-1980): National Science Foundation, *National Patterns of Science and Technology Resources*, annual.

NOTE: For the years before 1972 employment in federally funded R & D centers is included under Universities and colleges.

INVENTIVE EFFORT AND PATENT PROTECTION[3]

END OF GROWTH IN PATENT INVENTIONS?

Machlup noted an "amazing contrast" between the growth in research and development expenditures and personnel since 1920 and the absence of any increase in the number of patents sought over the same period. In absolute terms, this difference has diminished somewhat, as the number of patent applications has risen steadily over the period of our study. Machlup noted that the number of patent applications in 1959 was at its peak for that decade at 78,594. By the late 1970s this number had increased to over 110,000. But although the absolute number of patent applications increased over this period, they continued to decline in comparison with the financial and human resources invested in the research and development process.

This is illustrated in the following three tables. Table V-6 reports the number of patent applications filed per 100,000 in the overall population and per 100 technical workers. The number of patent applications per 100,000 population has, in fact, risen slightly from 1940 to 1980, from 39.6 to 45.7. Compared to the number of technical workers in the population, however, the number of patent applications declined between 1940 and 1980, from 0.80 per hundred to 0.65 per hundred.

Table V-7 refines the comparison somewhat, relating the number of scientists and engineers to the number of patents granted for several of the years of our study. The original Table V-7 showed a 92 percent decline in the number of patents issued relative to the number of scientists and engineers in the years

[3] See Machlup, *Production and Distribution of Knowledge*, pp. 161-176.

TABLE V-6

NUMBER OF DOMESTIC PATENT APPLICATIONS COMPARED WITH POPULATION AND NUMBER OF TECHNICAL WORKERS, 1940-1980

Year	Domestic patent applications 5-year averages (1)	Resident population (millions) (2)	Technical workers (millions) (3)	Patent applications per	
				100,000 population (4)	100 technical workers (5)
1940	52,200	131.95	6.59	39.57	0.80
1950	60,100	151.23	8.59	39.74	0.70
1960	82,573	183.28	13.90	45.05	0.60
1970	100,108	207.97	15.50	48.14	0.65
1980	103,460	226.55	16.00	45.66	0.65

SOURCES: U.S. Bureau of the Census, *Statistical Abstract of the United States* (Washington, D.C.: Government Printing Office, various years); Jacob Schmookler, "The Level of Inventive Activity," *Review of Economics and Statistics*, Vol. 36 (May 1954), p. 186.

from 1900 to 1954. Our Table V-7 shows a continuing decline in this statistic over the last two decades.

Table V-8, perhaps, best helps us to quantify these trends, showing the number of patent applications filed per 100 scientists and engineers engaged in research and development and per million dollars of expenditures for that activity. Unadjusted for inflation, the trend for expenditures is constantly downward, as fewer inventions are "purchased" each year by the expenditure of one million dollars. Because of the effects of inflation, this is not a terribly useful series, however.

TABLE V-7

NUMBER OF SCIENTISTS AND ENGINEERS COMPARED WITH NUMBER OF PATENTS, 1960-1980

Year	Scientists and engineers (1)	Index of growth of scientists and engineers (2)	Patents granted (3)	Index of growth of patents (4)	Index of relative growth of patents in relation to scientists and engineers (4) ÷ (2) × 100 (5)
1958	1,001,000	100	48,330	100	100
1963	1,280,000	127	45,699	94	74
1967	1,476,000	147	65,652	135	92
1972	1,817,000	182	74,808	155	85
1977	2,047,000	204	65,300	135	66
1980	2,316,000	232	61,800	128	55

SOURCES: (1958, 1963, 1967): National Bureau of Labor Statistics, *Employment of Scientists and Engineers*. (1972, 1977, 1980): National Science Foundation, *National Patterns of Science and Technology Resources 1980*; and U.S. Bureau of the Census, *Statistical Abstract of the United States*, annual ed.

TABLE V-8

PATENT APPLICATIONS FILED FOR INVENTIONS COMPARED WITH R & D SCIENTISTS AND
ENGINEERS AND R & D EXPENDITURES, 1960-1980

Patent applications filed			Reseach & development		Patent applications per 100 R & D	
			Scientists and engineers (thousands)	Expenditures (millions)	scientists and engineers (2) ÷ (4)	per million $ R & D expenditures (2) ÷ (5)
Period	Average	Year				
(1)	(2)	(3)	(4)	(5)	(6)	(7)
1960-62	82,573	1960	379.5	13,523	21.76	6.11
1961-63	84,617	1961	425.7	14,380	19.88	5.88
1962-64	86,116	1962	435.5	15,610	19.77	5.52
1963-65	89,317	1963	471.2	17,350	18.96	5.15
1964-66	90,174	1964	490.5	19,215	18.38	4.69
1965-67	90,265	1965	494.5	20,044	18.25	4.50
1966-68	89,767	1966	520.5	22,264	17.25	4.03
1967-69	93,131	1967	535.6	23,613	17.39	3.94
1968-70	98,130	1968	550.6	25,119	17.82	3.91
1969-71	101,940	1969	556.6	26,169	18.31	3.90
1970-72	102,121	1970	546.6	26,545	18.68	3.85
1971-73	102,396	1971	528.9	27,151	19.36	3.77
1972-74	101,607	1972	518.6	28,396	19.59	3.58
1973-75	102,305	1973	517.5	30,615	19.77	3.34
1974-76	101,840	1974	525.4	32,734	19.38	3.11
1975-77	101,405	1975	532.7	35,213	19.04	2.88
1976-78	101,367	1976	549.9	39,016	18.43	2.60
1977-79	101,767	1977	570.3	42,982	17.84	2.37
1978-80	101,900	1978	595.3	48,295	17.12	2.11
1979-81	103,260	1979	621.0	54,994	16.63	1.88
1980-82	105,230	1980	647.2	62,222	16.26	1.69

SOURCES: U.S. Bureau of the Census, *Statistical Abstract of the United States*, various years.

The number of patent applications per 100 R & D scientists and engineers, in contrast, is a picture unaffected by inflation. Here the downward trend remains, but it is much less severe than those found elsewhere in any of these three tables. The number of patent applications per 100 R & D scientists and engineers, which was 54.94 in 1941, had declined to 21.76 in 1966, and 16.26 in 1980.

The reader is directed to Machlup's original text for a discussion of possible explanations of this trend that is as cogent today as when written (Machlup, *Production and Distribution of Knowledge*, pp. 174-176).

THE SUPPLY OF SCIENTISTS AND ENGINEERS[4]

Although a detailed discussion of the marketplace for scientists and engineers is beyond the scope of this book, some useful observations are possible. We saw

[4] See Machlup, *Production and Distribution of Knowledge*, pp. 193-197.

in Table V-5 that the number of scientists and engineers involved in research and development has roughly doubled over the years of our study. This growth was uneven, with a period of actual decline in employment in these activities in the early 1970s, a time of retrenchment in federal funding of the space program.

There is one trend here that some observers may consider disturbing. As shown in Table V-9, the number of doctorates awarded in the scientific and engineering fields rose steadily from 1960 until 1971, from 6,407 to 16,392. A decline then began. From the 1971 peak of 16,392, the number of doctorates awarded dropped to about 14,000 per year in the late 1970s, and among physical scientists and engineers was especially severe.

TABLE V-9

NUMBER OF DOCTOR'S DEGREES AWARDED IN MATHEMATICS AND THE PHYSICAL, BIOLOGICAL, AND ENGINEERING SCIENCES, 1960-1980

Year	Total	Physical sciences[a]	Mathematics	Engineering	Life sciences[b]
1960	6,407	2,754	290	825	2,538
1961	6,035	1,995	362	1,006	2,672
1962	6,814	2,199	410	1,281	2,924
1963	7,633	2,514	538	1,454	3,127
1964	8,360	2,770	600	1,610	3,380
1965	9,116	2,865	685	2,073	3,493
1966	10,079	3,028	766	2,283	4,002
1967	11,296	3,478	828	2,581	4,409
1968	12,578	3,642	970	2,833	5,133
1969	14,042	3,901	1,063	3,234	5,844
1970	15,105	4,400	1,222	3,432	6,051
1971	16,392	4,494	1,236	3,495	7,167
1972	16,228	4,226	1,281	3,475	7,246
1973	15,594	4,101	1,222	3,338	6,933
1974	15,750	3,800	1,916	3,144	6,890
1975	15,008	3,749	1,149	2,959	7,151
1976	14,594	3,572	1,003	2,791	7,228
1977	14,236	3,410	959	2,641	7,226
1978	14,026	3,234	959	2,423	7,410
1979	14,368	3,321	977	2,494	7,576
1980	14,401	3,151	963	2,479	7,808

SOURCE: U.S. Bureau of the Census, *Statistical Abstract of the United States,* various years.

[a] Does not include mathematics or engineering; includes physical anthropology, archaeology, and geography.
[b] Includes psychology.

VI   The Media of
Communication

This chapter updates Chapter VI of *The Production and Distribution of Knowledge in the United States.* Seven major categories of communication media are covered here, containing detailed statistics on some nineteen specific media. The broad topics include: (1) printed matter, including books, pamphlets, periodicals, newspapers and other printed matter; (2) photography and phonography; (3) stage and cinema; (4) broadcasting, including radio and television, and also cable television; (5) advertising; (6) telephone, telegraph, and postal services; and (7) meetings and conventions.

Expenditures for each medium are presented for each of the economic census years after 1958, plus 1980. In addition, descriptions of the types of knowledge conveyed by each medium are presented where possible.

Summary Table VI summarizes total expenditures in the United States for the various media of communication included in our study. These expenditures increased from $37,234 million in 1958 to $227,135 million in 1980. This growth was reflected in a small increase in the percentage of GNP attributable to these media: 7.7 percent in 1958, rising to 8.0 percent by 1980. Over this period three groups of media increased at a faster rate than GNP, including photography and phonography; radio and television broadcasting; and telephone, telegraph and postal services. The remaining four media increased at a rate slower than GNP.

More than half of those expenditures that could be allocated were made by businesses. Personal consumption expenditures accounted for the bulk of the remainder, with government expenditures tallying less than 10 percent of the total. Within the category of personal consumption expenditures are purchases of printing and publishing services as described in Table VI-13; services of portrait studios; purchases of phonographic equipment and supplies; admissions to stage, screen and sporting events; expenditures for radio and TV sets and repairs; and for telephone and telegraph services as shown in Table VI-35. Governmental expenditures include purchases of printing and publishing goods and services as shown in Table VI-13; purchases of telephone and telegraph equipment as shown in Table VI-35; and purchases of postal services in the form of franked mail totaling $52 million in 1958, $89 million in 1963, $146 million in 1967, $294 million in 1972, $611 million in 1977 and $745 million in 1980. Except for purchases of photographic equipment and postal services that cannot be allocated, all remaining purchases have been made by business.

The remainder of this chapter explores these trends in more detail.

SUMMARY TABLE VI

The Media of Communication and GNP
(millions of dollars)

	1958	1963	1967	1972	1977	1980
Printed materials	12,112	15,281	20,184	28,195	44,520	61,458
Photography and phonography	2,307	2,853	4,872	9,947	17,817	23,191
Stage and cinema	1,538	1,820	2,404	3,487	4,997	6,424
Radio and television broadcast	3,239	4,562	7,494	10,675	17,099	24,163
Advertising	5,000	6,000	7,537	10,415	16,774	21,914
Telephone, telegraph, and postal	11,438	16,128	21,900	35,230	60,426	81,685
Conventions	1,600	2,000	2,600	2,900	5,086	8,300
Total	37,234	48,644	66,991	100,849	166,719	227,135
Percent of adjusted GNP	7.7	7.5	7.7	7.9	8.1	8.0
Paid for by						
Personal consumption expenditures	12,414	16,274	22,561	33,950	54,451	71,297
Government expenditures	2,083	3,567	6,035	10,476	14,286	15,692
Business expenditures	18,462	23,349	29,635	40,769	72,338	105,677
Unallocated	4,275	5,454	8,760	15,654	25,644	34,469

Source: Text and tables in Chapter VI of this text.

Printed Matter[1]

EXPENDITURES FOR BOOKS AND PAMPHLETS

Machlup estimated the total retail value of books and pamphlets for the years 1954 and 1958 by calculating the value of the markup applied to their wholesale value produced in the United States. This rather elaborate calculation requires statistics that allocate publishers' sales by customer class. This technique cannot be reproduced for the years of our study, however, since this allocation of sales is not available for any year after 1954. Whereas Machlup was able to use the 1954 data to estimate results for 1958, the difficulty affecting use of "old" numbers becomes progressively more severe in the later years of our study.

[1] See Fritz Machlup, *The Production and Distribution of Knowledge in the United States* (Princeton, N.J.: Princeton University Press, 1962), pp. 208-236.

Hence, a new technique is used in this statistical update to estimate expenditures for books and pamphlets. The assumption is made that 40 percent of personal consumption expenditures for books and pamphlets is retail markup, and the remaining 60 percent is the publisher's gross income. Using this assumption, we can separate the manufacturer's sales to consumers. This set of calculations for the years of our study are reproduced at Table VI-1A. In order to compare the results of the two techniques, data for 1958 have been recast. The results are gratifyingly similar. Using the original Machlup technique, we estimated the retail value of books and pamphlets in 1958 at $1,456 million. Using the new technique, we calculated the same value to be $1,469 million.

With the retail value of books and pamphlets established, only the value of government publications remains to be measured before the total value of these materials can be determined.

TABLE VI-1A

Books and Pamphlets: Total Expenditures Including Distribution Costs,
1958, 1963, 1967, 1972, 1977, and 1980
(millions of dollars)

		1958	1963	1967	1972	1977	1980
(1)	Manufacturers' total receipts	998	1,548	2,255	2,915	5,008	6,114
(2)	Consumers' expenditures	1,181	1,413	1,847	2,921	4,504	6,849
(3)	Deduct imports	4	40	70	136	171	368
(4)	Domestic sales by U.S. manufacturers	1,177	1,373	1,777	2,785	4,333	6,481
(5)	Deduct 40% retail markup	471	549	711	1,114	1,733	2,592
(6)	Manufacturers' sales for consumer use (4 minus 5)	706	824	1,066	1,671	2,600	3,889
(7)	Manufacturers' sales for business and government (1 minus 6)	292	724	1,189	1,244	2,408	2,225
(8)	Retail value of books and pamphlets (4 plus 7)	1,469	2,097	2,966	4,029	6,741	8,706
(9)	Government publications	179	261	288	347	647	833
(10)	Total value, books and pamphlets (8 plus 9)	1,648	2,358	3,254	4,376	7,388	9,539
(11)	Deduct exports	44	63	144	170	315	529
(12)	Add imports	4	40	70	136	171	368
(13)	Domestic use (Intake)	1,608	2,335	3,180	4,342	7,244	9,378
Paid for by							
(14)	Personal consumption expenditures	1,181	1,413	1,847	2,921	4,504	6,849
(15)	Government expenditures	343	615	977	1,080	1,956	1,536
(16)	Business expenditures	84	307	356	341	784	993

Sources: Table VI-1. See also discussion in this text. Line (9): For 1963 U.S. Department of Commerce, *Input-Output Structure of the U.S. Economy, 1963* (Washington, D.C.: Government Printing Office, 1969).

GOVERNMENT PUBLICATIONS

Machlup reported four elements in the calculation of federal government publications: the work done at the main plant of the Government Printing Office; the work done by some 320 executive branch printing plants; the cost of services provided by the Superintendent of Documents; and printing for the government performed by commercial printers. The value of these four elements came to $179 million in 1958.

Data for the fiscal year from July 1, 1963 to June 30, 1964 were compiled for the Joint Committee on Printing of the United States Congress in a special study entitled, *Federal Printing Program*.[2] In that year, total expenditures for printing by the federal government were reported to have risen to $261 million. Some $118 million of that amount was procured from commercial printers.

The remaining four years of our study, 1967, 1972, 1977, and 1980, are derived from the appropriate years' *Budget of the Government of the United States*.[3] The total procurement of government printing and the amount purchased from commercial printers for each of these years, in millions of dollars, is:

	Total Procurement	Purchased from Commercial Printers
1967	288	89
1972	347	130
1977	647	258
1980	833	470

In order to avoid double counting, government purchases from commercial printers are deducted from the total value of commercial printing and lithography calculated in Table VI-10A below.

Using the figures calculated in the previous two sections, we estimate that total expenditures in the United States for books and pamphlets rose from $1,608 million in 1958 to $9,378 million in 1980 (see row 13, Table VI-1A).

THE TYPES OF KNOWLEDGE CONVEYED BY BOOKS

Tables VI-2 through VI-4 present trends in classes of subject matter in book publishing over the last two decades. The total number of new books published per year tripled in the period of our study, going from 11,000 to over 34,000. The careful observer will note that these totals vary slightly from those reported on Table VI-1. The difference is that Table VI-1 reports the total of all books published in a given year; both new books and merely new editions of previously published books. Table VI-2, in contrast, reports only new books.

[2] *Federal Printing Program*, Joint Committee on Printing, U.S. Congress, 90th Congress, 1st Session (Washington, D.C.: Government Printing Office, 1967).
[3] An annual publication, Washington, D.C.: Government Printing Office, various years.

TABLE VI-1

BOOKS AND PAMPHLETS: NUMBERS PUBLISHED, SALES RECEIPTS, AND CONSUMER EXPENDITURES, 1914-1980

Year	Number of books published in U.S. (1)	Number of pamphlets, etc. printed and copyrighted in U.S.[d] (2)	Sales receipts of publishers for books and pamphlets (millions of dollars) (3)	Consumer expenditures for books and maps		
				(millions of dollars) (4)	(dollars per capita) (5)	(% of GNP) (6)
1914	12,010	17,021				
1919	8,594	28,261				
1929	10,187	40,245	n.a.	309	2.53	0.296
1939	10,640	44,046	155.0	226	1.73	0.248
1949	10,892	38,664	587.0	630	4.23	0.244
1959	14,876	39,418	1,134.3	1,088	6.12	0.225
1960	15,012	41,423	1,282.3	1,139	6.30	0.225
1961	18,060	43,942	1,365.0	1,212	6.60	0.234
1962	21,904	42,518	1,501.9	1,287	6.90	0.232
1963	25,784	43,268	1,549.1	1,413	7.47	0.239
1964	28,451	41,644	1,729.6	1,612	8.40	0.255
1965	28,595	42,245	1,817.6	1,648	8.48	0.240
1966	30,050	44,764	2,081.3	1,840	9.36	0.248
1967[a]	28,762	49,830	2,255.3	1,847	9.30	0.233
1968	30,387	49,120	2,388.9	2,006	10.00	0.232
1969	29,579	48,564	2,521.8	2,296	11.00	0.239
1970[b]	36,071	53,153	2,677.0	2,903	14.17	0.296
1971	37,692	55,704	2,814.1	2,955	14.27	0.278
1972	38,053	58,257	2,915.4	2,921	13.99	0.249
1973[c]	39,951	59,073	3,160.2	3,093	14.70	0.237
1974	40,846	61,762	3,407.7	3,303	15.59	0.234
1975	39,372	68,190	3,789.3	3,775	17.67	0.247
1976	41,698	72,148	4,179.7	3,866	17.96	0.227
1977	42,780	81,289	5,007.7	4,504	20.77	0.237
1978	41,216		5,640.6	5,435	24.87	0.255
1979	45,182		5,574.2	6,107	27.68	0.258
1980	42,377		6.114.4	6,849	30.08	0.261

SOURCES: Column (1): *The Bowker Annual of Library and Book Trade Information* (New York: R.R. Bowker Company, annual ed.). Column (2): Library of Congress, *Catalogue of the Register of Copyrights* (Washington, D.C.: Government Printing Office, annual ed.). Column (3): U.S. Bureau of the Census, *Annual Survey of Manufactures* (Washington, D.C.: Government Printing Office, annual ed.). Columns (4)-(6): U.S. Bureau of the Census, *Statistical Abstract of the United States* (Washington, D.C.: Government Printing Office, annual ed.).

[a] The decline in title output from 1966 to 1967 does not mean a decline in American book production output as such; rather it reflects a revision which was made in the method of counting at the beginning of 1967.

[b] The significant rise in the number of books for 1970 may not be due to an increase in books published, but to better reporting of it. (See *Publishers' Weekly* editorial, November 2, 1970, p. 32.)

[c] Data beginning in 1973 are derived by Bowker from Library of Congress MARC data primarily, consistent with *Weekly Record* listings. Not counted are U.S. government publications, or publications of many other governmental units, or university theses.

[d] Figure was obtained by reducing total number of copyrights for books and pamphlets by books manufactured abroad (except those registered for ad interim copyright). From this, the number of books published in the U.S. is substracted.

TABLE VI-2

BOOKS: NEW BOOKS PUBLISHED BY SUBJECT MATTER CLASSES AND TYPES OF KNOWLEDGE, AS A PERCENT OF TOTAL,
1958, 1963, 1967, 1972, 1977, AND 1980

	1958	1963	1967	1972	1977	1980
Practical	14.8	14.7	15.1	16.0	20.2	22.0
Agriculture	1.1	1.1	1.0	1.1	1.4	1.1
Business	2.6	2.1	2.3	2.0	2.5	2.7
Home economics	1.3	1.1	0.9	1.8	2.1	2.3
Law	2.2	1.4	1.8	1.6	2.2	2.4
Medicine and hygiene	3.6	3.9	4.3	5.2	6.7	7.8
Technical and military	4.0	5.1	4.8	4.4	5.4	5.7
Intellectual	52.0	57.0	59.8	62.1	57.5	57.2
Arts	3.7	3.5	3.9	4.1	4.4	4.2
Biography	5.5	3.6	3.6	4.0	4.7	4.1
Education	2.5	4.1	3.6	3.9	3.0	2.6
Literature	4.5	4.5	5.4	5.2	3.6	3.9
Geography and travel	2.5	3.1	3.5	3.6	1.0	1.2
History	6.8	4.4	4.6	3.4	4.3	4.6
Music	0.8	0.7	0.8	0.8	0.6	0.7
Philology	1.0	1.8	1.7	1.3	1.2	1.3
Philosophy	3.3	2.6	2.9	3.1	3.3	3.2
Poetry and drama	3.4	3.0	3.4	3.3	3.1	2.8
Science	7.1	8.7	8.4	8.0	7.4	7.5
Sociology and economics	4.5	10.2	12.6	17.4	16.8	17.3
Juvenile (one-half)	6.5	6.8	5.5	4.0	3.9	3.8
Pastime	22.7	18.8	16.3	14.4	13.6	11.8
Fiction	14.5	9.8	9.1	7.8	7.0	5.6
Games and sports	1.8	2.2	1.8	2.6	2.7	2.4
Juvenile (one-half)	6.5	6.8	5.5	3.9	3.9	3.9
Spiritual	8.5	7.7	6.9	4.6	5.2	4.8
Religion	8.5	7.7	6.9	4.6	5.2	4.8
Miscellaneous	1.9	1.8	1.9	2.9	3.5	2.9
Total percent	100.0	100.0	100.0	100.0	100.0	100.0
Total publications (thousands)	11,012	19,057	21,877	26,868	33,292	34,028

SOURCE: R. R. Bowker Co., New York, reproduced in the annual editions of the U.S. Bureau of the Census, *Statistical Abstract of the United States*. The subdivisions into four major groupings have been added to the list.

NOTE: Figures may not add up because they have been rounded off.

Among the four major categories set out by Machlup, two showed a substantial increase over the period of our study in their share of all titles published. Practical books increased from 14.8 percent of all new books published in 1958 to 22.0 percent in 1980. (See Tables VI-2 and VI-4.) Intellectual books showed a similar increase from 52 percent to 57.2 percent. The share of "pastime" books, however, declined by half, from 22.7 percent to 11.8 percent. Spiritual books declined from 8.5 percent to 4.8 percent. Within these broad categories, several classes of books have shown particularly notable changes.

TABLE VI-3

Books and Pamphlets: Quantity and Value of Sales by
Publishers, 1954, 1958, 1963, 1967, 1972, and 1977

	1954	1958	1963	1967	1972	1977
	Copies sold (in thousands)					
Textbooks, elementary and high school	81.8	99.5	135.7	163.0	158.1	153.3
Textbooks, college	15.8	22.6	33.5	57.9	57.1	80.8
Workbooks	59.4	82.6	106.3	124.3	97.1	84.0
Reference books	25.9	30.6	35.7	33.1	31.0	n.a.
Religious books	30.3[a]	70.8	59.4	57.1	93.9	99.7
Technical, scientific and professional books	19.2	23.7	31.4	36.1	46.5	61.7
General books, adult	274.6	340.9	406.2	529.6	702.7	917.3
General books, juvenile	220.1	172.9	175.6	209.6	63.8	114.6
All other books	43.8	56.6	41.4	47.3	44.2	29.5
Total books	770.8	900.2	1,025.2	1,258.0	1,294.4	1,540.9
Pamphlets	267.1	435.7	n.a.	n.a.	464.3	191.0
	Receipts (in millions of dollars)					
Textbooks, elementary and high school	101.7	148.1	241.0	342.5	365.1	558.0
Textbooks, college	51.7	84.1	146.6	259.3	322.4	579.0
Workbooks	26.9	43.3	61.1	88.6	88.7	220.8
Reference books	89.8	152.7	207.3	216.3	235.3	305.4
Religious books	36.0[a]	58.7	81.1	110.4	131.2	236.3
Technical, scientific and professional books	63.6	114.1	156.3	240.2	403.0	684.1
General books, adult	169.2	214.3	385.5	550.2	918.5	1,734.4
General books, juvenile	50.8	61.6	72.7	107.5	88.2	161.2
All other books	38.8	64.9	118.5	171.1	144.6	134.2
Total books	628.6	941.8	1,470.1	2,086.1	2,697.0	4,613.4
Pamphlets	25.1	31.1[b]	58.8[b]	72.2[b]	62.9[b]	76.2[b]
Unspecified receipts	11.8	25.5	18.9	97.0	155.5	318.1
Total receipts	665.4	998.4	1,547.8	2,255.3	2,915.4	5,007.7

Source: For all years, U.S. Bureau of the Census, *Census of Manufactures* (Washington, D.C.: Government Printing Office, quinquennial ed.).

Note: Because of sample limitations, the Census Bureau does not always report the quantity of books and pamphlets sold. Totals for books and pamphlets are thus, to some degree, undervaluations.

[a] For some categories of religious books, no data are available for 1954. The figures in the table include the residue taken from the official tabulation.
[b] "Standardized tests" are merged with "pamphlets" for all years, despite being listed by the Bureau of the Census among books in each year from 1958.

Fiction has declined from 14.5 percent to only 5.6 percent of all books published. Sociology and economics titles increased almost fourfold, increasing to 17.3 percent from 4.5 percent. Yet agriculture titles remained unchanged at 1.1 percent.

Surprisingly, these trends are not corroborated by the statistics on copies sold

TABLE VI-4

BOOKS: PERCENT DISTRIBUTION OF TITLES PUBLISHED, COPIES
SOLD, AND DOLLARS RECEIVED AMONG TYPES OF KNOWLEDGE,
1954, 1958, 1963, 1967, 1972, AND 1977

	1954	1958	1963	1967	1972	1977
			Titles published			
Practical	15.7	14.8	14.7	15.1	16.0	20.2
Intellectual	48.1	52.0	57.0	59.8	62.1	57.5
Pastime	25.2	22.7	18.8	16.3	14.4	13.6
Spiritual	7.5	8.5	7.7	6.9	4.6	5.2
Not allocated	3.5	1.9	1.8	1.9	2.9	3.5
	100.0	100.0	100.0	100.0	100.0	100.0
			Copies sold			
Practical	19.3	21.7	24.4	23.8	21.3	17.4
Intellectual	42.5	39.5	39.9	41.0	40.5	41.9
Pastime	34.0	30.4	29.6	30.5	30.7	34.1
Spiritual	4.2	8.4	6.1	4.7	7.5	6.6
	100.0	100.0	100.0	100.0	100.0	100.0
			Sales receipts			
Practical	36.0	39.9	38.1	38.5	37.3	36.3
Intellectual	39.3	37.7	39.1	38.5	37.8	37.2
Pastime	18.6	15.7	16.9	17.2	19.9	21.2
Spiritual	6.1	6.7	5.9	5.8	5.1	5.3
	100.0	100.0	100.0	100.0	100.0	100.0

SOURCES: Tables VI-2 and VI-3 in this book.

NOTE: Figures may not add because they have been rounded off.

and sales receipts that are reported in Table VI-3. The problem may simply be that our arbitrary division into major categories is not comparable among the different data sources. This is borne out to some extent by the substantial category of spiritual books, which is the only clearly comparable category among our various data series. The trends among all three series are consistent for spiritual books. Each of our other three categories of books shows erratic trends among titles published, copies sold, and sales receipts.

PERIODICALS

Tables VI-5 and VI-6 present our findings on periodicals such as magazines, journals, and bulletins. Over the twenty-two years of our study the number of periodicals published in this country has grown from 8,074 to 10,236. Most of this growth can be attributed to an increase in the number of bimonthly and quarterly publications, which tallied 1,473 in 1958, but 2,558 in 1980. In contrast, the number of weekly and monthly publications remained relatively sta-

TABLE VI-5

PERIODICALS: NUMBER OF TITLES AND ISSUES AND RECEIPTS FROM SALES, SUBSCRIPTIONS, AND ADVERTISING, 1958-1980

Year	Number of periodicals published (1)	Number of issues copyrighted (2)	Total receipts (millions of dollars) (3)	Receipts from sales and subscriptions (millions of dollars) (4)	Receipts from advertising* (millions of dollars) (5)
1958	8,074	60,691	1,639.1	582.8	1,056.3
1963	8,758	69,682	2,035.5	741.1	1,294.4
1967	9,238	81,647	2,668.2	930.1	1,738.1
1972	9,062	84,686	3,187.0	1,298.3	1,888.7
1977	9,732		5,528.8	2,278.5	3,250.3
1980	10,236		8,418.7	3,469.5	4,949.2**

SOURCES: Column (1): *Ayer Directory Publications* (Bala Cynwyd, Pa.: Ayer Press, annual ed.); Column (2): Library of Congress, *Annual Report of the Register of Copyrights* (Washington, D.C.: Government Printing Office, annual ed.); Columns (3)-(5): U.S. Bureau of the Census, *Census of Manufactures*, quinquennial ed. and the *1980 Annual Survey of Manufactures*, 1981.

NOTE: Changes in the copyright laws make comparisons impossible for the years 1977 to 1980 with earlier years.

* Small amounts of "miscellaneous" receipts have been added to "advertising" receipts.

** For 1980, allocation of receipts between "sales and subscriptions" and "advertising" is made in the same proportion as that reported for 1977 by the Bureau of the Census.

ble, the latter rising from 3,925 to 3,985, and the former from 1,619 to 1,716.[4]

Publishers' receipts from periodicals increased five-fold over the years of our study, rising from $1,639 million to $8,419 million. Somewhat more of this revenue came from advertising than from sales and subscriptions; 64 percent of the total in 1958, and 59 percent in 1980.

Some sense of the types of knowledge conveyed by periodicals can be obtained by repeating Machlup's exercise of dividing the various types of periodicals into four groups: Practical, intellectual, pastime, and spiritual. Impressionistic rather than statistically rigorous, the results of the exercise nonetheless are interesting. Drawing from Machlup's work and our Table VI-6, we see for example that "spiritual" publications ranged from 10.4 percent to 4.5 percent of all titles at different times between 1963 and 1977. "Practical" works ranged between 38.4 percent and 38.8 percent of the total, while "intellectual" works were between 12.9 percent and 23.6 percent at various times. "Pastime" publications fluctuated most over the years of our study, between 27.2 percent and 44.2 percent.

NEWSPAPERS

The number of newspapers in the United States has declined substantially over the last several years of our study, after remaining extremely stable for al-

[4] U.S. Bureau of the Census, *Census of Manufactures* (Washington, D.C.: Government Printing Office, quinquennial eds.).

TABLE VI-6

PERIODICALS: RECEIPTS FROM SALES AND SUBSCRIPTIONS BY MAJOR
SUBJECTS AND TYPES OF KNOWLEDGE CONVEYED, 1963 AND 1977
(millions of dollars)

Major Subject Matter	Total	Practical	Intellectual	Pastime	Spiritual
1963					
Agriculture and Farm	8	8			
Business and Finance	13	13			
Comics	11			11	
General Interest	279	93	93	93	
General News	39	13	13	13	
Professional and Technical	56	28	28		
Religious	66				66
Scientific and Engineering	30	15	15		
Trade	20	20			
Women's Fashion and Service	110	55		55	
All other and unspecified	109				
Total without unclassified	632	245	149	172	66
Percent Distribution		38.8	23.6	27.2	10.4
1977					
Agriculture and Farm	15	15			
Business and Finance	37	37			
Comics	33			33	
Fraternal and Club	99			99	
General Interest	488	163	162	163	
General News	259	86	87	86	
Professional and Technical	102	51	51		
Religious	104				104
Sports, Outdoor, Hobby	454			454	
Trade	349	349			
Women's Fashion and Service	382	191		191	
All other and unspecified	41				
Total without unclassified	2,322	892	300	1,026	104
Percent Distribution		38.4	12.9	44.2	4.5

SOURCE: U.S. Bureau of the Census, *Census of Manufactures*, 1963 and 1977.

most two decades. Table VI-7 indicates that the total number of newspapers published declined slightly between 1963 and 1977, dropping from 11,311 to 11,089. The following three years, however, have witnessed the number of papers plummet to 9,620. While the recent death of prominent dailies, such as *The Washington Star*, has attracted the bulk of the media attention, it has been the attrition among the weekly papers that has caused the major part of the decline. Weekly papers have diminished in number from 8,915 in 1963 to 7,159 in 1980. At the same time, the number of dailies has declined only from 1,754 to 1,745.

TABLE VI-7

NEWSPAPERS: NUMBER AND RECEIPTS FROM SALES, SUBSCRIPTIONS,
AND ADVERTISING, 1958, 1963, 1967, 1972, 1977, AND 1980

	Number of papers			Receipts (millions of dollars)		
Year	Total[a]	Daily	Weekly	Semi-weekly	Total	Sales and subscriptions	Advertising[b]
1958		1,756			3,458.3	979.3	2,479.0
1963	11,311	1,754	8,915	370	4,254.7	1,147.3	3,107.4
1967	11,307	1,749	8,915	366	5,549.8	1,387.3	4,162.5
1972	11,299	1,761	8,682	398	7,901.1	1,852.9	6,048.2
1977	11,089	1,753	8,506	550	12,468.1	2,801.7	9,666.4
1980	9,620	1,745	7,159	537	17,155.7	3,855.0	13,300.7[c]

SOURCES: For number of papers, see *Ayer Directory Publications*. For receipts, see U.S. Bureau of the Census, *Census of Manufactures*, quinquennial ed. and U.S. Bureau of the Census, *1980 Annual Survey of Manufactures*.

[a] Because of the existence of "other" newspapers not classified above, the sum of daily, weekly, and semiweekly will not add to total.

[b] Small amounts of "miscellaneous" receipts have been added to "advertising" receipts.

[c] For 1980 allocation of receipts between "sales and subscriptions" and "advertising" is made in the same proportions as that reported for 1977 by the Bureau of the Census.

The relative stability of daily papers is further shown by the circulation trend of these newspapers, in the aggregate, on a per issue basis. Table VI-8 shows that the per issue circulation of daily newspapers has increased only slightly between 1958 and 1980, rising from 57.6 million to 62.2 million. Unfortunately, no similar statistics are available for the circulation of weekly and semiweekly papers.

Due in large part no doubt to inflation, newspaper revenues have steadily increased, rising from $3,458.3 million in 1958 to $17,155.7 million in 1980. Receipts from sales and subscriptions have increased fourfold over this period, from $979.3 million to $3,855.0 million, while receipts from advertising have increased more than fivefold, from $2,479.0 million to $13,300.7 million.

Table VI-9 replicates Machlup's exercise of dividing the subject matter of newspaper reports into the four types of knowledge: Practical, intellectual, pastime, and spiritual. The two studies reported upon in Table VI-9, which measure the amount of space accorded various types of news stories, were separated by a period of almost two decades, occurring in 1954 and 1973. Unfortunately, complete comparability between the two studies is prevented since the 1973 study reported "news photographs" as a separate category, whereas the 1954 study included them under whatever type of news story they accompanied. Even so, it would appear that "practical" stories grew slightly in the space accorded them over the two decades of our study, mostly at the expense of intellectual and pastime stories.

TABLE VI-8

NEWSPAPERS: CIRCULATION OF DAILY AND SUNDAY PAPERS, COMPARED WITH NUMBER OF HOUSEHOLDS, 1955-1980

Year	Total circulation		Number of households	Per household	
	Dailies	Sundays	(millions)	Dailies	Sundays
	(millions)				
	(1)	(2)	(3)	(4)	(5)
1955	56.1	46.4	47.9	1.17	0.969
1956	57.3	47.2	48.9	1.17	0.965
1957	58.0	47.1	49.7	1.17	0.948
1958	57.6	47.0	50.5	1.14	0.931
1959	58.3	47.8	51.4	1.13	0.930
1960	58.9	47.7	52.8	1.12	0.903
1961	59.3	48.2	53.3	1.11	0.904
1962	59.8	48.9	54.7	1.09	0.894
1963	58.9	46.8	55.2	1.07	0.848
1964	60.4	48.4	56.0	1.08	0.864
1965	60.4	48.6	57.4	1.05	0.847
1966	61.4	49.2	58.1	1.06	0.847
1967	61.6	49.2	58.8	1.05	0.837
1968	62.5	49.7	60.4	1.03	0.823
1969	62.1	49.7	61.8	1.00	0.804
1970	62.1	49.2	63.4	0.979	0.776
1971	62.2	49.7	64.7	0.961	0.768
1972	62.5	49.3	66.7	0.937	0.739
1973	63.1	51.7	68.3	0.924	0.757
1974	61.9	51.7	69.9	0.886	0.740
1975	60.6	51.1	71.1	0.852	0.719
1976	61.0	51.6	72.9	0.837	0.708
1977	61.5	52.4	74.1	0.830	0.707
1978	62.0	54.0	76.0	0.816	0.711
1979	62.2	54.4	77.3	0.805	0.704
1980	62.2	54.7	79.1	0.786	0.692

SOURCES: *Editor and Publisher International Yearbook* figures reproduced in the U.S. Bureau of the Census, *Statistical Abstract of the United States*, annual ed.; and U.S. Bureau of the Census, *Current Population Reports*, Series P-25 (Washington, D.C.: Government Printing Office, published intermittently, 1955-1980).

EXPENDITURES FOR PERIODICALS AND NEWSPAPERS

Table VI-10 presents computation of the distribution cost of newspapers and periodicals. When added to publishers' receipts from domestic sales and receipts from advertising, the result is total domestic expenditures for these items.

Total expenditures for periodicals increased from $1,796 million in 1958 to $8,632 million in 1980. (See Row 17, Table VI-10.) Over the same time period, total domestic expenditures for newspapers increased from $3,789 million to $18,078 million. (See Row 28, Table VI-10.)

OTHER PRINTED MATTER

Tables VI-10A, VI-11, and VI-12 report expenditures for commercial printing and lithography and stationery and other office supplies. Table VI-10A re-

TABLE VI-9

NEWSPAPERS: DISTRIBUTION OF SPACE, EXCLUSIVE OF ADVERTISING,
AMONG VARIOUS SUBJECT MATTER CLASSES AND TYPES OF KNOWLEDGE,
1954 AND 1973

Subject matter and type	1954 Percent of total		1973 Percent of total	
Practical		7.9		11.7
Home and garden	3.8		5.2	
Economics (one half)	4.1		6.5	
Intellectual		33.4		21.0
Politics	2.0			
Government	11.5		10.6	
Foreign	5.4		2.6	
Economics (one half)	4.1		6.5	
Education, science, etc.	7.3		0.6	
Serious arts	0.9		0.7	
Information features	2.2			
Pastime		51.4		44.4
Crime and vice	4.0		2.7	
Accidents and disaster	3.6		1.4	
Popular entertainment	3.6		5.2	
Comics	8.4		8.9	
Personalities	1.8		3.3	
Society	12.7		8.3	
Sports	13.0		13.2	
Human interest	4.3		1.4	
Spiritual		2.0		1.0
Churches, religion	2.0		1.0	
Unclassified		5.3		21.9
		100.0		100.0

SOURCES: Charles E. Swanson, "What They Read in 130 Daily Newspapers," *Journalism Quarterly*, Vol. 32, No. 3 (1955), pp. 411-421; and David H. Weaver and L. E. Mullins, "Content and Format of Competing Newspapers," *Journalism Quarterly*, Vol. 52, No. 3 (1975), pp. 257-264.

produces in tabular form information that Machlup presented textually. Federal purchases of commercial printing and lithography are debited from the whole in order to avoid double counting as they were previously tallied under books and pamphlets in Table VI-1. Domestic use of commercial printing and lithography increased from $3,058 million in 1958 to $15,643 million in 1980. (See Row 12, Table VI-10A.)

Tables VI-11 and VI-12 replicate Machlup's original tables faithfully, with the exception that expenditures by individuals, government, and business are reported here in detail, rather than in Table VI-13. Table VI-12 shows that total expenditures for stationery and other office supplies increased from $1,863 million in 1958 to $9,673 million in 1980.

TABLE VI-10

PERIODICALS AND NEWSPAPERS: CONSUMPTION EXPENDITURES,
PUBLISHERS' RECEIPTS, EXPORTS, IMPORTS, DISTRIBUTION
COST, AND TOTAL COST, 1958, 1963, 1967, 1972, 1977, AND 1980
(millions of dollars)

	1958	1963	1967	1972	1977	1980
(1) Personal consumption expenditures for periodicals and newspapers*	2,061	2,467	3,207	4,659	6,456	8,562
(2) Imports	11	4	8	31	63	102
(3) Personal consumption expenditures for domestic periodicals and newspapers [(1) + (2)]	2,050	2,463	3,199	4,628	6,393	8,460
Publishers' receipts from sales and subscriptions						
(4) Periodicals, total	583	741	930	1,298	2,279	3,470
(5) Exports	32	46	77	98	185	312
(6) Domestic sales and subscriptions [(4) − (5)]	551	695	853	1,200	2,094	3,158
(7) Newspapers, total	979	1,147	1,387	1,853	2,802	3,855
(8) Exports	4	2	3	2	7	10
(9) Domestic sales and subscriptions [(7) − (8)]	975	1,145	1,384	1,851	2,795	3,845
(10) Periodicals and newspapers, total domestic sales and subscriptions [(6) + (9)]	1,526	1,840	2,237	3,051	4,889	7,003
(11) Distribution cost, total [(3) − (10)]	524	623	962	1,577	1,504	1,457
(12) Periodicals	189	224	346	568	541	525
(13) Newspapers	335	399	616	1,009	963	932
Periodicals						
(14) Distribution cost [from (12)]	189	224	346	568	541	525
(15) Publishers' receipts from domestic sales [from (6)]	551	695	853	1,200	2,094	3,158
(16) Publishers' receipts from advertising	1,056	1,294	1,738	1,889	3,250	4,949
(17) Cost of domestic production for domestic use [(14) + (15) + (16)]	1,796	2,213	2,937	3,657	5,885	8,632
(18) Add imports	7	2	4	19	29	67
(19) Domestic use (intake) [(17) + (18)]	1,803	2,215	2,941	3,676	5,914	8,699
Paid for by						
(20) Personal consumption expenditures	747	921	1,203	1,787	2,664	3,750
(21) Government expenditures						
(22) Business expenditures	1,056	1,294	1,738	1,889	3,250	4,949
Newspapers						
(23) Distribution cost [from (13)]	335	399	616	1,009	963	932
(24) Publishers' receipts from domestic sales [from (9)]	975	1,145	1,384	1,851	2,795	3,845
(25) Publishers' receipts from advertising	2,479	3,107	4,163	6,048	9,666	13,301

TABLE VI-10 (con't)

	1958	1963	1967	1972	1977	1980
(26) Cost of domestic production for domestic use [(23) + (24) + (25)]	3,789	4,651	6,163	8,908	13,424	18,078
(27) Add imports	4	2	4	12	34	35
(28) Domestic use (intake) [(26) + (27)]	3,793	4,653	6,167	8,920	13,458	18,113
Paid for by						
(29) Personal consumption expenditures	1,314	1,546	2,004	2,872	3,792	4,812
(30) Government expenditures						
(31) Business expenditures	2,479	3,107	4,163	6,048	9,666	13,301

SOURCES: U.S. Bureau of Economic Analysis, *The National Income and Product Accounts of the United States, 1929-1976* (Washington, D.C.: Government Printing Office, 1976); U.S. Bureau of Economic Analysis, *Survey of Current Business* (Washington, D.C.: Government Printing Office, July 1982); U.S. Bureau of the Census, *Census of Manufactures*, quinquennial ed.; and U.S. Bureau of the Census, *1980 Annual Survey of Manufactures*. Also, rows (4) and (16) from Table VI-5 and rows (7) and (25) from Table VI-7.

* Includes sheet music.

Table VI-13 summarizes our findings for all printed materials for each year of our study. In Row 1 we see that total domestic expenditures for all printed matter increased from $12,202 million in 1958 to $61,954 million in 1980.

PHOTOGRAPHY AND PHONOGRAPHY[5]

PHOTOGRAPHY

The difficulties in preparing a statistical story of the role of photography in this country's economy have not lessened since Machlup wrote; however, the importance of this category has been enhanced by new technological innovation. It is a quirk of our economic statistics that paper copiers—the ubiquitous xerox machines—are counted among photographic goods rather than among office machines and equipment by the Bureau of the Census. Furthermore, it is not possible to separate paper copiers from other photographic equipment and supplies, since the Census Bureau has generally withheld data on the paper copier industry in order to protect the confidentiality of the data provided to it by the industry leader. Data are typically available only for the total production of the photography industry, plus a few of its components, but not in great detail.

Our method of measuring this industry is different from Machlup's, who felt able to omit most of the industry for lack of data. He reported only on personal consumption. We shall use a method Machlup rejected, which is to report on production statistics, corrected for export and import data. We recognize that these statistics will underestimate the market value of these goods and services

[5] See Machlup, *Production and Distribution of Knowledge*, pp. 236-241.

TABLE VI-10A

COMMERCIAL PRINTING AND LITHOGRAPHY: 1958, 1963, 1967, 1972, 1977, AND 1980
(millions of dollars)

	1958	1963	1967	1972	1977	1980
(1) Gross receipts of commercial printers	2,428	2,711	2,835	3,381	4,621	5,705
(2) Receipts of printers from newspapers, etc.	613	743	594	476	570	784
(3) Net receipts of commercial printers [(1) minus (2)]	1,815	1,968	2,241	2,905	4,051	4,921
(4) Gross receipts of lithographic printing	1,366	2,025	2,982	4,920	8,980	13,353
(5) Receipts from newspapers, periodicals	84	158	313	762	1,522	2,094
(6) Net receipts of lithographic printing [(4) minus (5)]	1,282	1,867	2,669	4,158	7,458	11,259
(7) Total printing and lithography [(3) plus (6)]	3,097	3,835	4,910	7,063	11,509	16,180
(8) Federal purchases of printing and lithography	27	118	89	130	258	470
(9) Net national output, printing and lithography [(7) minus (8)]	3,070	3,717	4,821	6,933	11,251	15,710
(10) Deduct exports	31	65	51	68	168	246
(11) Add imports	19	18	20	61	134	179
(12) Domestic use	3,058	3,670	4,790	6,926	11,217	15,643
Paid for by						
(13) Personal consumption expenditures						
(14) Government expenditures						
(15) Business expenditures	3,058	3,670	4,790	6,926	11,217	15,643

SOURCES: Rows (1), (2), (4), and (5): U.S. Bureau of the Census, *Census of Manufactures*, for various years, and the *1980 Annual Survey of Manufactures*. Row (8): U.S. Office of Management and Budget, *The Budget of the Government of the United States* (Washington, D.C.: Government Printing Office, annual ed.).

NOTE: Receipts of commercial printers and lithographers from newspapers, for 1980, are estimated from the ratio of 1977 receipts to total receipts of newspaper publishers.

since the "value added" of wholesale and retail distribution will not be captured, and further, that we will not be able to allocate most of these expenditures among business, government, and personal consumption expenditures. We feel, however, that these limitations should not invalidate those available data.

Total domestic production of photographic goods and services, corrected for imports and exports, rose from $1,272 million in 1958 to $1,339 million in

TABLE VI-11

STATIONERY: PAPER PRODUCTS, CARDS, BLANK BOOKS, AND OTHER
OFFICE SUPPLIES, 1958, 1963, 1967, 1972, 1977, AND 1980
(millions of dollars)

	1958	1963	1967	1972	1977	1980
Printed products						
Greeting cards	277	310	441	584	765	1,096
Other cards (including picture postcards)	6	12	15	13	15	
Blank books and paper ruling	118	124	187	320	606	950
Loose-leaf binders and devices	95	120	154	210	346	539
Business services, indexes, etc.	73	102	123	242	417	562
Paper products						
Die-cut office supplies	56	68	93	130	200]	
Die-cut cards (including machine tabulation cards)	88	143	158	131	140]	745
Stationery tablets, and related products	151	202	257	422	631	841
Business machines paper supplies	45	100	72	77	201	
Office supplies						
Pens, mechanical pencils, and parts	147	178	211	312	563	786
Lead pencils, leads and crayons	65	69	74	63	91	175
Hand stamps and stencils	59	107	131	164	216	271
Carbon paper, stencil paper, and inked ribbon	119	161	222	318	489	632
Total manufacturers' sales	1,299	1,696	2,138	2,986	4,680	6,597
Personal consumption expenditures for stationery and writing supplies	954	1,259	1,757	2,424	3,748	5,707
Retailers' markup (40%)	382	504	703	970	1,499	2,283
Manufacturers' sales for consumers' use	572	755	1,054	1,454	2,249	3,424
Manufacturers' sales for business and government use	727	941	1,084	1,532	2,431	3,173
Total manufacturers' sales	1,299	1,696	2,138	2,986	4,680	6,597

SOURCES: U.S. Bureau of the Census, *Census of Manufactures*, 1963, 1967, 1972, 1977, and 1980; and U.S. Bureau of Economic Analysis, *Survey of Current Business*, July issues of 1959, 1964, 1968, 1973, 1978, and 1981.

NOTE: Other miscellaneous office supplies were withheld to avoid disclosing figures for individual companies.

1963; $3,052 million in 1967; $7,194 million in 1972; and $12,130 million and $17,061 million in 1977 and 1980 respectively, according to statistics reported by the U.S. Bureau of the Census.[6]

[6] See the quinquennial editions of the *Census of Manufactures*, plus the *1980 Annual Survey of Manufactures*, all published by Government Printing Office, Washington, D.C.

TABLE VI-12

STATIONERY AND OTHER OFFICE SUPPLIES: TOTAL EXPENDITURES
INCLUDING DISTRIBUTION COSTS, 1958, 1963, 1967, 1972,
1977, AND 1980
(millions of dollars)

	1958	1963	1967	1972	1977	1980
Manufacturers' sales for government and business use	727	941	1,084	1,532	2,431	3,173
Add 25% for distribution cost	182	236	271	383	608	793
Expenditures by government and business	909	1,177	1,355	1,915	3,039	3,966
Personal consumption expenditures	954	1,259	1,757	2,424	3,748	5,707
Total expenditures of stationery and office supplies (output)	1,863	2,436	3,112	4,339	6,787	9,673
Deduct exports	15	30	34	43	183	159
Add imports	2	2	28	35	83	111
Domestic use (intake)	1,850	2,408	3,106	4,331	6,687	9,625
Paid for by						
Personal consumption expenditures	954	1,259	1,757	2,424	3,748	5,707
Government expenditures	182	235	271	383	608	793
Business expenditures	727	942	1,084	1,532	2,431	3,173

SOURCE: See Table VI-11 in this book.

TABLE VI-13

TOTAL EXPENDITURES FOR ALL PRINTED MATTER AND WRITING
SUPPLIES: 1958, 1963, 1967, 1972, 1977, AND 1980
(millions of dollars)

	1958	1963	1967	1972	1977	1980
National production (output)	12,202	15,423	20,367	28,313	44,927	61,954
Deduct exports	126	206	309	381	858	1,256
Add imports	36	64	126	263	451	760
Domestic use (intake)	12,112	15,281	20,184	28,195	44,520	61,458
Paid for by						
Personal consumption expenditures	4,196	5,139	6,811	10,004	14,708	21,118
Government expenditures	525	850	1,248	1,463	2,564	2,329
Business expenditures	7,391	9,292	12,125	16,728	27,248	38,011

SOURCES: See previous tables and discussions in this book.

PHONOGRAPHY

Tables VI-14 and VI-15 describe the growth of phonography over the years of our study. Table VI-14 shows that expenditures for phonograph records have increased steadily from their level of $390 million in 1958 to $2,450 million in 1980. Table VI-15 shows that expenditures for portable and console pho-

TABLE VI-14

PHONOGRAPH RECORDS: RETAIL SALES, 1921-1980
(millions of dollars)

Year	Sales	Year	Sales
1921	105.6	1951	178.5
1922	92.4	1952	189.0
1923	79.2	1953	191.1
1924	68.2	1954	182.7
1925	59.4	1955	235.2
1926	70.4	1956	312.6
1927	70.4	1957	400.0
1928	72.6	1958	390.0
1929	74.8	1959	462.0
1930	46.2	1960	521.0
1931	17.6	1961	587.0
1932	11.0	1962	651.0
1933	5.5	1963	658.0
1934	6.6	1964	693.0
1935	8.8	1965	789.0
1936	11.0	1966	959.0
1937	13.2	1967	1,051.0
1938	26.4	1968	1,124.0
1939	44.0	1969	1,170.0
1940	48.4	1970	1,182.0
1941	50.6	1971	1,251.0
1942	55.0	1972	1,383.0
1943	66.0	1973	1,436.0
1944	66.0	1974	1,550.0
1945	99.0	1975	1,668.0
1946	198.0	1976	1,908.0
1947	203.7	1977	2,440.2
1948	172.2	1978	2,733.6
1949	157.5	1979	2,411.2
1950	172.2	1980	2,450.0

SOURCE: U.S. Bureau of the Census, *Statistical Abstract of the United States*, annual ed.

nographs, tape recorders, and component systems have increased from $645 million in 1958 to $3,680 million in 1980. (See Column 9, Table VI-15.)

STAGE AND CINEMA[7]

Table VI-16 presents personal consumption expenditures for attendance at motion pictures, theaters, concerts, and spectator sports for the years of our study. Machlup's original Table VI-16 contained information on receipts for various aspects of the motion picture industry, including production, distribution, and theaters. This created some inconsistency, since our GNP ac-

[7] See Machlup, *Production and Distribution of Knowledge*, pp. 241-250.

TABLE VI-15

PHONOGRAPHS AND TAPE RECORDERS: RETAIL SALES, 1958-1980

Year	Portable and table Phonographs		Console phonographs		Tape recorders		Component systems		Total Retail Sales**
	Number (thousands) (1)	Retail sales (millions of dollars) (2)	Number (thousands) (3)	Retail sales (millions of dollars) (4)	Number (thousands) (5)	Retail sales (millions of dollars) (6)	Number (thousands) (7)	Retail sales (millions of dollars) (8)	(millions of dollars) (9)
1958	4,096*	575.0*			400	70.0			645.0
1959	4,275*	544.0*			400	56.0			600.0
1960	2,958	585.0*	1,375		425	75.0			660.0
1961	2,452	567.0*	1,461		600	90.0			657.0
1962	3,411	737.0*	1,675		720	105.0			842.0
1963	3,372	777.0*	1,770			79.0			856.0
1964	3,363	615.0*	1,859			97.0			712.0
1965	4,436	271.0	1,809	525.0	3,445	122.0			918.0
1966	4,432	248.0	1,810	483.0	5,000	113.0			844.0
1967	3,986	215.0	1,496	437.0	4,025	117.0			769.0
1968	4,020	233.0	1,586	457.0	5,573	160.0			850.0
1969	3,495	252.0	1,379	455.0	6,929	198.0			905.0
1970	2,856	174.0	1,004	331.0	8,459	244.0			749.0
1971	3,500	210.0	1,062	334.0	8,747	707.0			1,251.0
1972	4,256	213.0	928	296.0	10,268	861.0			1,370.0
1973	5,235	246.0	900	228.0	12,000	998.0			1,472.0
1974	3,942	355.0	865	235.0	10,400	886.0			1,476.0
1975	3,491	681.0	523	149.0	11,200	687.0	10,105	1,017.0	2,534.0
1976	3,582	716.0	654	215.0	11,700	679.0	10,891	1,143.0	2,753.0
1977	4,508	915.0	725	254.0	12,905	754.0	12,045	1,324.0	3,247.0
1978	4,474	963.0	600	186.0	13,963	872.0	13,190	1,497.0	3,518.0
1979	4,341	939.0	540	108.0	14,240	877.0	14,562	1,705.0	3,629.0
1980	3,851	813.0	470	99.0	15,600	996.0	14,700	1,772.0	3,680.0

SOURCES: *Merchandising Annual Statistical and Marketing Reports* (New York: Gralla Publications, Inc., annual ed.), except for retail value of tape recorders, 1963 through 1972, which was taken from *Television Factbook* (Washington, D.C.: Television Digest, Inc., 1974).

* For the years 1958 through 1964, retail sales values for various types of phonographs were not reported separately.
** Column (9) is the sum of Columns (2), (4), (6), and (8).

counting for the knowledge industry uses personal consumption expenditures to measure the value of theaters, concerts, and spectator sports. Thus, Table VI-16 has been recast. Personal consumption expenditures for motion pictures increased from $992 million in 1958 to $2,822 million in 1980; for theaters and concerts, from $297 million to $1,318 million; and for spectator sports from $249 million to $2,284 million. As these figures show, the popularity battle between the theater and sports noted by Machlup has been decisively won over the last two decades by spectator sports.

TABLE VI-16

PERSONAL CONSUMPTION EXPENDITURES FOR MOTION PICTURES, THEATERS AND CONCERTS,
AND SPECTATOR SPORTS, 1950-1980
(millions of dollars)

Year	Motion pictures	Theaters and concerts	Spectator sports
1950	1,376	183	222
1955	1,326	245	230
1956	1,394	268	237
1957	1,126	287	242
1958	992	297	249
1959	954	317	300
1960	956	342	354
1961	955	327	403
1962	945	350	462
1963	942	356	522
1964	951	383	588
1965	1,067	388	668
1966	1,119	432	759
1967	1,128	474	802
1968	1,294	488	871
1969	1,400	516	987
1970	1,521	556	1,064
1971	1,626	570	1,163
1972	1,644	632	1,211
1973	1,766	670	1,223
1974	2,034	717	1,265
1975	1,480	667	1,444
1976	1,742	929	1,555
1977	2,376	868	1,753
1978	2,442	1,064	1,944
1979	2,562	1,230	2,139
1980	2,822	1,318	2,284

SOURCE: U.S. Bureau of Economic Analysis, *Survey of Current Business*, monthly eds. Annual data are normally reported in the July issue.

The interrelated structure of the motion picture industry is depicted by Table VI-17, which sets out the distribution of revenues among the parts of the industry. Wholesale distribution of motion pictures has become an increasingly large factor in the years from 1941 to 1977.

In part, this result may be a statistical quirk, but it also reflects the increased market for motion pictures outside of the traditional cinema, particularly in television. Table VI-18 further amplifies this theme, showing that the number of films produced in the United States has declined substantially over the last two decades. At the same time, for the years before 1969 when data are available, imports were becoming a more significant factor in the national market. Both of these influences, the television broadcast of movies and the greater ap-

TABLE VI-17

Motion Pictures: Distribution of Gross Receipts, 1941, 1958, 1963, 1967, 1972, and 1977
(percent of total)

	1941	1958	1963	1967	1972	1977
Gross box office receipts	100.0	100.0	100.0	100.0	100.0	100.0
Payroll	16.0	23.1	23.5	21.7	20.8	17.7
Local advertising	8.0				3.8	4.2
Other	41.0	40.3	34.6	34.1	36.5	29.9
Profit			5.6	5.6	3.5	
Total local theater	65.0	63.4	63.7	61.4	64.6	51.8
Wholesale distribution	10.0	17.6	18.6	20.2		34.8
Film production	25.0	19.0	17.7	18.4		13.4

Sources: U.S. Bureau of the Census, *Census of Business* (Washington, D.C.: Government Printing Office, quinquennial ed.);
U.S. Bureau of the Census, *Census of Service Industries* (Washington, D.C.: Government Printing Office, quinquennial ed.);
and U.S. Internal Revenue Service, *Statistics of Income* (Washington, D.C.: Government Printing Office, annual ed.).

peal of foreign films, would correlate the increased importance—and revenue—of the motion picture wholesaler.

BROADCASTING[8]

A statistical presentation of the maturation of the radio and television broadcast
industries is presented in Tables VI-19 through VI-21. Further, the emergence
of cable television and public broadcasting are documented separately.

BROADCAST RADIO AND TELEVISION

Table VI-19 shows that in the years from 1958 to 1980, the number of
broadcast radio stations more than doubled, climbing from 3,948 to 8,886. A
major factor in this growth was the conscious policy of the Federal Communications Commission to encourage the proliferation of FM broadcast stations.
This growth in stations was paralleled by a revenue growth for radio stations
from $523 million in 1958 to $3,206 million in 1980.

Over the same time period considered above, the number of television
broadcast stations increased from 588 to 1,013. In part, this growth can be attributed to another policy decision of the Federal Communications Commission, in this case to encourage the exploitation of the UHF television channel
frequencies. Revenues expanded from $1,030 million in 1958 to $8,808 million in 1980.

The cumulative gross investment in all broadcasting stations rose from $856
million in 1958 to $5,529 million in 1980. This figure was erroneously re-
ported by Machlup to have been the annual investment in these stations. Un-

[8] See Machlup, *Production and Distribution of Knowledge*, pp. 250-265.

TABLE VI-18

MOTION PICTURES: RELEASES OF U.S.- PRODUCED AND IMPORTED FEATURES, 1939-1980

Year	Total releases	U.S.-produced	Imported
1939	761	483	278
1949	479	356	123
1950	622	383	239
1951	654	391	263
1952	463	324	139
1953	534	344	190
1954	427	253	174
1955	392	254	138
1956	479	272	207
1957	533	300	233
1958	507	241	266
1959	439	187	252
1960	406	154	252
1961	364	131	233
1962	478	147	331
1963	401	121	280
1964	440	141	299
1965	514	153	361
1966	451	156	295
1967	462	178	284
1968	454	180	274
1969		177	
1970		231	
1971		223	
1972		224	
1973		201	
1974		179	
1975		161	
1976		188	
1977		157	
1978		162	
1979		167	
1980			

SOURCES: (1939-1968): *Yearbook of Motion Pictures* (New York: Film Daily, annual ed.). (1969-1980): Patrick Robertson, *Movie Facts and Feats* (New York: Sterling Publishing, 1980).

NOTE: After 1968 the *Yearbook of Motion Pictures* did not report "Total Releases" and "Imported" statistics. The yearbook was discontinued in 1970.

der these circumstances, and in the absence of any alternative data, no entry is made in our GNP accounts under the heading of investments in broadcast equipment. Rather, the annual investment in broadcast equipment will be reported in the chapter on "Information Machines."

CABLE TELEVISION

The emergence of cable television, or CATV, has been one of the more dramatic developments in the field of telecommunications since the publication

TABLE VI-19

GROWTH OF RADIO AND TELEVISION BROADCASTING, 1921-1980

Year	Number of households with Radio sets (thousands) (1)	TV sets (thousands) (2)	Number of stations Radio (thousands) (3)	TV (thousands) (4)	Revenues of stations Total (millions of dollars) (5)	Radio (millions of dollars) (6)	TV (7)	Cumulative gross investment in broadcasting stations Total (millions of dollars) (8)	Radio (millions of dollars) (9)	TV (10)
1921			1							
1922	60		30							
1923	400		556							
1929	10,250		606							
1930	13,750		618							
1932	18,450		604							
1935	21,456		585		86.5	86.5				
1940	28,500		765		147.1	147.1		70.9	70.9	
1941	29,300		836	2	168.8	168.8		78.0	78.0	
1942	30,600		894	4	178.8	178.8		81.3	81.3	
1943	30,800		928	4	215.4	215.3	0.1	81.1	81.1	
1945	33,100		971	6	299.6	299.3	0.3	88.1	88.1	
1946	33,998	8	1,002	6	323.3	322.6	0.7	107.8	107.8	
1947	35,900	14	1,210	7	365.6	363.7	1.9	150.0	150.0	
1948	37,623	172	2,017	17	415.7	407.0	8.7	201.8	201.8	
1949	39,300	940	2,777	69	449.5	415.2	34.3	286.5	230.6	55.9
1950	40,700	3,875	2,897	104	550.4	444.5	105.9	314.7	244.4	70.3
1951	41,900	10,320	3,013	107	686.1	450.4	235.7	347.7	254.7	93.0
1952	42,800	15,300	3,076	108	793.9	469.7	324.2	391.5	267.4	124.1
1953	44,800	20,400	3,144	199	908.0	475.3	432.7	509.3	276.2	233.1
1954	45,100	26,000	3,253	408	1,042.5	449.5	593.0	593.8	278.8	315.0
1955	45,900	30,700	3,396	469	1,198.1	453.4	744.7	649.4	284.7	364.7
1956	46,800	34,900	3,552	516	1,377.5	480.6	896.9	727.2	297.5	429.7
1957	47,700	38,900	3,744	545	1,460.5	517.2	943.3	805.8	328.2	477.6
1958	48,500	41,925	3,948	588	1,553.1	523.1	1,030.0	856.0	333.3	522.7
1959	49,450	43,950	4,153	609	1,723.9	560.0	1,163.9	936.6	373.4	563.2
1960	50,193	45,750	4,389	626	1,866.3	597.7	1,268.6	1,015.6	422.8	592.8
1961	50,695	47,200	4,677	607	1,909.0	590.7	1,318.3	1,056.5	425.5	631.0
1962	51,305	48,855	4,958	630	2,122.3	636.1	1,486.2	1,138.6	466.1	672.5
1963	52,630	50,300	5,201	651	2,278.3	681.1	1,597.2	1,215.8	492.7	723.1
1964	55,225	51,600	5,400	661	2,525.3	732.0	1,793.3	1,301.8	521.1	780.7
1965	58,156	52,700	5,630	681	2,757.3	792.5	1,964.8	1,426.6	566.8	859.8
1966	58,550	53,850	5,881	721	3,075.1	872.1	2,203.0	1,636.4	623.0	1,013.4
1967	59,761	55,130	6,161	753	3,182.7	907.3	2,275.4	1,855.7	671.0	1,184.7
1968	61,112	56,670	6,401	811	3,543.9	1,023.0	2,520.9	2,030.1	723.3	1,306.8
1969	62,511	58,250	6,647	857	3,882.0	1,085.8	2,796.2	2,225.4	780.2	1,445.2
1970	63,897	59,550	6,830	881	3,939.1	1,136.9	2,802.2	2,319.5	822.2	1,497.3
1971	65,419	61,600	7,054	890	4,008.3	1,258.0	2,750.3	2,441.8	877.2	1,564.6
1972	67,240	63,500	7,240	909	4,586.4	1,407.0	3,179.4	2,573.2	934.8	1,638.4
1973	69,379	65,600	7,438	929	4,966.2	1,501.4	3,464.8	2,616.3	885.7	1,730.6
1974	70,837	66,800	7,640	939	5,379.4	1,603.1	3,776.3	2,765.0	933.4	1,831.6
1975	72,600	68,500	7,903	949	5,819.1	1,725.0	4,094.1	2,982.0	1,004.0	1,978.0
1976	74,000	71,460	8,144	961	7,217.9	2,019.4	5,198.5	3,192.0	1,050.0	2,142.0
1977	75,800	73,100	8,387	984	8,163.5	2,274.5	5,889.0	3,436.0	1,097.5	2,338.5
1978	76,000	74,700	8,577	988	9,585.1	2,635.3	6,949.8	4,201.7	1,510.3	2,691.4
1979	77,300	76,240	8,739	1,002	10,748.5	2,873.5	7,875.0	4,774.2	1,655.5	3,118.7
1980	79,100	76,300	8,886	1,013	12,013.7	3,206.0	8,807.7	5,529.4	1,912.1	3,617.3

SOURCES: Columns (1) and (2): *Merchandising Annual Statistical and Marketing Reports*, annual ed. Columns (3) through (10): *Report of the Federal Communications Commission* (Washington, D.C.: Government Printing Office, annual ed.).

of *The Production and Distribution of Knowledge in the United States* in 1962. For the purposes of analysis in this book, CATV is listed under the category of "broadcasting" despite the mixture of techniques that cable television employs.

"Cable" television aptly describes the technology that underlies this industry, for unlike broadcast television, where signals are carried into individual homes through electronic signals captured by antenna, the messages of CATV are carried by wire directly to each user, somewhat like a telephone system. And soon, perhaps very soon, a CATV system will be able to operate with each member of the audience able to talk back to a central station where all programming originates. In the early development of CATV, a community antenna was often used to capture signals transmitted to it by microwave. More recently, CATV signals have been broadcast via communications satellite to community receivers. But regardless of the method by which those signals reach a CATV operating system, they are then "translated" for home use and are distributed by cable.

CATV originated as a means of bringing television service to communities that were outside the reception area of any television station; however, today it is gaining considerable popularity even in communities that are rich in broadcast stations. The CATV system, which is available for a monthly fee, offers viewers an even greater variety of choice than does standard broadcast television. Specialized networks featuring sports, recent movies, 24-hour news and so on, all help to attract subscribers.

The consumer attractiveness of CATV may be immeasurably increased as its capabilities as a two-way communications link become available. A new technology, called Videotex, offers computer services to the home market through cable links between the computer and the home television via cable and is the logical next step for the marketing of CATV.

The future of CATV is conjecture; the past is documented in Table VI-19A, which presents statistics on the number of CATV systems, the number of subscribers, and total revenues of CATV systems. The first two sets of data are presented from 1952 to 1980, whereas the third offers data for a more limited number of years where information is available. In the 28 years for which data are available, the number of subscribers to CATV services has grown from 14 thousand to 15.5 million and the number of systems has risen from 70 to over 4000. In 1980 CATV systems generated revenues of $2,238 million.

PUBLIC BROADCASTING SYSTEMS

Machlup described the group of 50 odd educational television stations (ETV) that broadcasted over the UHF frequency in the early 1960s. By 1980 the number of such stations had risen to 267, the beneficiaries of the FCC decision described earlier in this section that required all new televisions to be equipped to receive the UHF channels. As Machlup noted, to have equipped all existing televisions in New York City with the adapters to receive UHF would have cost $120 million; not surprisingly, the FCC order applied only to

TABLE VI-19A

CABLE TELEVISION SYSTEMS: SUBSCRIBERS AND
REVENUES, 1952-1980

Year	Operating systems (1)	Total subscribers (thousands) (2)	Total revenues cable television systems (millions of dollars) (3)
1952	70	14	
1953	150	30	
1954	300	65	
1955	400	150	
1956	450	300	
1957	500	350	
1958	525	450	
1959	560	550	
1960	640	650	
1961	700	725	
1962	800	850	
1963	1,000	950	
1964	1,200	1,085	
1965	1,325	1,275	
1966	1,570	1,575	
1967	1,770	2,100	150.0
1968	2,000	2,800	
1969	2,260	3,600	245.0
1970	2,490	4,500	295.0
1971	2,639	5,300	340.0
1972	2,841	6,000	410.0
1973	2,991	7,300	490.0
1974	3,158	8,700	590.0
1975	3,506	9,800	895.0
1976	3,681	10,800	1,000.0
1977	3,832	11,900	1,206.0
1978	3,875	13,000	1,511.0
1979	4,150	14,100	1,817.0
1980	4,225	15,500	2,238.0

SOURCES: Columns (1) and (2): *Television Factbook*, annual ed. Column (3): Prior to 1975, U.S. Department of Commerce estimates reported in *U.S. Industrial Outlook* (Washington, D.C.: Government Printing Office, annual ed.); and after 1975, the U.S. Federal Communications Commission, *Cable Television Revenues* (Washington, D.C.: Government Printing Office, annual ed.).

newly manufactured televisions. Table VI-19B reports the funding levels of these stations for the years 1972 to 1980. In order to avoid double counting, these figures are not included in our GNP accounts of the knowledge industries.

RADIO AND TELEVISION RECEIVERS

Table VI-20 presents the domestic consumption and total retail value of radios, televisions, and video cassette recorders, as well as repair expenses paid

TABLE VI-19B

PUBLIC BROADCASTING SYSTEMS: INCOME BY SOURCE, 1972-1980
(millions of dollars)

Year	Federal government	State and local government	Subscribers	Business	Foundations	Other	Total
1972	60	108	18	*	25	24	235
1973	56	127	25	10	20	17	255
1974	67	139	32	16	18	19	291
1975	92	157	42	21	29	24	365
1976	130	176	54	29	23	21	433
1977	135	191	64	40	23	29	482
1978	161	218	75	49	17	32	552
1979	163	241	86	58	20	30	598
1980	192	266	102	72	23	42	697

SOURCE: Corporation for Public Broadcasting, press release dated September 9, 1982, "Status of Federal Funding for Public Broadcasting," Washington, D.C.

* "Business" figure included in "Other" for 1972.

for those items. In 1958 these expenditures totalled $1,688 million and had risen to $9,911 million by 1980.

Table VI-21 summarizes all expenditures for radio and television services for each of the years of our study and compares it to total GNP. Expenditures for these services have consistently been under one percent of GNP, ranging between 7/10 and 9/10 of one percent of GNP.

We shall not attempt to update Machlup's discussion of the types of knowledge broadcast over radio and television, nor shall we update Tables VI-22 and VI-23, which are not presented in this book.

ADVERTISING[9]

In the last two decades, total advertising expenditures have risen from $10,302 million to $54,590 million. The distribution of these expenditures among the various media, however, has shifted very slowly as shown by the figures in Table VI-24. For example, newspapers have retained their very substantial market share, declining only from 31 percent to 28.5 percent. At the same time, television's share of the advertising market increased from 13 percent to 20.7 percent, a shift that moved television into the position of the second most used medium. Direct mail advertising declined to third place, despite the fact that its share of the advertising market declined only slightly, from 15.4 percent to 13.9 percent. Radio improved its position one notch, on an increase in market share from 6 percent to 7 percent. Other forms of advertising, including

[9] See Machlup, *Production and Distribution of Knowledge*, pp. 265-275.

TABLE VI-20

EXPENDITURES FOR RADIO AND TELEVISION
RECEIVERS, 1946-1980

	Radios		Televisions		Video Cassette Recorders				
Year	Production and imports for domestic consumption, net of exports (thousands) (1)	Retail value (millions of dollars) (2)	Production and imports for domestic consumption, net of exports (thousands) (3)	Retail value (millions of dollars) (4)	Sales (thousands) (5)	Retail value (millions of dollars) (6)	Total domestic expenditures* (millions of dollars) (7)	Private households annual repair bills for radio and TV sets (millions of dollars) (8)	Total current expenditures** (millions of dollars) (9)
1946	14,031	702.0	6	1.0			703.0	115.0	818.0
1947	16,961	926.0	179	50.0			976.0	140.0	1,116.0
1948	13,108	692.0	970	226.0			918.0	174.0	1,092.0
1949	7,972	345.0	2,970	574.0			919.0	202.0	1,121.0
1950	9,849	434.0	7,355	1,397.0			1,831.0	283.0	2,114.0
1951	8,084	277.0	5,312	944.0			1,221.0	353.0	1,574.0
1952	7,692	261.0	6,194	1,064.0			1,325.0	393.0	1,718.0
1953	8,186	269.0	6,870	1,170.0			1,439.0	434.0	1,873.0
1954	10,243	189.0	7,410	1,042.0			1,231.0	482.0	1,713.0
1955	14,190	233.0	7,758	1,078.0			1,311.0	516.0	1,827.0
1956	14,008	276.0	7,451	980.0			1,256.0	573.0	1,829.0
1957	15,448	303.0	6,473	868.0			1,171.0	682.0	1,799.0
1958	14,512	287.0	5,131	720.0			1,007.0	681.0	1,688.0
1959	21,273	325.0	6,368	843.0			1,168.0	714.0	1,882.0
1960	24,463	314.0	5,829	797.0			1,111.0	774.0	1,885.0
1961	29,222	362.0	6,315	814.0			1,174.0	825.0	1,999.0
1962	32,030	332.0	7,134	1,005.0			1,337.0	862.0	2,199.0

Year	(1)	(2)	(3)	(4)	(5)	(6)	(7)	(8)	(9)
1963	31,548	282.0	7,983	1,099.0			1,381.0	904.0	2,285.0
1964	31,871	472.0	9,764	1,384.0			1,856.0	930.0	2,786.0
1965	41,726	576.0	11,447	1,869.0			2,441.0	933.0	3,374.0
1966	44,173	613.0	12,714	2,617.0			3,230.0	946.0	4,176.0
1967	41,211	592.0	11,564	2,570.0			3,162.0	999.0	4,161.0
1968	46,832	701.0	13,211	2,677.0			3,378.0	1,057.0	4,435.0
1969	51,353	738.0	13,308	2,585.0			3,323.0	1,082.0	4,405.0
1970	44,427	651.0	12,220	2,202.0			2,853.0	1,079.0	3,932.0
1971	47,610	802.0	14,921	2,976.0			3,778.0	1,137.0	4,915.0
1972	55,311	983.0	17,084	3,474.0			4,457.0	1,222.0	5,679.0
1973	50,198	963.0	17,368	3,657.0			4,620.0	1,334.0	5,754.0
1974	43,992	929.0	15,279	3,201.0			4,130.0	1,408.0	5,538.0
1975	34,515	724.0	10,637	2,492.0			3,216.0	1,483.0	4,699.0
1976	44,101	895.0	14,131	3,380.0	43.0	52.0	4,327.0	2,415.0	6,742.0
1977	52,926	1,043.0	15,431	3,811.0	225.0	247.0	5,103.0	2,626.0	7,729.0
1978	48,035	1,067.0	17,407	4,308.0	402.0	356.0	5,731.0	2,823.0	8,554.0
1979	40,029	1,063.0	16,617	4,180.0	478.0	431.0	5,674.0	2,975.0	8,649.0
1980	37,726	1,248.0	17,508	4,620.0	804.0	700.0	6,568.0	3,343.0	9,911.0

SOURCES: Columns (1), (3), and (4): *Television Factbook*, annual ed. Column (2): Prior to 1964, *Merchandising Annual Statistical and Marketing Reports*, annual ed.; and after 1964, *Television Factbook*, annual ed. Column (5): *Merchandising Annual Statistical and Marketing Reports*, annual ed.

* Column (7) is the sum of Columns (2), (4), and (6).

** Column (9) is the sum of Columns (7) and (8).

TABLE VI-21

Expenditures for Radio and Television Services: 1958, 1963, 1967, 1972, 1977, and 1980
(millions of dollars)

Year	Total revenues of broadcast radio and TV stations (1)	Total revenues of CATV systems (2)	Expenditures on radio and TV receivers (3)	Current expenditures (1)+(2)+(3) (4)	Current expenditures as a percent of GNP (5)
1958	1,553		1,688	3,241	0.72
1963	2,278		2,285	4,563	0.76
1967	3,183	150	4,161	7,494	0.94
1972	4,586	410	5,679	10,675	0.91
1977	8,164	1,206	7,729	17,099	0.90
1980	12,014	2,238	9,911	24,163	0.92

Sources: Tables VI-19, VI-19A, and VI-20 in this book.

magazines, saw an overall decline in market share from 34.5 percent to 29.9 percent.

One surprising aspect of our findings is that the shift to national advertising noted by Machlup has, to some extent, reversed itself. Whereas national advertising accounted for 61.4 percent of all advertising in 1958 and displayed a consistent trend upward, its share peaked in 1963 at 62.2 percent and has declined ever since, reaching 55.4 percent in the late 1970s. This shift may be explained partly by the resurgence in radio caused by the popularity of automobile radios and also by the emergence of "national" magazines with advertising tailored to one or another region.

Table VI-25 replicates Machlup's 1958 comparison between the advertising receipts and expenditures of various media. Discrepancies first noted by Machlup have remained with surprising consistency. For example, expenditures have consistently exceeded receipts for newspapers, radio, and television. We accept Machlup's explanation that "the differences are evidently 'value added by the advertising industry,' that is, the fees and commissions collected by advertising agencies and public relations firms." Conversely, publishers' revenues seem to have consistently exceeded advertisers' expenditures for magazines and periodicals; but as Machlup originally noted "the expenditures are only for *magazine* advertisements, while the receipts are for periodicals of any sort" (*Production and Distribution of Knowledge*, p. 268).

THE ADVERTISERS

The shifts in advertising by different industries is beyond the scope of this study. Table VI-26, however, presents some suggestive evidence that advertising policy among large firms changes very slowly. Seven of the top ten advertising spenders in 1960 were still in that group in 1977. Even the banning of

TABLE VI-24

ADVERTISING, BY SCOPE AND MEDIUM, 1900-1980
(millions of dollars)

Year	National	Local	Total	News-papers	Maga-zines	Radio	Television	Direct mail	Other
1900			542						
1914			1,302						
1920			2,935						
1930			2,607						
1940	1,163	925	2,088	815	198	216		334	525
1950	3,257	2,453	5,710	2,076	515	605	171	803	1,540
1958	6,331	3,971	10,302	3,193	767	616	1,354	1,589	2,783
1959	6,835	4,420	11,255	3,546	866	656	1,494	1,688	3,005
1960	7,296	4,636	11,932	3,703	941	692	1,590	1,830	3,176
1961	7,270	4,575	11,845	3,623	924	683	1,691	1,850	3,074
1962	7,683	4,698	12,381	3,681	973	736	1,897	1,933	3,161
1963	8,148	4,959	13,107	3,804	1,034	789	2,032	2,078	3,370
1964	8,745	5,410	14,155	4,148	1,108	846	2,289	2,184	3,580
1965	9,398	5,857	15,255	4,457	1,199	917	2,515	2,324	3,843
1966	10,213	6,457	16,670	4,896	1,291	1,010	2,823	2,461	4,189
1967	10,250	6,616	16,866	4,942	1,280	1,031	2,889	2,488	4,236
1968	10,883	7,244	18,127	5,265	1,318	1,190	3,231	2,612	4,511
1969	11,518	7,964	19,482	5,753	1,376	1,264	3,585	2,670	4,834
1970	11,485	8,115	19,600	5,745	1,323	1,278	3,665	2,734	4,855
1971	11,775	8,965	20,740	6,215	1,405	1,380	3,520	2,950	5,270
1972	13,030	10,270	23,300	7,008	1,440	1,555	4,091	3,350	5,856
1973	13,775	11,345	25,120	7,595	1,448	1,690	4,460	3,698	6,229
1974	14,760	12,020	26,780	8,001	1,504	1,837	4,851	3,986	6,601
1975	15,410	12,820	28,230	8,442	1,465	1,980	5,263	4,181	6,899
1976	18,585	15,135	33,720	9,910	1,789	2,330	6,721	4,813	8,157
1977	21,055	17,065	38,120	11,132	2,162	2,634	7,612	5,333	9,247
1978	23,990	19,980	43,970	12,707	2,597	3,052	8,979	5,987	10,648
1979	27,070	22,650	49,720	14,493	2,930	3,385	10,195	6,650	12,067
1980	30,240	24,350	54,590	15,541	3,149	3,827	11,295	7,596	13,182

SOURCES: U.S. Bureau of the Census, *Historical Statistics of the United States, Colonial Times to 1970* (Washington, D.C.: Government Printing Office, 1975); and *Advertising Age* (New York: Crain Communications, Inc., weekly eds.).

NOTE: Among "Other" advertising media are regional farm publications, business papers, outdoor advertising, and miscellaneous advertising expenditures.

cigarette advertisements on television in the early 1970s did not reduce the aggregate expenditures for advertising by, for example, the R. J. Reynolds Industries. Reynolds' expenditures shifted massively to newspapers and magazines, but never let up.

NET ADVERTISING EXPENDITURES

For our GNP accounting purposes, the total advertising expenditures paid in each of the years of our study must be reduced by the amount of advertising receipts being counted elsewhere, to avoid double counting, as shown in Table

TABLE VI-25

Advertising: Expenditures by Advertising and Receipts
by Media, 1958, 1963, 1967, 1972, and 1977
(millions of dollars)

Advertising	Magazines or periodicals	Newspapers	Radio	TV
1958				
Expenditures	767	3,193	616	1,354
Receipts	1,017	2,444	1,523	1,030
Difference	− 250	749	93	324
Percent of expenditures	− 33	23	15	24
1963				
Expenditures	1,034	3,804	789	2,032
Receipts	1,242	3,024	681	1,597
Difference	− 208	780	108	435
Percent of expenditures	− 20	21	14	21
1967				
Expenditures	1,280	4,942	1,031	2,889
Receipts	1,547	3,896	907	2,275
Difference	− 267	1,046	124	614
Percent of expenditures	− 21	21	12	21
1972				
Expenditures	1,440	7,008	1,555	4,091
Receipts	1,693	5,600	1,407	3,179
Difference	− 253	1,408	148	912
Percent of expenditures	− 18	20	10	22
1977				
Expenditures	2,162	11,132	2,634	7,612
Receipts	2,559	8,875	2,275	5,889
Difference	− 397	2,257	359	− 1,723
Percent of expenditures	− 18	20	14	23

Sources: "Expenditures" from Table VI-24; and "Receipts" from Tables VI-5, VI-7, and VI-19.

VI-27. Deducted are advertising receipts of periodicals, newspapers, radio, and television. Also deducted are all third-class postal revenues, which we attribute to direct mail advertising. Advertising revenues, under this scheme, increased from $5,000 million in 1958 to $21,914 million in 1980.

Telephone, Telegraph, and Postal Service[10]

TELEPHONE

The last two decades have witnessed the achievement of truly "universal" telephone service in the United States. Machlup observed that the portion of

[10] See Machlup, *Production and Distribution of Knowledge*, pp. 275-291.

TABLE VI-26

ADVERTISING: THE TEN LARGEST SPENDERS, BY
SELECTED MEDIA, 1960, 1970, AND 1977

Company	Total (1)	News-papers (2)	General maga-zines (3)	Farm and business publica-tions (4)	Spot TV (5)	Network TV (6)	Outdoor (7)	Radio (8)
1960								
(1) General Motors Corporation	122	40	38	4	23	6	11	
(2) Proctor & Gamble Company	109	4	4		46	55		
(3) General Foods Company	65	16	9		19	19	2	
(4) American Home Products Company	55	4	7	2	33	9		
(5) Ford Motor Company	54	19	11	2	11	5	6	
(6) Lever Brothers Company	54	5	3		29	17		
(7) Chrysler Corporation	43	18	13	1	8	2	1	
(8) Colgate-Palmolive	41	5	3		22	11		
(9) R.J. Reynolds Industries	34	9	5		16	4		
(10) General Mills, Inc.	30	7	5	1	15	2		
1970								
(1) Proctor & Gamble Company	188	1	7	1	51	128		
(2) General Foods Company	122	9	12		49	45		6
(3) General Motors Corporation	119	20	24	5	9	35	5	24
(4) Bristol-Myers Company	90	2	20	4	2	57	1	4
(5) Colgate-Palmolive	101	3	5		37	47		10
(6) American Home Products Company	91	3	7		26	41		12
(7) R.J. Reynolds Industries	84	2	10		14	52		5
(8) Ford Motor Company	80	11	15	3	8	31	3	9
(9) Sterling Drug, Inc.	73	1	10		13	41		7
(10) Warner-Lambert Pharmaceuticals	73		3	4	18	46		
1977								
(1) Proctor & Gamble Company	372	1	21		115	235		
(2) General Foods Corporation	247	2	29		72	143		1
(3) General Motors Corporation	175	4	44		27	91	6	3
(4) Bristol-Myers Company	157	1	23		19	114		
(5) American Home Products Company	153		6		35	108		3
(6) Sears Roebuck & Company	149		41		22	80		5
(7) General Mills, Inc.	144	1	16		44	83		1
(8) R.J. Reynolds Industries	127	24	60		5	5	34	
(9) Philip Morris, Inc.	124	11	48		10	32	22	
(10) Ford Motor Company	121		25		28	66	1	1

SOURCES: (1960): *Advertising Age*, Vol. 32, June 5, 1961. (1970): *Advertising Age*, Vol. 42, June 21, 1971. (1977): *Advertising Age*, Vol. 49, May 1, 1978.

households with telephone service had risen from 35 percent in 1920 to 78 per-cent in 1958. Table VI-28 shows that this trend continued in the 1960s and 1970s, so that by 1977 fully 96 percent of all households in the United States enjoyed telephone service. Equally startling is the continuing growth in the number of telephones in the United States, which nearly tripled between 1958

TABLE VI-27

ADVERTISING: EXPENDITURES NET OF PAYMENTS ACCOUNTED FOR IN THE COST OF
ADVERTISING MEDIA, 1958, 1963, 1967, 1972, 1977, AND 1980
(millions of dollars)

	1958	1963	1967	1972	1977	1980
Total advertising expenditures, all media	10,302	13,107	16,866	23,300	38,120	54,590
Receipts from advertising						
Periodicals	1,017	1,242	1,547	1,693	2,559	4,949
Newspapers	2,444	3,024	3,896	5,600	8,875	13,301
Radio	523	681	907	1,407	2,275	3,206
Television	1,030	1,597	2,275	3,179	5,889	8,808
Total accounted for	5,014	6,544	8,625	11,879	19,598	30,264
Other advertising expenditures, all media	5,288	6,563	8,241	11,421	18,522	24,326
Deduct for postage	288	563	704	1,006	1,748	2,412
Net expenditures	5,000	6,000	7,537	10,415	16,774	21,914

SOURCES: Tables VI-5, VI-7, VI-24, and VI-25 in this book.

and 1980. The 180.4 million telephones connected at the end of 1980 represented 790 telephones per 1,000 population, a more than doubling from the
379.5 per thousand recorded by Machlup in 1958.

Telephone usage has increased with the rise in the availability of the equipment. The average number of local calls placed daily has risen in roughly the
same proportion as the number of installed telephones, nearly tripling from
242 million daily in 1958 to 717 million in 1980. In contrast, the growth in
long-distance toll calls has grown at more than double the rate of installed telephones. From 1958 to 1980 the average daily number of toll calls increased
sevenfold, rising from 10.5 million to 70 million.

The increasing availability and usage of telephone service over the last two
decades has been reflected in the operating revenues of the various telephone
companies. Annual revenues have risen from $7.64 billion in 1958 to $61.0
billion in 1980. These revenues have risen slowly but steadily as a percentage
of GNP, increasing from 1.73 percent to 2.32 percent in the years from 1958
to 1980.

The Bell System, with slight erosion, has remained the dominant provider
of telephone services in the years from 1958 to 1980. Although this situation
will be altered radically by the breakup of the Bell System required by the 1982
antitrust settlement, the Bell monolith was basically unaffected over the years
of our study. That is, as shown in Table VI-29, the Bell System enjoyed a mo-
nopolist's share of revenues, some 83.3 percent in 1980, albeit representing a
slight decline from the 90.8 percent share observed by Machlup in 1958. As

TABLE VI-28

TELEPHONE: NUMBERS OF TELEPHONES AND CALLS, OPERATING REVENUES, AND RELATED DATA, 1880-1980

Year	Total telephones Number (thousands)	Per 1000 population	Percentage of house-holds with telephone service	Dial telephones as percentage of all telephones**	Average daily calls* Local (thousands)	Toll (thousands)	Operating revenues (million dollars)	Operating revenues (as per-centage of GNP)
	(1)	(2)	(3)	(4)	(5)	(6)	(7)	(8)
1880	54	1.1					3	0.03
1890	234	3.7					16	0.12
1900	1,356	17.6			7,689	193	46	
1910	7,635	82.0			35,299	862	164	
1920	13,329	123.9	35.0	3.6	50,207	1,607	529	0.60
1930	20,202	163.4	40.9	27.7	80,225	3,295	1,186	1.30
1940	21,928	165.1	37.0	53.6	95,150	3,150	1,286	1.28
1950	43,004	280.9	63.0	70.7	164,400	6,200	3,611	1.27
1960	74,342	407.8	78.3	95.9	273,322	12,064	9,015	1.79
1961	77,422	418.0	78.9	97.2	284,497	12,613	9,608	1.85
1962	80,969	430.7	80.2	98.1	303,100	13,406	10,312	1.84
1963	84,453	442.9	81.4	98.9	314,682	14,184	11,044	1.87
1964	88,793	459.5	82.8	99.3	329,700	15,500	11,936	1.89
1965	93,656	479.0	84.6	99.6	350,800	17,000	12,850	1.88
1966	98,787	499.6	86.3	99.8	370,800	18,700	14,154	1.89
1967	103,752	519.3	87.1	99.8	385,700	20,300	15,184	1.91
1968	109,256	541.5	88.5	99.9	404,600	22,300	16,581	1.92
1969	115,222	565.2	89.8	99.9	435,400	24,800	18,520	1.99
1970	120,218	583.4	90.5	100.0	458,400	26,700	20,160	2.05
1971	125,141	601.0	92.0	100.0	488,000	29,000	22,154	2.08
1972	131,602	628.0	92.0	100.0	513,000	33,000	25,049	2.14
1973	138,288	655.0	94.0	100.0	539,000	37,000	28,295	2.17
1974	143,970	677.0	94.0	100.0	574,000	39,000	31,514	2.23
1975	149,008	695.0	94.0	100.0	585,000	42,000	34,894	2.28
1976	155,173	718.0	95.0	100.0	599,000	45,000	39,572	2.33
1977	162,072	744.0	96.0	100.0	629,000	50,000	44,164	2.33
1978	169,027	770.0	96.0	100.0	680,000	56,000	49,807	2.34
1979	175,535	793.0	96.0	100.0	692,000	64,000	54,481	2.30
1980	180,424	790.2	96.0	100.0	717,000	70,000	61,041	2.32

SOURCE: U.S. Federal Communications Commission, *Statistics of Communications Common Carriers* (Washington, D.C.: Government Printing Office, annual ed.).

* Figures represent average daily conversations. For annual total, multiply by 365.
** Figure includes dial and touch-tone telephones.

Machlup also observed, Bell's share in total operating revenues has been con-sistently above its share in the number of telephones.

The increasing importance of long-distance service was suggested in our ear-lier finding that such calls were growing at a higher rate than local calls. Table VI-30 permits us to examine this trend in more detail. In 1976 long-distance toll charges produced more revenue than did local service, the first time this had ever occurred. Toll charges had amounted to 38 percent of revenue in

TABLE VI-29

Telephone: Share of Bell System and Independent Companies in Total Number
of Telephones and Operating Revenues, 1895-1980

Year	Number of telephones				Operating revenues			
	Total (thou- sands)	Inde- pendent companies (thou- sands)	Bell System (thou- sands)	Bell System (percent- age of total)	Total (millions of dol- lars)	Inde- pendent companies (millions of dol- lars)	Bell System (millions of dol- lars)	Bell System (per- centage of total)
	(1)	(2)	(3)	(4)	(5)	(6)	(7)	(8)
1895	340	30	310	91.2			24.0	
1900	1,356	520	836	61.7			46.0	
1905	4,127	1,842	2,285	55.4			97.0	
1907	6,119	3,106	3,013	49.2			128.0	
1908	6,484	3,308	3,176	49.0			137.0	
1910	7,635	3,702	3,933	51.5			164.0	
1916	11,241	4,696	6,545	58.2	312.0	49.0	263.0	84.3
1920	13,329	4,995	8,334	62.5	529.0	81.0	448.0	84.7
1930	20,202	4,520	15,682	77.6	1,186.0	91.0	1,095.0	92.3
1940	21,928	3,862	18,066	82.4	1,286.0	81.0	1,205.0	93.7
1950	43,004	6,526	36,478	84.8	3,611.0	270.0	3,341.0	92.5
1958	66,645	9,886	56,759	84.6	7,642.0	704.0	6,938.0	90.8
1959	70,820	10,710	60,110	84.9	8,371.2	801.3	7,569.9	90.4
1960	74,342	11,353	62,989	84.7	9,014.5	905.7	8,108.8	90.0
1961	77,422	11,915	65,507	84.6	9,608.1	993.8	8,614.3	89.7
1962	80,969	12,576	68,393	84.5	10,312.0	1,119.5	9,192.5	89.1
1963	84,453	13,301	71,152	84.3	11,043.9	1,267.6	9,796.3	88.7
1964	88,793	14,134	74,659	84.1	11,935.5	1,386.1	10,549.4	88.4
1965	93,656	15,024	78,632	84.0	12,850.0	1,529.7	11,320.3	88.1
1966	98,789	15,976	82,813	83.8	14,153.5	1,734.3	12,419.2	87.7
1967	103,752	16,976	86,776	83.6	15,183.5	1,872.9	13,310.6	87.7
1968	109,256	18,134	91,122	83.4	16,581.2	2,152.3	14,428.9	87.0
1969	115,222	19,279	95,943	83.3	18,519.5	2,461.8	16,057.7	86.7
1970	120,218	20,315	99,903	83.1	20,159.8	2,791.3	17,368.5	86.2
1971	125,141	21,443	103,698	82.9	22,154.3	3,202.3	18,952.0	85.5
1972	131,603	22,792	108,811	82.7	25,048.9	3,660.9	21,388.0	85.4
1973	138,288	24,353	113,935	82.4	28,294.9	4,187.7	24,107.2	85.2
1974	143,972	25,826	118,146	82.1	31,513.6	4,713.6	26,800.0	85.0
1975	149,008	26,820	122,188	82.0	34,893.9	5,293.9	29,600.0	84.8
1976	155,173	28,209	126,964	81.8	39,572.0	6,072.0	33,500.0	84.7
1977	158,513	29,675	128,838	81.3	44,164.4	6,864.4	37,300.0	84.5
1978	169,072	31,594	137,478	81.3	49,806.8	7,806.8	42,000.0	84.3
1979	175,536	33,226	141,700	81.1	54,481.1	9,073.1	45,408.1	83.3
1980	180,424	34,548	145,876	80.9	61,040.6	10,176.7	50,863.8	83.3

Source: U.S. Federal Communications Commission, Statistics of Communications Common Carriers, annual ed.

TABLE VI-30

TELEPHONE: OPERATING REVENUES FROM LONG-DISTANCE AND LOCAL SERVICE, 1935-1980
(millions of dollars)

	Local service			Long-distance service			Percent of total		
Year	Total	Bell System	Inde-pendent com-panies	Total	Bell System	Inde-pendent com-panies	Total	Local charges	Toll charges
1935	687	641	46	286	273	13	100	70.6	29.4
1940	871	811	60	380	361	19	100	69.6	30.4
1945	1,157	1,073	84	893	845	48	100	56.4	43.6
1950	2,167	1,996	171	1,300	1,208	92	100	62.5	37.5
1955	3,497	3,168	329	2,155	2,000	155	100	61.8	38.2
1956	3,829	3,458	371	2,399	2,220	179	100	61.5	38.5
1958	4,509	4,049	460	2,760	2,543	217	100	62.0	38.0
1959	4,881	4,362	519	3,097	2,843	254	100	61.2	38.8
1960	5,250	4,665	585	3,348	3,058	290	100	61.1	38.9
1961	5,561	4,921	640	3,604	3,284	320	100	60.7	39.3
1962	5,929	5,219	710	3,916	3,544	372	100	60.2	39.8
1963	6,306	5,528	778	4,243	3,814	429	100	60.0	40.0
1964	6,628	5,779	849	4,783	4,291	492	100	58.1	41.9
1965	7,031	6,114	917	5,267	4,706	561	100	57.2	42.8
1966	7,517	6,517	1,000	6,047	5,378	669	100	55.4	44.6
1967	7,983	6,910	1,073	6,582	5,852	730	100	54.8	45.2
1968	8,545	7,366	1,179	7,364	6,472	892	100	53.7	46.3
1969	9,293	7,979	1,314	8,505	7,451	1,054	100	52.2	47.8
1970	10,139	8,685	1,454	9,274	8,042	1,232	100	52.2	47.8
1971	11,051	9,426	1,625	10,296	8,835	1,461	100	51.8	48.2
1972	12,453	10,630	1,823	11,692	9,983	1,709	100	51.6	48.4
1973	13,748	11,712	2,036	13,538	11,524	2,014	100	50.4	49.6
1974	15,374	13,131	2,243	15,056	12,729	2,327	100	50.5	49.5
1975	16,920	14,400	2,520	16,815	14,200	2,615	100	50.2	49.8
1976	18,800	16,000	2,800	19,493	16,400	3,093	100	49.1	50.9
1977	20,597	17,500	3,097	22,070	18,500	3,570	100	38.3	51.7
1978	22,543	19,200	3,343	25,443	21,200	4,243	100	47.0	53.0
1979	24,550	20,800	3,750	28,873	23,800	5,073	100	46.0	54.0
1980	27,256	23,027	4,229	32,639	26,674	5,965	100	45.5	54.5

SOURCES: U.S. Federal Communications Commission, *Statistics of Communications Common Carriers*, annual ed.; and *Statistics of the Independent Telephone Industry* (Washington, D.C.: United States Independent Telephone Association, annual ed.).

1958, but rose to 54.5 percent by 1980. This trend correlates with our finding that true universal telephone service has been achieved in the United States. Decisions over the last twenty years by the Federal Communications Commission and the various state public utility commissions have encouraged the subsidization of local telephone service by long-distance toll service. In effect, local telephone rates have been kept lower than they would otherwise have been, in order to permit a larger portion of the population to be able to afford telephone service. Conversely, long-distance rates have been higher than would otherwise be the case. Heavy long-distance users have subsidized local telephone service.

TELEGRAPH

The decline in the telegraph industry that was evident to Machlup in 1958 has continued over the last two decades and, perhaps, has bottomed out. According to Table VI-31, in 1958 some 158.7 million telegraphic messages were sent in the United States, 131.8 million of which were to domestic destinations and 26.9 to foreign points. Domestic messages decreased over the following

TABLE VI-31

TELEGRAPH: NUMBERS OF TELEGRAMS AND OPERATING EXPENSES, 1870-1980

Year	Messages handled (in thousands)			Operating revenues (in millions of dollars)			Operating revenues as percentage of GNP
	Domestic	Inter-national	Total	Domestic	Inter-national	Total	
	(1)	(2)	(3)	(4)	(5)	(6)	(7)
1870			9,158			6.7	0.10
1880			31,703			16.7	0.18
1902			91,655			39.5	0.25
1912			109,378			62.8	0.17
1920	155,884	4,387	160,271	124.4	40.5	164.9	0.19
1930	211,971	20,409	232,380	148.2	35.4	183.6	0.20
1940	191,645	16,619	208,264	114.6	32.1	146.7	0.15
1950	178,904	22,578	201,482	178.0	50.3	228.3	0.08
1958	131,867	26,875	158,742	240.4	77.3	317.7	0.07
1959	130,993	28,133	159,126	260.8	84.4	345.2	0.07
1960	124,319	28,278	152,597	262.4	87.0	349.4	0.07
1961	117,263	28,345	145,608	265.7	90.1	355.8	0.07
1962	112,407	28,568	140,975	264.1	92.4	356.5	0.06
1963	104,220	29,390	133,610	286.8	97.8	384.6	0.07
1964	97,448	30,102	127,550	299.4	107.6	407.0	0.06
1965	94,302	28,830	123,132	305.6	106.7	412.3	0.06
1966	92,682	29,925	122,607	319.3	121.5	440.8	0.06
1967	89,078	29,953	119,031	335.0	132.4	467.4	0.06
1968	85,645	30,705	116,350	358.2	153.6	511.8	0.06
1969	77,059	32,235	109,294	391.3	180.0	571.3	0.06
1970	69,679	32,241	101,920	402.5	193.8	596.3	0.06
1971	44,103	31,049	75,152	396.8	207.4	604.2	0.06
1972	39,826	29,098	68,924	431.8	227.6	659.4	0.06
1973	37,572	29,862	67,434	454.7	263.3	718.0	0.05
1974	42,079	29,257	71,336	483.9	298.9	782.8	0.06
1975	41,968	26,096	68,064	504.8	316.1	820.9	0.05
1976	43,032	24,130	67,162	527.5	343.8	871.3	0.05
1977	45,306	22,756	68,062	554.9	396.7	951.6	0.05
1978	50,398	21,870	72,268	576.5	455.0	1,031.5	0.05
1979	55,148	21,065	76,213	636.1	496.7	1,132.8	0.05
1980	55,014	20,456	75,470	697.0	534.8	1,231.8	0.05

SOURCE: U.S. Federal Communications Commission, *Statistics of Communications Common Carriers*, 1980.

two decades to a low of 39.8 million in 1972 and recovered somewhat by 1980 to the level of 55.0 million. In contrast, messages to foreign destinations initially increased throughout the 1960s, rising to a historic peak of 32.2 million in 1969 and 1970. Since that time, however, international messages have declined steadily, so that by 1980 the 20.5 million messages sent were the lowest recorded in almost four decades.

Despite this erratic record, total operating revenues have risen steadily over the last two decades, without ever showing a year-to-year decline. By 1980 these revenues stood at $1,231.8 million, divided between $697.0 million from domestic messages and $534.8 million for international messages.

POSTAL SERVICE

Perhaps the major development over the last two decades insofar as the U.S. Postal Service is concerned has been the termination of domestic airmail services as a special class of mail. A governmental reorganization that removed the postmaster general from the president's cabinet, strikes or threatened strikes by postal employees, and an effort to "balance" the Post Office's budget have had little effect on the consuming public—other than in continually escalating postage rates. As for airmail service, virtually all first-class mail now travels by air, thus eliminating the need for a special designation. Trends in postal usage are shown in Table VI-32, which depicts a steady rise in the number of pieces of mail handled over the two decades of our study. By 1980 over 60 billion pieces of mail were being handled annually, double the number in 1958.

As shown in Table VI-33, in the years from 1958 to 1980 total expenses of the U.S. Postal Service increased from $3,478 million to $19,412 million. No adjustment has been made here for parcel post expenditures unrelated to the transportation of printed or recorded information, since there are no data available upon which to base such a charge. In order to preserve compatibility across years, the 1958 data have been appropriately restated.

TELEPHONE, TELEGRAPH, AND FIRST CLASS MAIL COMPARED

Table VI-34 shows that in terms of physical volume the telephone has increased its share of the communications media discussed in this chapter. Already in a dominant position in 1958 when it enjoyed 73 percent of the market among these media, the telephone has increased that share to fully 83 percent in 1980. This growth has reduced the share of first-class letters from 27 percent to 17 percent over the same time period. The division of revenues among these media is similar to that of message volume.

The final statistical estimation in this section is to separate the parts of total expenditures that were made by business, government, and consumers. These estimations are presented in Table VI-35, which directly follows the original formulations by Machlup.

TABLE VI-32

POSTAL SERVICE: FIRST CLASS MAIL AND DOMESTIC AIRMAIL, 1930-1980

| | First class mail | | Domestic airmail | | Total revenue from first class and domestic airmail | |
| | Pieces (millions) | Revenues (millions of dollars) | Pieces (millions) | Revenues (millions of dollars) | (millions of dollars) | Percent of GNP |
Year	(1)	(2)	(3)	(4)	(5)	(6)
1930	16,832	359	69	5	364	0.40
1940	15,224	413	259	19	432	0.43
1950	24,500	741	853	74	815	0.29
1958	32,218	1,092	1,435	151	1,243	0.28
1959	32,274	1,439	1,368	153	1,592	0.33
1960	33,235	1,510	1,356	157	1,667	0.33
1961	34,289	1,558	1,453	171	1,729	0.33
1962	35,333	1,615	1,545	185	1,800	0.32
1963	35,833	1,824	1,545	200	2,024	0.34
1964	36,943	2,109	1,505	216	2,325	0.37
1965	38,068	2,193	1,629	243	2,436	0.36
1966	40,422	2,334	1,828	277	2,611	0.35
1967	41,998	2,442	2,111	329	2,771	0.35
1968	43,183	2,722	2,065	425	3,147	0.36
1969	46,411	3,135	1,836	485	3,620	0.39
1970	48,690	3,290	1,718	484	3,774	0.38
1971	50,036	3,506	1,457	198	3,704	0.35
1972	48,933	4,379	1,360	210	4,589	0.39
1973	50,965	4,578	1,327	213	4,791	0.37
1974	51,595	5,019	1,335	231	5,250	0.37
1975	51,373	5,798	1,109	219	6,017	0.39
1976	52,108	6,734	352	84	6,818	0.40
1977	53,654	7,831	13	6	7,837	0.41
1978	55,981	8,575			8,575	0.40
1979	57,926	9,733			9,733	0.41
1980	60,276	10,146			10,146	0.39

SOURCE: U.S. Postal Service, *Annual Report of the Postmaster General* (Washington, D.C.: Government Printing Office, various years).

CONVENTIONS[11]

This section reports on expenditures to attend conventions in the United States, including travel, hotel, and meal expenses of the participants, and expenses directly involved in staging these affairs. Machlup reported on estimates that conventions were attended by perhaps 10,000,000 members or delegates to some 20,000 conventions in the year 1957. Expenditures came to perhaps $1,600 million in that year. Similar estimates for 1968 state that 12,000,000 people attended 35,130 conventions, spending $2,200 million in the proc-

[11] See Machlup, *Production and Distribution of Knowledge*, pp. 291-294.

TABLE VI-33

POSTAL SERVICE: APPORTIONED EXPENDITURES AND PIECES OF MAIL, 1958, 1963, 1967, 1972, 1977, AND 1980

	1958	1963	1967	1972	1977	1980
Pieces of mail (in millions)						
First class mail	32,218	35,834	44,109	50,293	53,668	60,332
Second class mail	7,148	8,227	8,711	9,494	8,673	8,446
Third class mail	15,849	18,407	20,985	21,908	24,050	30,381
Fourth class mail	1,170	1,076	1,070	914	762	633
Domestic airmail	1,435	1,545				
International mail	534	538	637	914	885	963
Other mail	1,776	2,225	2,855	3,633	4,186	5,555
Total	60,130	67,852	78,367	87,156	92,224	106,310
Expenses (in millions of dollars)						
First class mail	1,232	1,691	2,407		6,561	
Second class mail	352	454	551		759	
Third class mail	612	874	1,116		1,913	
Fourth class mail	702	806	933		1,029	
Domestic airmail	142	172	271			
International mail	97	139	186		373	
Other mail	57	179	297		565	
Special services	258	287	345		582	
Unassignable expenses	26	97	143	n.a.	3,528	n.a.
Total	3,478	4,699	6,249	9,522	15,310	19,412

SOURCE: U.S. Postal Service, *Annual Report of the Postmaster General*, various years.

NOTES: Separate statistics on domestic airmail are not available after 1966. Also, detailed expenses were not reported for 1972 or 1980.

ess.[12] In addition, perhaps another 400 million could be attributed to travel expenses.

A series of biennial surveys conducted by the magazine *Meetings and Conventions* provides further insight in the business of conventions for the mid and later 1970s. These studies, conducted between 1976 and 1980, show the number of major trade association conventions at 11,500 in 1976; 10,300 in 1978; and 10,550 in 1980. Attendance increased from almost 8,000,000 in 1978 to 9,500,000 in 1980.[13] Expenditures, including an estimate for travel, came to about $5,100 million in 1978 and $8,300 in 1980.

These figures, however, are not directly comparable with those for 1957 and 1968. Whereas the earlier data include both national and regional conventions, the latter reports only on national conventions. Thus, what appears to be a major drop in the number of conventions between 1968 and 1976 is in fact a discontinuity in our statistics. Nor is this our only problem. No data are

[12] "The Great American Get-Together," *Forbes*, 103 (February 15, 1969), p. 28.
[13] "$24 Billion-Market," *Meetings and Conventions*, (January 1982), pp. 49, 54.

TABLE VI-34

COMMUNICATIONS: DOMESTIC MESSAGES HANDLED AND REVENUES
COLLECTED BY TELEPHONE, TELEGRAPH, AND POSTAL SERVICE,
1926-1980

	NUMBER OF MESSAGES HANDLED							
	Total		Telephone		Telegraph		First class and airmail	
Year	Millions	Percent	Millions	Percent	Millions	Percent	Millions	Percent
1926	41,450	100	25,981	62.68	203	0.49	15,266	36.83
1930	47,598	100	30,485	64.05	212	0.45	16,901	35.51
1935	40,503	100	27,740	68.49	176	0.43	12,587	31.08
1940	51,555	100	35,880	69.60	192	0.37	15,483	30.03
1945	62,747	100	40,625	64.74	236	0.38	21,886	34.88
1950	87,801	100	62,269	70.92	179	0.20	25,353	28.88
1955	105,086	100	74,752	71.13	154	0.15	30,180	28.72
1956	110,776	100	79,059	71.37	152	0.14	31,565	28.49
1957	120,713	100	87,525	72.51	144	0.12	33,044	27.37
1958	125,221	100	91,436	73.02	132	0.11	33,653	26.87
1959	132,086	100	98,313	74.43	131	0.10	33,642	25.47
1960	138,881	100	104,166	75.00	124	0.09	34,591	24.91
1961	144,304	100	108,445	75.15	117	0.08	35,742	24.77
1962	152,515	100	115,525	75.75	112	0.07	36,878	24.18
1963	157,518	100	120,036	76.20	104	0.07	37,378	23.73
1964	164,543	100	125,998	76.57	97	0.06	38,448	23.37
1965	174,038	100	134,247	77.14	94	0.05	39,697	22.81
1966	184,511	100	142,168	77.05	93	0.05	42,250	22.90
1967	192,388	100	148,190	77.03	89	0.05	44,109	22.93
1968	201,153	100	155,819	77.46	86	0.04	45,248	22.50
1969	216,297	100	167,973	77.66	77	0.04	48,247	22.31
1970	227,540	100	177,062	77.82	70	0.03	50,408	22.15
1971	240,242	100	188,705	78.55	44	0.02	51,493	21.43
1972	249,623	100	199,290	79.84	40	0.02	50,293	20.15
1973	262,570	100	210,240	80.07	38	0.01	52,292	19.92
1974	276,717	100	223,745	80.86	42	0.02	52,930	19.13
1975	281,379	100	228,855	81.33	42	0.01	52,482	18.65
1976	287,563	100	235,060	81.74	43	0.01	52,460	18.24
1977	301,547	100	247,835	82.19	45	0.01	53,667	17.80
1978	324,671	100	268,640	82.74	50	0.02	55,981	17.24
1979	333,921	100	275,940	82.64	55	0.02	57,926	17.35
1980	347,586	100	287,255	82.64	55	0.02	60,276	17.34
1926	1,367	100	896	65.55	150	10.97	321	23.48
1930	1,698	100	1,186	69.85	148	8.72	364	21.44
1935	1,451	100	996	68.64	106	7.31	349	24.05
1940	1,833	100	1,286	70.16	115	6.27	432	23.57
1945	2,992	100	2,114	70.66	182	6.08	696	23.26
1950	4,604	100	3,611	78.43	178	3.87	815	17.70
1955	7,253	100	5,927	81.72	229	3.16	1,097	15.12
1956	7,924	100	6,536	82.48	238	3.00	1,150	14.51
1957	8,567	100	7,102	82.90	246	2.87	1,219	14.23
1958	9,125	100	7,642	83.75	240	2.63	1,243	13.62
1959	10,224	100	8,371	81.88	261	2.55	1,592	15.57
1960	10,944	100	9,015	82.37	262	2.39	1,667	15.23
1961	11,603	100	9,608	82.81	266	2.29	1,729	14.90
1962	12,376	100	10,312	83.32	264	2.13	1,800	14.54
1963	13,355	100	11,044	82.70	287	2.15	2,024	15.16

TABLE VI-34 *(cont.)*

	AMOUNTS OF REVENUES COLLECTED							
	Total		*Telephone*		*Telegraph*		*First class and airmail*	
Year	Millions dollars	Percent	Millions dollars	Percent	Millions dollars	Percent	Millions dollars	Percent
1964	14,560	100	11,936	81.98	299	2.05	2,325	15.97
1965	15,592	100	12,850	82.41	306	1.96	2,436	15.62
1966	17,083	100	14,153	82.85	319	1.87	2,611	15.28
1967	18,290	100	15,184	83.02	335	1.83	2,771	15.15
1968	20,086	100	16,581	82.55	358	1.78	3,147	15.67
1969	22,531	100	18,520	82.20	391	1.74	3,620	16.07
1970	24,337	100	20,160	82.84	403	1.66	3,774	15.51
1971	26,255	100	22,154	84.35	397	1.51	3,704	14.11
1972	30,070	100	25,049	83.30	432	1.44	4,589	15.26
1973	33,541	100	28,295	84.36	455	1.36	4,791	14.28
1974	37,248	100	31,514	84.61	484	1.30	5,250	14.09
1975	41,416	100	34,894	84.25	505	1.22	6,017	14.53
1976	46,918	100	39,572	84.34	528	1.13	6,818	14.53
1977	52.556	100	44,164	84.03	555	1.06	7,837	14.91
1978	58,959	100	49,807	84.48	577	0.98	8,575	14.54
1979	64,850	100	54,481	84.01	636	0.98	9,733	15.01
1980	71,884	100	61,041	84.92	697	0.97	10,146	14.11

SOURCES: (Telephone Messages): Table VI-28, Column 5 plus Column 6 × 365. (Telegraph Messages): Table VI-31, C olumn 1. (Postal Messages): Table VI-32, Column 1 plus Column 3;

(Telephone Revenues): Table VI-28, Column 7. (Telegraph Revenues): Table VI-31, Column 4. (Postal Revenues); Table VI-32, Column 5.

available either for 1963 or 1972, and we must use 1968 data to report on 1967, and the same for 1976 and 1977.

For the purposes of establishing trend data for this book, we shall accept these irregularities in our statistics and shall interpolate for the years 1963 and 1972, estimating expenditures at \$2,000 million and \$2,900 million respectively.

TABLE VI-35

TELEPHONE AND TELEGRAPH: EXPENDITURES BY CONSUMERS,
BUSINESS, AND GOVERNMENT, 1958, 1963, 1967, 1972,
1977, AND 1980
(millions of dollars)

	1958	1963	1967	1972	1977	1980
Operating revenues						
(1) Telephone	7,642	11,044	15,184	25,049	44,164	61,041
(2) Telegraph	318	385	467	659	952	1,232
(3) Total	7,960	11,429	15,651	25,708	45,116	62,273
Consumer expenditures						
(4) Telephone and telegraph	3,892	5,524	7,668	12,386	21,152	26,985
(5) Excise taxes*	358	503	698	1,127	1,007	530
(6) Net of excise taxes	3,534	5,021	6,970	11,259	20,145	26,455
(7) Telephone	3,393	4,852	6,762	10,981	19,720	25,932
(8) Telegraph	141	169	208	278	425	523
Business and government expenditures						
(9) Telephone and telegraph [(3) minus (6)]	4,426	6,408	8,681	14,449	24,971	35,818
Excise taxes						
(10) Total	650	881	1,102	1,700	1,700	994
(11) Consumer excise taxes	358	503	698	1,127	1,007	530
(12) Business excise taxes [(10) minus (11)]	292	378	404	573	693	464
Business expenditures						
(13) Telephone and telegraph	2,920	3,780	4,040	5,730	13,860	23,200
(14) Telephone	2,831	3,684	3,953	5,633	13,688	22,741
(15) Telegraph	89	96	87	97	172	459
Government expenditures						
(16) Telephone and telegraph [(9) minus (13)]	1,506	2,628	4,641	8,719	11,111	12,618
(17) Telephone	1,418	2,508	4,469	8,435	10,877	12,368
(18) Telegraph	88	120	172	284	234	250

SOURCES: Rows (1) and (2): Tables VI-29 and VI-31. Row (4): U.S. Bureau of Economic Analysis, *Survey of Current Business*, data are from various monthly issues. Row (10): U.S. Treasury Department, Internal Revenue Service, *Annual Report of the Commissioner* (Washington, D.C.: Government Printing Office, various annual eds.).

* Excise taxes were 10 percent of gross expenditures until 1973, when they were reduced one percent per year until the rate reached one percent in 1981.

CHAPTER VII   Information Machines

This chapter updates four statistical elements of Chapter VII of *The Production and Distribution of Knowledge in the United States.* Among the topics covered are: (1) the investment of the various knowledge industries in information machines; (2) the sales value of signaling devices; (3) the production of measuring and controlling instruments; and (4) the production of office and computing equipment. Each of these topics is treated statistically for each of the economic census years since 1958, plus 1980.

Summary Table VII presents a summary of expenditures in the United States for information machines and reports the share of these expenditures as a percentage of Gross National Product for the years of our study. The dollar value of those expenditures has increased from $9,878 million in 1958 to $90,210 million in 1980. Expenditures for information machines as a percentage of GNP have increased from 2 percent in 1958 to 3.2 percent in 1980.

These expenditures have mostly been made by businesses; for example, some $76,064 million in 1980 out of a total of $90,210 million. The allocation of expenditures is as follows: Consumers are tallied for the purchase of musical

SUMMARY TABLE VII

INFORMATION MACHINES AND GNP
(millions of dollars)

	1958	1963	1967	1972	1977	1980
Communications equipment	1,834	2,632	4,054	6,131	11,037	17,522
Signaling devices	130	166	231	336	847	1,193
Measuring and controlling instruments	6,509	10,079	12,806	14,815	27,005	41,358
Computing, office and store machines	1,405	2,362	5,605	7,867	15,529	30,137
Total	9,878	15,239	22,696	29,149	54,418	90,210
Information machines as a percent of adjusted GNP	2.0	2.4	2.6	2.3	2.6	3.2
Paid for by						
Government expenditures	53	580	1,452	1,271	1,957	5,285
Business expenditures	9,015	13,647	19,004	24,285	45,741	76,064
Consumer expenditures	810	1,012	1,499	1,912	3,144	3,641
Unallocated expenditures			741	1,681	3,576	5,220

SOURCES: Tables VII-1 through VII-3 in this book.

instruments and some measuring and controlling instruments, as described in Table VII-2; government expenditures are for computers and other office machinery, which is calculated from statistics provided by the Bureau of Economic Analysis; and business expenditures constitute the remainder of expenditures that can be allocated.

INFORMATION MACHINES FOR KNOWLEDGE INDUSTRIES[1]

The problem of double counting noted by Machlup in the treatment of information machines has grown no less difficult with the passage of time. Information machines are used in education, in research and development, and in the communications industries. Further, technological developments in the last decade have made possible the widespread use of information machines in various service industries. Word-processing equipment, small office computers and electronic calculators are ubiquitous in all knowledge-producing industries. These machines are no less common in law offices or engineering and architectural firms than in research laboratories or the telecommunications industry. Sorting out the expenditures of these industries for information machines, so as to avoid double counting, is a major challenge.

Machlup approached this problem in two ways. The first approach was used in the communications industries, where he drew a distinction between those industries whose investment outlay had been counted earlier and those for which no such count had been made. The result was a statistical table that accounted for all investments in information machinery by the communications industry, segregated so as to avoid double counting. Machlup used a second approach in the education, and research and development industries. These industries posed greater difficulties in measuring investments in information machines, and Machlup chose to accept some double counting rather than attempt an extremely rough estimate of expenditures that, compared to the total, were negligible in any case.

This study follows the procedures established by Machlup. Expenditures for information machines in the education, research and development, and now, information service industries cannot be accurately documented. Rather than attempt estimates that would be little more than guesses, we will accept this double counting as a limitation on the accuracy of our work. Hence, no estimates are provided of the expenditures of those industries for information machines.

Consistent with Machlup's approach, the investment outlays by the communications industries are presented in Table VII-1, divided up between outlays counted earlier in our study and those not previously included. Our results show that total investment by the communications industry for information

[1] See Fritz Machlup, *The Production and Distribution of Knowledge in the United States* (Princeton, N.J.: Princeton University Press, 1962), pp. 295-299.

TABLE VII-1
INFORMATION MACHINES USED IN COMMUNICATIONS INDUSTRIES:
ESTIMATES OF INVESTMENT OUTLAYS, 1958, 1963, 1967, 1972,
1977, AND 1980
(millions of dollars)

Communications industry	Information machines	1958	1963	1967	1972	1977	1980
	Investment outlay included in communications chapter						
Photography	Photographic equipment	997	972	2,155	5,417	9,217	13,970
Radio and TV	Receiving sets	1,007	1,381	3,162	4,457	5,103	6,568
Phonography	Phonographs	645	856	769	1,370	3,247	3,680
Total, previously included		2,649	3,209	6,086	11,244	17,567	24,218
	Investment outlay in communications equipment not previously included						
Radio and TV	Broadcast equipment	54	150	344	430	568	1,148
Books, pamphlets, periodicals, newspapers, other printing	Printing machinery	311	403	656	737	1,287	2,053
Plays and concerts	Musical instruments	242	319	401	525	879	1,091
Motion pictures	Motion picture equipment	148	128	194	192	178	251
Telephone and telegraph	Telephone and telegraph equipment	1,079	1,538	2,248	3,974	7,119	11,162
	Microwave and mobile telephone equipment		65	166	148	695	919
	Communication satellites		29	45	125	311	898
Postal service	Postage meters, etc.						
Conventions	Microphones, etc.						
Total, not included yet		1,834	2,632	4,054	6,131	11,037	17,522
Total investment outlays		4,483	5,841	10,140	17,375	28,604	41,740

SOURCES: (1958-1977): U.S. Bureau of the Census, *Census of Manufacturers* (Washington, D.C.: Government Printing Office, quinquennial ed.). (1980): U.S. Bureau of the Census, *1980 Annual Survey of Manufactures* and *Current Industrial Reports* (Washington, D.C.: Government Printing Office, annual ed.).

machines increased almost tenfold from 1958 to 1980, going from $4,483 million in 1958 to $41,740 million in 1980. The amount that had not been included previously in our calculations in Chapter VI increased from $1,834 million to $17,522 million over the same time period.

Several changes are noteworthy in the presentation of Table VII-1, compared to the original by Machlup. In a number of instances, 1958 statistics have been recalculated to take advantage of revisions by the Census Bureau in its earlier published data. Further, the category "broadcast equipment" has been moved into those outlays not included previously. This is consistent with our omission, in Chapter VI, of the entry for investment in radio and television stations. Finally, corrections of the data for the cost of installation and transportation have been omitted because of unavailability of data upon which to base such changes.

SIGNALING DEVICES[2]

Machlup noted that the *Census of Manufactures* ceased to report signaling devices as a separate category in 1958. Fortunately, it reappeared in the same year under the title, "interconnection equipment," and contained essentially the same elements as the former industry. The following sales values of these devices was reported in the various economic censuses: for 1958, $130 million; for 1963, $166 million; for 1967, $231 million; for 1972, $336 million; for 1977, $847 million; for 1980, $1,193 million.

No estimates are made here for distribution or installation costs.

THE PRODUCTION OF MEASURING AND CONTROLLING INSTRUMENTS[3]

Table VII-2 reproduces the annual sales receipts for the industries that produce measuring and controlling instruments, as reported by the Bureau of the Census for the years 1958, 1963, 1967, 1972, 1977, and 1980. The underlying classification system used by the Bureau of the Census has changed repeatedly over the course of the five economic censuses reported here. Thus, the data have been revised to make them comparable over time, and these changes are explained in the footnotes accompanying the table. The reader should also note that the 1958 data originally reported by Machlup have been revised as well, to reflect subsequent revisions by the Bureau of the Census. Also, several types of instruments have been added to the table, including electronic navigation aids, radar and sonar, and guidance systems for missiles and satellites.

The convention adopted by Machlup for dividing the manufacturer's sales of measuring and controlling instruments between personal consumption expenditures and business investments is repeated here. That is, the arbitrary as-

[2] See Machlup, *Production and Distribution of Knowledge*, p. 299.
[3] See Machlup, *Production and Distribution of Knowledge*, pp. 299-304.

TABLE VII-2
MEASURING AND CONTROLLING INSTRUMENTS: MANUFACTURERS'
SALES, 1958, 1963, 1967, 1972, 1977, AND 1980
(millions of dollars)

		1958	1963	1967	1972	1977	1980
(1)	Electrical measuring instruments[a]	673	736	1,137	1,330	2,566	4,340
(2)	Electrical control apparatus[b]	1,375	1,722	2,670	3,304	5,727	8,507
(3)	Scientific and professional instruments	1,000	689	1,049	1,106	1,850	2,518
(4)	Electronic navigation aids	425	1,295	1,215	1,072	1,214	1,842
(5)	Radar, sonar and other search and detection apparatus	1,016	1,615	1,671	2,264	5,134	9,498
(6)	Missile-borne navigation and guidance systems		973	849	778	1,080	1,218
(7)	Mechanical measuring instruments[c]	1,086	1,671	2,073	2,366	4,874	6,966
(8)	Optical instruments and lenses[d]	103	377	559	585	1,300	2,788
(9)	Ophthalmic goods	194	244	378	484	844	1,051
(10)	Watches and clocks[e]	335	407	663	828	1,265	1,206
(11)	Watch cases	35	29	45	53	67	92
(12)	Scales and balances	78	90	131	182	329	482
(13)	Total	6,320	9,848	12,440	14,352	26,250	40,508
(14)	Business investment	5,941	9,386	11,708	13,428	24,740	38,808
(15)	Personal consumption	568	693	1,098	1,387	2,265	2,550
(16)	Total outlay	6,509	10,079	12,806	14,815	27,005	41,358

SOURCES: (1958 to 1977): U.S. Bureau of the Census, *Census of Manufactures*, quinquennial ed. (1980): U.S. Bureau of the Census, *Annual Survey of Manufactures for 1980*.

[a] In 1972, SIC 3611, "Electrical Measuring Instruments," was divided into two parts, one of which became new SIC 3825, "Instruments to Measure Electricity," while the other was incorporated into SIC 3612, "Transformers." Thus, 1972 and 1977 are not directly comparable to the earlier years; however, new SIC 3825 seems to be a somewhat more pure measure of an "Information" machine than was SIC 3611.

[b] In 1958, SIC 3616, "Electrical control Apparatus," was broken into SIC 3613, "Switchgear, Switchboard Apparatus," and SIC 3622, "Industrial Controls."

[c] In 1972, SIC 3821, "Mechanical Measuring Devices" was broken up into SIC 3823, "Process Control Instruments," SIC 3824, "Fluid Meters and Counting Devices," and SIC 3829, "Measuring and Controlling Devices, Nec."

[d] In 1972, part of SIC 1941, "Sighting and Fire Control Equipment" was added to SIC 3831, forming SIC 3832, "Optical Instruments and Lenses."

[e] In 1972, SIC 3873, "Watches, Clocks and Watch Cases" was formed from SIC 3831, "Watches and Clocks," and SIC 3832, "Watch Cases."

sumption is made that consumers buy all of the ophthalmic goods and one half of all watches and clocks, and pay an additonal 50 percent for retail markups. The computations are also presented in Table VII-2.

Using the techniques described above, we find that the total outlay for measuring and controlling instruments in 1980 amounted to $41,358 million, compared to $6,509 million in 1958.

Office Computing Machines[4]

The final entry in this chapter is our measurement of computing, office, and store machinery. The task of forming statistical measures is greatly compounded here by the frenetic pace of technological innovation in these industries. Electronic computers, for example, have grown from a $324 million industry in 1958 to a $25 billion industry in 1980, in large measure because of the revolutionary path of the underlying technology. Machines that once utilized electronic vacuum tubes, and as a result were massive in size and generated great amounts of heat, now use semiconductors, making miniaturization possible. Computers are now sold for personal use that contain, in the space of a desk top, more computational power than the state-of-the-art machines of the early 1950s.

The pace of technological change has been equally great in the other machines we are considering here; i.e., the electronic calculator, the typewriter, and a variety of accounting machines. The common denominator of each of these machines is their evolution from mechanical devices to electronic devices that rely upon the semiconductor. Electronic word processors are replacing mechanical and electric typewriters today. These devices store the text of documents electronically, allowing the operator to retrieve documents quickly and correct errors without retyping the entire document. Equally familiar today are hand-held calculators that offer many of the computational features of small computers. The list of examples goes on at length, but the point is already well made.

The problem, then, is to accommodate these technological changes into the analytic framework originally set forth by Machlup. Several premises can aid our decisions. First, whenever an information product is used exclusively as an input into another industry's product, that input is not counted separately, thus avoiding double counting. The semiconductor, as we have already described, is an input into a variety of other information machines. The output of the semiconductor industry is not separately accounted for here, but rather is included in the product of the computer, electronic calculator, and other industries. A second premise is that new, electronic, products that perform the same function as older mechanical machines will be counted in the same general category. Thus, "typewriters" will include not only mechanical typewriters, but also electric typewriters and word processors; "electronic computers" will include CPU's, peripheral devices, and small home computers; and "calculators" will include a variety of new, semiconductor-based products.

Table VII-3 presents our findings. Manufacturers' sales of computing, office, and store machinery increased 20-fold over the years of our study, growing from $1,405 million in 1958 to $30,137 million in 1980. This growth was

---

[4] See Machlup, *Production and Distribution of Knowledge*, pp. 304-322.

TABLE VII-3

Computing, Office, and Store Machines: Manufacturers' Sales, 1958, 1963, 1967, 1972, 1977, and 1980
(millions of dollars)

	1958	1963	1967	1972	1977	1980
Electronic computers	324	880	4,049	6,108	12,673	25,658
Calculating and accounting machines	709	970	630	694	836	1,233
Typewriters	189	265	508	580	1,102	1,909
Other office machines	183	247	418	485	918	1,337
Total	1,405	2,362	5,605	7,867	15,529	30,137

Sources: (1958, 1963, 1967, 1972, and 1977): U.S. Bureau of the Census, *Census of Manufactures*, quinquennial ed. (1980): U.S. Bureau of the Census, *Annual Survey of Manufactures for 1980*.

paced by the electronic computer industry, which experienced a dramatic 80-fold increase over the period of the study, increasing from $324 million in 1958 to $25,658 million in 1980.

Machlup's 1962 tables VII-4 through VII-6 have not been updated by this study and do not appear in this book.

CHAPTER **VIII**   Information Services

This chapter presents a statistical update of Chapter VIII of *The Production and Distribution of Knowledge in the United States*. As in the original text, five broad classes of information services are measured, plus one addition: (1) professional knowledge services; (2) information and financial services as joint products; (3) the intelligence service of wholesale traders; (4) data-processing services; (5) miscellaneous service industries; and (6) government as knowledge industry. Within these six broad categories there are fourteen separate industries or economic activities.

In the twenty years since the publication of the original volume, there have been significant changes in both the marketplace for information services and in the economic statistics we use to portray that marketplace. Several new information services have emerged since 1962 and are described here. Among these new entries are services made possible by the technological advances in electronic data processing, including the widespread use of credit cards, and the offering of new business services that also employ those media. The quality of the statistics has improved as well, allowing us to measure several activities that were present when Machlup wrote the earlier version of this statistical work, but which could not then be quantified because of the absence of reliable data.

Summary Table VIII presents total expenditures for information services for the years 1958, 1963, 1967, 1972, 1977, and 1980. Expenditures for information services rose from $23.8 billion in 1958 to over $156 billion in 1977 and are estimated at about $237 billion in 1980. More startling is the growth of those expenditures as a percent of adjusted Gross National Product, rising steadily from 4.9 percent in 1958 to 7.6 percent in 1977, to over 8.4 percent by 1980. (The reader should refer to Chapter III for a discussion of the adjustments made in GNP.)

Concurrent with increases in the total expenditures for information services, rapid increases have taken place in the expenditures by businesses for information services, increasing from about 39 percent of the total in 1958 to almost 54 percent in 1980. The share of information services purchased by consumers declined steadily over the same time period, going from 44 percent of the total to only 32 percent in 1980, while the government share also declined, from 17 percent to 14 percent. For the purpose of these computations, business expenditures include all purchases of engineering and architectual services, all accounting services, all costs of credit-card handling, all costs of wholesale

SUMMARY TABLE VIII
Total Expenditures for Information Services: 1958,
1963, 1967, 1972, 1977, and 1980
(millions of dollars)

	1958	1963	1967	1972	1977	1980
Professional knowledge						
services	7,971	10,958	17,992	29,995	55,267	85,067
Financial services	8,742	12,367	16,279	26,707	49,716	78,311
Wholesale trading	1,529	1,893	2,479	3,595	6,066	
Computer and						
data processing				3,411	7,476	13,365
Miscellaneous						
information services	1,548	3,080	5,314	8,440	15,516	26,064
Government	3,974	5,505	7,334	12,994	22,624	34,173
Total	23,764	33,803	49,398	85,142	156,665	236,980
Percent of						
adjusted GNP	4.9	5.2	5.7	6.7	7.6	8.4
Paid for by						
Government						
expenditures	3,974	5,505	7,334	12,994	22,624	34,173
Business						
expenditures	9,260	15,116	22,762	42,410	85,329	127,313
Consumer						
expenditures	10,530	13,182	19,302	29,738	48,712	75,494

Sources: Text and tables within Chapter VIII of this book.

trading, all computer services and all miscellaneous business services. Consumer expenditures include all purchases of medical services, all purchases of stock brokerage services, and those parts of legal, real estate, insurance, and banking services not paid for by business.

Professional Knowledge Services

This section reports on national expenditures for four types of professional knowledge services, presenting data for each of the economic census years, including 1958, 1963, 1967, 1972, and 1977, and for the latest year available, 1980. The four service industries studied are: (1) legal services; (2) engineering and architectural services; (3) accounting and auditing services; and (4) medical services.

The data presented here are consistent with the earlier version of this book; however, the source of the underlying data has been changed in order to make full use of new materials that were not available in 1960. The data sources used in this section are examined in detail below, as a prelude to the report of our findings.

COMPARISON OF DATA SOURCES

This section describes recently available data sources that make possible more accurate measurement of the expenditures for several professional knowledge services, including legal, architectural and engineering, and accounting services. In Machlup's original work, the data source for expenditures for these services was an annual publication of the Internal Revenue Service (the "IRS") entitled *Statistics of Income*.

Unfortunately, the statistical techniques employed by the IRS yielded a substantial underestimate of the value of the activities that we are seeking to measure. These difficulties do not, however, affect the statistics that are compiled every five years by the Census Bureau and that are published as the *Census of Services*. Of course, the Census data have their own drawbacks, the most basic being that only one year in five is reported.

Each of our statistical sources, the IRS and the Census Bureau, reports on the total revenues of a given industry, broken down into three segments that correspond to the three organizational forms of business, including sole proprietorships, partnerships, and corporations or "professional associations." The findings reported by our two sources are in considerable agreement on the revenues enjoyed by proprietors and partnerships, but diverge widely in their findings on the revenues of corporations. The IRS statistics severely understate the gross receipts of professional associations when compared to the data compiled in the *Census of Services*.

This shortcoming in the IRS statistics has become progressively more serious as the trend away from the use of the partnership organizational form has accelerated in recent years. Since the mid-1960s there has been a growing trend toward the corporate form for businesses that were traditionally organized as partnerships. These professional associations offer the dual benefits of reduced personal liability for the individuals involved in the business, as well as attractive pension benefits available only to corporations under the tax laws. In short, professional associations are now common in the legal, accounting, and engineering industries where the partnership form once predominated.

The undercount in IRS statistics arises from the fact that the IRS material is an estimate that is created by extrapolating from a survey based upon stratified samples. For example, in 1967, the sample for corporations was 126,695 returns out of a population of 1.7 million returns; however, for returns of corporations with assets under 100,000 dollars, only 2.3 percent of the population was sampled. The problem is that the sample for a given industry is often so small as to be statistically insignificant. When this happens, the IRS aggregates the data on that industry into the catch-all "other services" industry, effectively precluding its measurement. A similar problem is avoided in the IRS data for proprietors and partnerships since a much greater percentage of the population is covered by the sample for those organizational forms.

The severity of this problem can be understood by looking at several examples. In 1977 for engineering and architectural services, the *Census of Services* reported total receipts of 14,737.2 million dollars, of which $11,000 million came from corporations. In comparison, IRS reported total revenues to $3,533 million, with no corporate revenues reported. In accounting and auditing services, the IRS reported no corporate revenues, while Census reported $1,245.7 million from corporate revenues. In both industries, IRS and Census data for partnerships and sole proprietors matched very closely.[1]

The net result is a substantial dilemma for the researcher. The IRS data constitute our only opportunity for annual time-series statistics for the three industries in question, but involve a serious undercount. On the other hand, the Census data, while considerably more accurate, are only available for a very few years. The results from each data source are summarized in Table VIII-A.

Since the Census Bureau began to collect data on engineering and architec-

TABLE VIII-A
COMPARISON OF INFORMATION FROM TWO SOURCES

Year	Corporate Revenues		Total Revenues	
	Census	IRS	Census	IRS
Legal Services				
1958		0		3,025
1963		127		4,596
1967		0	6,334	6,254
1972	2,142	928	10,938	10,534
1977	3,864		18,695	
Engineering and Architectural Services				
1958		0		1,249
1963		0		1,563
1967	2,533	0	4,510	2,294
1972	5,400	0	7,186	2,724
1977	11,536	0	14,049	3,533
Accounting and Auditing Services				
1958		0		1,410
1963		0		1,615
1967		0		2,547
1972		0		4,126
1977	1,245	0	7,990	6,620

SOURCES: Internal Revenue Service, *Statistics of Income* (Washington, D.C.: Government Printing Office, annual ed.), and U.S. Bureau of the Census, *Census of Business* and *Census of Services* (Washington, D.C.: Government Printing Office, quinquennial eds.).

[1] See Internal Revenue Service, *Statistics of Income*, annual editions, and the Business of the Census, *Census of Business*, quinquennial editions for 1958, 1963, and 1967; and *Census of Service Industries*, quinquennial editions for 1972 and 1977. All of these are publications of the Government Printing Office, Washington, D.C.

tural services in 1967, legal services in 1972, and accounting and auditing services in 1977, the IRS is our only source for data on these industries before those years. Under the circumstances we will use both data sources, in any particular instance choosing the source that best meets our needs.

LEGAL SERVICES[2]

Table VIII-1 presents the gross receipts of the legal services industry for the years 1958, 1963, 1967, 1972, 1977, and 1980. For the first three of those years, the data source is the IRS publication *Statistics of Income*, the same source used by Machlup. Data from the *Census of Services* is used in the two years for which it is available, 1972 and 1977, since it provides a more accurate accounting of the gross revenues of professional corporations. The data source for 1980 is Bureau of the Census unpublished data.

TABLE VIII-1
LEGAL SERVICES: GROSS RECEIPTS OF LAW FIRMS AND PERSONAL
CONSUMPTION EXPENDITURES, 1958, 1963, 1967, 1972, 1977
AND 1980
(millions of dollars)

Gross receipts of	1958	1963	1967	1972	1977	1980
(1) Single proprietorships	1,487	1,985	2,853	2,285	4,739	
(2) Partnerships	1,538	2,484	3,481	5,911	10,093	
(3) Professional corporations		127		1,056	3,864	
(4) Other				1,086		
(5) Total	3,025	4,596	6,334	10,338	18,696	23,424
(6) Personal consumption expenditures	1,531	2,308	3,163	5,435	9,008	13,070
(7) Business expenses for legal services	1,494	2,288	3,171	4,903	9,688	10,354

SOURCES: Lines (1) through (4), (1958 to 1963): U.S. Internal Revenue Service, *Statistics of Income* (Washington, D.C.: Government Printing Office, annual ed.); (1967): U.S. Bureau of the Census, *Census of Business* (Washington, D.C.: Government Printing Office, quinquennial ed.); (1972 and 1977): U.S. Bureau of the Census, *Census of Service Industries* (Washington, D.C.: Government Printing Office, quinquennial ed.), Line (5), (1980); U.S. Bureau of the Census, *Current Business Reports* (Washington, D.C.: Government Printing Office, monthly ed.). Line (6): U.S. Bureau of Economic Analysis, *Survey of Current Business* (Washington, D.C.: Government Printing Office, monthly ed.). Line (7): Line 5 minus Line 6.

Of the $18,696 million that this industry is credited with in 1977, $9,008 million was for personal consumption expenditures and $9,688 million was for business expenses. The Bureau of the Census estimates that the legal services industry enjoyed total receipts of $23,424 million in 1980.

[2] See Fritz Machlup, *The Production and Distribution of Knowledge in the United States* (Princeton, N.J.: Princeton University Press), p. 328.

ENGINEERING AND ARCHITECTURAL SERVICES[3]

Table VIII-2 presents the gross receipts of the engineering and architectural service industries for the years 1958, 1963, 1967, 1972, and 1977. In the original volume, Machlup noted that these two services were classified together with educational services and could not be separated. Machlup argued, however, that a measurement of the two industries could be approximated by assuming that educational services were sold exclusively by corporations and that the receipts of proprietors and partnerships corresponded to the total receipts of the engineering and architectural service industries.

Since the date of Machlup's preparation of his earlier text, two data sources have become available that allow us to separate educational services from the two industries of interest here. IRS *Statistics of Income*, which was relied upon by Machlup, has reorganized its classification system in such a way that educational services are now reported separately from engineering and architectural services. The reader will note in Table VIII-2 that the 1958 data have been revised to take advantage of this newer material and consequently do not agree with the figures reported by Machlup. In addition, the *Census of Services* reports comparable statistics for the years 1967, 1972, and 1977. Following the pattern established in our treatment of legal services, these two sources are used to obtain the best possible statistic picture of the engineering and architectural service industries. Thus, the IRS material is used for 1958 and 1963, and the Census material for 1967, 1972, and 1977. For 1977 the gross receipts of engineering and architectural services amounted to $14,049 millions. Table VIII-2 reports this in more detail.

The Bureau of the Census reports that the total receipts of this industry amounted to $25,713 million in 1980. No detail by organizational form is available.

TABLE VIII-2

ENGINEERING AND ARCHITECTURAL SERVICES: GROSS RECEIPTS OF ENGINEERING AND ARCHITECTURAL PARTNERSHIPS, PROPRIETORSHIPS, AND CORPORATIONS, 1958, 1963, 1967, 1972, AND 1977
(millions of dollars)

Gross receipts of	1958	1963	1967	1972	1977
(1) Single proprietorships	563	759	973	664	1,075
(2) Partnerships	686	804	1,004	1,122	1,438
(3) Corporations			2,534	5,400	11,536
(4) Total	1,249	1,563	4,511	7,186	14,049

SOURCES: (1958 and 1963): U.S. Internal Revenue Service, *Statistics of Income*, annual ed. (1967, 1972, and 1977): U.S. Bureau of the Census, *Census of Services Industries*, quinquennial ed.

[3] See Machlup, *Production and Distribution of Knowledge*, p. 329.

ACCOUNTING AND AUDITING SERVICES[4]

At the time of the publication of the original work, Professor Machlup reported that statistics on this industry were sparse and was able to report its gross receipts only for 1957. Since that time, the IRS publication *Statistics of Income* has reported gross receipts for this industry on a regular basis, and data are now available for the years 1958, 1963, 1967, 1972, and 1977. In addition, the *Census of Services* has reported in detail on 1977. Table VIII-2A reports the gross receipts for this industry for five separate years, using the various data sources as indicated. For 1977, the most recent year for which data are available, the gross receipts amounted to $7,991 million.

The authors have used data reported in *County Business Patterns 1980: United States*, a publication of the Census Bureau, to estimate that this industry's gross receipts came to $12,625 million in 1980. The estimate is calculated from ratios of the industry's payroll in the years 1977 and 1980.

TABLE VIII-2A

ACCOUNTING AND AUDITING SERVICES: GROSS RECEIPTS OF ACCOUNTING AND AUDITING PARTNERSHIPS, PROPRIETORSHIPS, AND CORPORATIONS, 1958, 1963, 1967, 1972, AND 1977
(millions of dollars)

Gross receipts of	1958	1963	1967	1972	1977
(1) Single proprietorships	719	652	933	1,208	1,758
(2) Partnerships	691	963	1,614	2,918	4,987
(3) Corporations					1,246
(4) Total	1,410	1,615	2,547	4,126	7,991

SOURCES: (1958, 1963, 1967, and 1972): U.S. Internal Revenue Service, *Statistics of Income*, annual ed. (1977): U.S. Bureau of the Census, *Census of Service Industries*, quinquennial ed.

MEDICAL SERVICES[5]

This section uses the technique described by Machlup to measure the value of the information services provided by medical practitioners. Personal consumption expenditures for the services of physicians are divided evenly in two, as an estimate of those medical services that are knowledge producing and those that are not. Consultation and diagnosis are considered knowledge producing in this activity. Our findings for the census years are reported in Table VIII-2B. In 1980 the value of these services came to $23,305 million.

[4] See Machlup, *Production and Distribution of Knowledge*, p. 329.
[5] See Machlup, *Production and Distribution of Knowledge*, p. 330.

TABLE VIII-2B

MEDICAL SERVICES: PERSONAL CONSUMPTION EXPENDITURES, 1958, 1963, 1967, 1972, AND 1977

(millions of dollars)

	1958	1963	1967	1972	1977
(1) Personal expenditures					
physicians and surgeons	4,574	6,366	9,361	15,489	29,066
(2) Deduct non-knowledge					
components	2,287	3,183	4,681	7,745	14,533
(3) Consultation and advice	2,287	3,183	4,680	7,744	14,533

SOURCE: U.S. Department of Commerce, *Survey of Current Business.* These data appeared in the July issue for various years.

INFORMATION AND FINANCIAL SERVICES AS JOINT PRODUCTS

Machlup identified a number of industries that produced information as a joint product with the other financial services they provide. Included in this group were: (1) check-deposit banking; (2) security and commodity brokers, dealers, and exchanges; (3) insurance carriers and other financial services; and (4) real estate brokerage.

An additional activity, not significant at the time of Machlup's work, has grown substantially over the last twenty years and must be included here. The use of credit cards has experienced a phenomenal growth in the last two decades, accounting for a steadily increasing portion, nationally, of consumer credit. An estimate of the cost of processing charge accounts to business and to the American consumer will be presented in the following pages.

Machlup reported in detail the difficulties a researcher encounters in attempting to provide estimates of the information portions of these financial activities. Whereas recent improvements in data sources make our task somewhat easier, the remaining obstacles will be described below.

CHECK-DEPOSIT BANKING[6]

Machlup's observation that the major difficulty in measuring the value of check-deposit banking is the statistically and analytically embarrassing fact that banks do not collect payment for all the services they render is as true today as it was when it was written. Expenditures for the operation of checking accounts are not directly reported by any source. Further, surrogate measures of these expenditures are unsatisfactory for a variety of reasons. For example, the difficulties Machlup describes in the use of "imputed payments" of interest by banks; that is, interest that is earned by the depositor but that is retained by the

[6] See Machlup, *Production and Distribution of Knowledge,* p. 331.

bank to pay for other services, continues to hold. As Machlup noted, these imputed payments are "at best a measure of the value of the capital services to bank borrowers and debtors, but not a measure of the value of the check-deposit services to depositors or of their costs to banks."

The current expenses of member banks of the Federal Reserve System would serve our purposes well if expenditures for check-deposit banking could be separated from those for other tasks. Unfortunately, no such separation is available in these aggregate statistics.

The solution of these difficulties rests upon a series of annual studies that have been conducted by the Federal Reserve Board entitled *Functional Cost Analysis.*[7] These studies are designed to allow the management of a particular bank to compare its performance with that of an "average" bank, in order to identify and remedy inefficient portions of the particular bank's operation. The costs, by function, for participating banks, are reported in considerable detail. The number of participating banks has varied widely over the more than twenty years the studies have been conducted, ranging from a low in recent years of about 600 to over a thousand.

The major drawback besetting use of the data from the *Functional Cost Analysis* for our purposes is, in fact, in its participants. Unscientifically selected, since participation is entirely voluntary, the participants in the studies do not necessarily constitute a representative sample of the universe of commercial banks. In 1980, for example, the participants accounted for about 6 percent of all commercial banks and held roughly the same percentage of demand deposits. There were three strata of participants, including those with deposits under $10 million, those between $10 million and $200 million, and those over $200 million. The decision to use these data is largely the judgment that they are better than no data at all.

Table VIII-3 presents data for the years 1959 to 1980 from the *Functional Cost Analysis,* reporting income and expenses for participating banks for the operation of demand deposit accounts. The figures in the table are dollars of income or expense per $100 of demand deposits held by the "average" bank. Per $100 demand deposit, the average total expenses were $2.05 in 1959, but had risen to $4.34 by 1980. This increase was paced by a rise of employee salaries from $.80 to $2.03 over the same period. Nonetheless, the operation of demand deposit accounts has become progressively more profitable, net earnings before taxes per $100 deposit rising from $1.25 in 1959 to $4.57 by 1980. The major source of income has consistently been portfolio income, with service charges a distant second.

Table VIII-3A presents our estimates of the total annual cost of demand deposit accounts, obtained by multiplying total annual demand deposits by the

[7] *Functional Cost Analysis* is an annual publication of the Federal Reserve Board which reports on the various operating expenses of member banks.

TABLE VIII-3

INCOME AND EXPENSES OF COMMERCIAL BANKS IN THE OPERATION
OF DEMAND DEPOSIT ACCOUNTS, DOLLARS PER $100 OF DEMAND
DEPOSITS, 1959-1980

Year	Income	Portfolio income	Service charges	Total expenses	Employee salaries	Other expenses	Net earnings before taxes
1959	3.30	2.63	0.67	2.05	0.80	1.25	1.25
1960	3.72	2.93	0.79	2.24	0.92	1.32	1.48
1961	3.92	3.07	0.85	2.27	0.99	1.28	1.65
1962	4.06	3.22	0.84	2.30	1.00	1.30	1.76
1963	4.19	3.23	0.96	2.61	1.21	1.40	1.58
1964	4.33	3.36	0.97	2.65	1.24	1.41	1.68
1965	4.13	3.32	0.81	2.44	1.14	1.30	1.69
1966	4.37	3.72	0.65	1.96	1.03	0.93	2.41
1967	4.54	3.87	0.67	2.10	1.13	0.97	2.44
1968	4.99	4.27	0.72	2.29	1.18	1.11	2.70
1969	5.46	4.70	0.76	2.47	1.29	1.18	2.99
1970	5.74	5.01	0.73	2.55	1.32	1.23	3.19
1971	5.20	4.50	0.70	2.45	1.17	1.28	2.75
1972	5.16	4.44	0.72	2.50	1.18	1.32	2.66
1973	5.69	5.01	0.68	2.66	1.25	1.41	3.03
1974	6.47	5.72	0.75	2.92	1.42	1.50	3.55
1975	6.00	5.26	0.74	3.08	1.49	1.59	2.92
1976	6.05	5.32	0.73	3.30	1.61	1.70	2.75
1977	6.12	5.33	0.79	3.38	1.65	1.73	2.74
1978	6.53	5.77	0.76	3.43	1.69	1.74	3.10
1979	7.76	6.75	1.01	3.90	1.88	2.02	3.86
1980	8.91	7.69	1.22	4.34	2.03	2.31	4.57

SOURCE: Federal Reserve Board, *Functional Cost Analysis* (Washington, D.C., annual ed.).

NOTE: Data for the years 1966 to 1980 have been revised to make them comparable with figures for earlier years.

cost percentages in Table VIII-3. Since no separate figures are available for 1958, cost ratios for 1959 were used for both years. In 1980 the expense of commercial banks for demand deposit accounts was $11,588 million.

Personal consumption expenditures accounted for about one-half of the total cost of these services over most of the years of our study, with business paying for the remainder according to statistics reported by the Commerce Department.[8] Consumers spent $810 million in 1958 for demand deposit account services; $1,050 million in 1963; $1,585 million in 1967; $2,319 million in 1972; $3,517 million in 1977; and $5,590 million in 1980. Comparable expenditures by businesses were $1,445 million in 1958, increasing to $2,150 million in 1963; decreasing, probably in a statistical quirk, to $1,408 million

[8] These personal consumption expenditures are reported in various issues of the monthly *Survey of Current Business*, compiled by the Bureau of Economic Analysis and published by the Government Printing Office, Washington, D.C.

TABLE VIII-3A

Bank Expenses for Check-Deposit Banking, 1958-1980
(millions of dollars)

Year	Demand deposits (1)	Processing expenses of demand deposits (% of total demand deposits) (2)	Cost of processing demand deposits [(1) × (2)]/100 (3)
1958	110,000	2.05	2,255
1959	114,700	2.05	2,351
1960	114,500	2.24	2,565
1961	117,400	2.27	2,665
1962	119,600	2.30	2,751
1963	122,600	2.61	3,200
1964	126,800	2.65	3,360
1965	131,800	2.44	3,216
1966	137,400	1.96	2,693
1967	142,500	2.10	2,993
1968	152,900	2.29	3,501
1969	161,700	2.47	3,994
1970	166,800	2.55	4,253
1971	177,700	2.45	4,354
1972	190,400	2.50	4,760
1973	204,000	2.66	5,426
1974	212,800	2.92	6,214
1975	218,500	3.08	6,730
1976	227,400	3.30	7,504
1977	242,600	3.38	8,200
1978	259,600	3.43	8,904
1979	263,000	3.90	10,257
1980	267,000	4.34	11,588

Sources: Column (1): Bureau of Economic Analysis, *Business Statistics*, 1979 (Washington, D.C.: Government Printing Office, 1980), and U.S. Bureau of Economic Analysis, *Survey of Current Business*, July 1981. Column (2): Table VIII-3. Column (3): Column 1 multiplied by Column 2.

in 1967, then rising steadily from $2,441 million to $4,683 million to $5,598 million over the remaining years of our study.

COST OF PROCESSING CREDIT CARD ACCOUNTS[9]

In the last twenty years credit cards have become a major medium of consumer credit. This financial instrument has been built about the provision of information services by the card operators to merchants and their customers. The use of credit cards is attractive to the consumer for the convenience and safety it offers and useful to merchants since the card payments are guaranteed. The costs and risk of credit collection are effectively transferred from the merchant

[9] This is a new topic not treated by Machlup.

to the card operator by the use of credit cards. It is this "middleman" function that we seek to measure, and particularly that part of the operation which can be attributed to the processing of information: the crediting and debiting of customer accounts and the tallying of income due to individual merchants.

The expansion of the credit card industry is indicated by several consumer surveys showing that the use of credit cards has risen from 50 percent of the nation's families in 1970 to 62 percent by 1978 and that the use of bank cards in particular has risen from 16 percent to 38 percent over the same time period. [10] These surveys, however, do not do full justice to the story. The portion of consumer installment credit extensions accounted for by the use of credit cards provides a more accurate picture. Interpreting Table VIII-3B, we see that credit cards have risen from 14 percent of the total in 1961 to close to 45 percent in 1980. Out of total consumer credit extensions of $306.1 billion in 1980, credit cards accounted for $128.1 billion.

The story within a story in the credit card industry is the growth of bank credit cards. In 1973, the first year for which statistics are available, bank cards accounted for about 8 percent of all consumer installment credit extensions. By 1980 the figure was over 20 percent. The growth of the use of credit cards as an element of consumer installment credit is shown in Table VIII-3B, which presents data from the years 1958 to 1981.

Estimates of expenditures for the processing of credit card accounts are calculated using methods similar to those used to derive figures for demand deposits. Table VIII-3C uses statistics from the *Functional Cost Analysis* studies first described in the last section to show expenses as a percent of credit extensions for the years 1971 to 1981. The assumption is made here that the expenses underlying a bank card operation are the same as those required to operate a retail card or a gasoline card. Expense figures for 1963 and 1967, unavailable from the *Functional Cost Analysis*, are taken from *Study of Customer Credit Costs in Department Stores, 1963*, which was compiled by the accounting firm, Touche, Ross, Bailey & Smart, for the National Retail Merchants Association. [11] Where otherwise unavailable, expenses attributable to bad debts are assumed to be 2 percent of total credit extended, and are deducted from the information processing expenses. The percentages from *Functional Cost Analysis* are multiplied by total extensions of credit by use of credit cards. The result is our estimate of expenditures by credit card operators for information services.

According to our calculations, expenditures by credit card operators for information services were $725 million in 1963; $1,158 million in 1967; $3,288 million in 1972; $8,409 million in 1977; and $15,240 million in 1980.

---

[10] See Thomas A. Durkin, "Credit Card Holding and Use Among American Families: Results of National Surveys," *Journal of Retail Banking*, June 1980, pp. 19-26.

[11] Touche, Ross, Bailey, and Smart, *Study of Customer Credit Costs in Department Stores, 1963* (New York: National Retail Merchants Association, 1963).

TABLE VIII-3B

CONSUMER INSTALLMENT CREDIT EXTENSIONS, 1958-1981
(billions of dollars)

Year	Total revolving credit extended (2)+(3)+(4) (1)	Bank credit cards (2)	Retail credit cards (3)	Gasoline credit cards (4)	Other credit extensions* (5)	Total credit extended (6)
1958						41,290
1959						43,395
1960						47,022
1961	7,736		7,736		40,660	48,396
1962	9,659		9,659		46,532	56,191
1963	11,327		11,327		52,264	63,591
1964	13,310		13,310		57,360	70,670
1965	14,430		14,430		64,156	78,586
1966	16,494		16,494		66,338	82,832
1967	18,090		18,090		69,081	87,171
1968	19,122		19,122		80,862	99,984
1969	20,240		20,240		88,906	109,146
1970	21,526		21,526		90,632	112,158
1971	22,143		22,143		102,138	124,281
1972	24,541		24,541		118,410	142,951
1973	39,302	13,862	25,440		125,225	164,527
1974	44,132	17,098	27,034		115,876	160,008
1975	47,477	20,428	27,049		116,006	163,483
1976	73,381	30,547	29,447	13,387	151,034	224,415
1977	87,596	38,256	34,723	14,617	170,004	257,600
1978	105,125	51,333	37,775	16,017	192,543	297,668
1979	120,174	61,048	41,121	18,005	204,603	324,777
1980	128,068	61,593	44,222	22,253	178,008	306,076
1981	140,135	67,370	47,863	24,902	196,206	336,341

SOURCE: *Federal Reserve Bulletin*, a monthly publication of the Federal Reserve Board, Washington, D.C.

* Automobile loans, etc.

SECURITY AND COMMODITY BROKERS, DEALERS, AND EXCHANGES[12]

The difficulties reported by Machlup in measuring the expenditures for security and commodity brokers, dealers, and exchanges have not declined in the last two decades. Indeed, although new sources of information have become available in that period, the problems they solve have been replaced by new problems. The industry group "security and commodity brokers, dealers, and exchanges" consists of five subgroups: (1) security brokers and dealers; (2) commodity brokers and dealers; (3) exchanges and exchange clearing houses; (4) quotation services; and (5) investment advisors.

[12] See Machlup, *Production and Distribution of Knowledge*, p. 334.

TABLE VIII-3C

YIELDS AND EXPENSES FROM THE OPERATION OF BANK CREDIT
CARDS, DOLLARS PER $100 OF CREDIT EXTENDED, 1971-1981

Year	Gross yields	Merchant discount	Finance charges	Total expenses	Bad debts	Gross earnings before cost of money	Net earnings
1971	19.0			16.7		2.3	−1.2
1972	19.7			15.4		4.2	.7
1973	19.5			13.7		5.7	1.1
1974	19.4			13.0		6.4	.9
1975	18.7			12.4		6.3	1.7
1976	19.5			12.0		7.6	3.0
1977	19.6			11.6		7.9	3.3
1978	19.3			11.1		8.2	2.9
1979	19.6			11.4	2.0	8.2	2.8
1980	20.7	4.6	16.1	14.6	2.7	5.2	−1.8
1981	23.3	5.8	17.5	12.6	2.4	10.8	1.3

SOURCE: Federal Reserve Board, *Functional Cost Analysis*, annual ed.

Recognizing that available statistics hopelessly entangle the data for each of these subgroups, Machlup chose to estimate expenditures for the entire group. The income originating in the industry, as reported by the Department of Commerce, was used as a surrogate for the total expenditures for the industry's services. At the same time, Machlup noted that much of the income received by brokers was not a payment for information services at all. Rather, brokers received income for interest on margin accounts and from various types of investments. A partially successful correction for these data deficiencies was carried out by reducing the income originating by an estimate of interest payments made by individuals to brokers on margin accounts.

These problems are partially overcome by statistics, unavailable to Machlup, which are now collected by the Securities and Exchange Commission (SEC). In 1961 the SEC began to report in detail on the total revenue of all security and commodity brokers and dealers. Although there has been some change in detail and format over the years, Table VIII-4 presents these SEC data in time-series form. The revenue sources are listed by six categories, only one of which represents payments for information services. Aside from securities commissions, none of the income sources are payment for information services.

The major difficulty affecting the SEC statistics is their apparent incompleteness. The Internal Revenue Service publication *Statistics of Income* reports gross receipts for the broadly defined group of industries in the securities brokerage area. As a subset of that group, the revenues of the brokers reported

TABLE VIII-4

Security and Commodity Brokers and Dealers: Revenue by Source, 1961-1980
(millions of dollars)

Year	Total revenue	Securities commissions	Profit on trading accounts	Profit on investment accounts	Profit from underwriting	Margin interest	Other
1961	1,047	613	106	23	90	114	101
1962	1,464	856	129	15	122	191	151
1963	1,576	916	125	23	109	232	171
1964	1,801	1,054	150	32	123	263	179
1965	2,320	1,413	169	35	169	264	270
1966	2,851	1,766	186	34	208	337	320
1967	3,992	2,520	356	75	315	346	380
1968	5,403	3,245	641	133	462	445	477
1969	5,822	2,930	706	151	645	474	916
1970	4,800	2,185	847	66	625	380	697
1971	6,869	3,405	1,101	251	982	364	766
1972	7,022	3,533	1,039	210	939	527	774
1973	5,544	2,954	606	14	509	621	840
1974	5,065	2,438	722	54	496	622	733
1975	7,373	3,378	1,202	132	930	476	1,255
1976	8,915	3,657	1,828	269	1,035	557	1,569
1977	8,931	3,334	1,691	353	991	782	1,780
1978	11,197	4,498	2,053	394	949	1,223	2,080
1979	14,528	4,825	3,183	740	943	1,652	3,185
1980	20,715	6,876	4,717	797	1,627	2,089	4,609

Sources: Securities and Exchange Commission, *Statistical Bulletin*, various issues; and Securities and Exchange Commission, *Annual Report* (Washington, D.C.: Government Printing Office, various years).

by the SEC should be less than those reported by the IRS for the larger group. The sorry tale, however, is that in some years, the SEC figures are greater than the IRS figures. For example, in 1967, the SEC reported broker's income at $3,992 million whereas the IRS reported income of $3,307 million for the larger industry that allegedly included all brokers. The weakness noted earlier in this chapter in the IRS collection of data on corporations may account for this difficulty. In later years, the IRS and SEC statistics have reached closer conformity, with the SEC broker data running about 75 to 85 percent of the IRS data for the larger industry.

To measure the size of the knowledge industries we use the SEC data on securities commissions paid to brokers. In 1961 that figure came to $613 million and increased steadily to $6,876 million by 1980.

INSURANCE CARRIERS AND AGENTS[13]

Out of the larger group of activities that make up the insurance industry, Machlup recognized only "insurance agents and combination offices" as an

[13] See Machlup, *Production and Distribution of Knowledge*, p. 337.

industry specializing in "information" services. Gross receipts for this activity being unavailable at the time, Machlup used income originating as the value of its services, which was reported as $2,173 million in 1958.

Subsequent publications of the Internal Revenue Service have reported the gross receipts of this activity for a number of years, from 1958 to the late 1970s. Table VIII-5 presents these data for the years of our study. The reader should note that Machlup's original data for 1958 have been revised to take advantage of this new data source. In 1977 gross receipts of insurance agents and brokers came to $19,263 million.

Using methods that have been described earlier in this chapter and based upon data reported in the Census Bureau publication, *County Business Patterns 1980: United States*, the authors estimate that gross receipts of this industry totaled $29,447 million in 1980.

TABLE VIII-5

INSURANCE AGENTS, BROKERS, AND SERVICES: GROSS RECEIPTS, 1958, 1963, 1967, 1972, AND 1977
(millions of dollars)

Gross receipts of	1958	1963	1967	1972	1977
(1) Single proprietorships	1,620	1,878	2,333	3,559	5,431
(2) Partnerships	656	646	648	1,342	2,284
(3) Corporations	1,194	2,314	2,622	5,333	11,548
(4) Total	3,470	4,838	5,603	10,234	19,263

SOURCE: U.S. Internal Revenue Service, *Statistics of Income*, annual ed.

REAL ESTATE[14]

As Machlup noted, the broad category "real estate" is subdivided into a variety of groups, mostly relating to the operation of owned or leased real property. Only the group consisting of real estate agents and brokers can be considered to qualify as a knowledge-producing industry.

Data sources have improved somewhat in the intervening years since Machlup recorded an "n.a." for this industry in his calculations because of the unavailability of specific information on this activity. Table VIII-5A presents statistics on the gross receipts of real estate agents and brokers by organizational form for the years 1958 to 1977, as reported in the Internal Revenue Service publication, *Statistics of Income*. These data have some serious limitations, but are included here because they offer at least a rough estimate of this industry's magnitude. The major difficulty with the data source is that statistics for the gross receipts of corporations are only available up to 1970. At that time, a redefinition of the industries reported by the IRS eliminated the corporate activities of real estate agents and brokers as an identifiable category.

[14] See Machlup, *Production and Distribution of Knowledge*, p. 340.

TABLE VIII-5A

REAL ESTATE AGENTS, BROKERS, AND MANAGERS: GROSS RECEIPTS, 1958, 1963, 1967, 1972, 1977, AND 1980
(millions of dollars)

Gross receipts of	1958	1963	1967	1972	1977	1980
(1) Single proprietorships	739	1,459	1,861	4,107	8,475	
(2) Partnerships		264	384	785	2,035	
(3) Corporations		966	1,760			
(4) Total	739	2,689	4,005	4,892	10,510	15,160
(5) Personal consumption expenditures	414	1,629	1,948	2,881	6,272	7,564
(6) Business expenditures	325	1,060	2,057	2,011	4,238	7,596

SOURCE: U.S. Internal Revenue Service, *Statistics of Income,* annual ed.

NOTE: Data on corporations not available for 1972 and 1977. Allocations between business and consumer expenditures are made in the same proportions as total purchases of real estate, as reported by the Bureau of Economic Analysis.

Using data reported by the Census Bureau in *County Business Patterns 1980,* the authors estimate the receipts of this industry for the year 1980 were $15,160 million.

THE INTELLIGENCE SERVICE OF WHOLESALE TRADERS[15]

Machlup observed that among the activities in the category of wholesale trade, only "agents and brokers" belong on the list of knowledge industries. Unfortunately, as Machlup reported, no statistics on the total of brokerage and commission fees for this industry have been gathered since 1954. Table VIII-5B presents operating expenses of wholesale agents, brokers, and commission merchants for each of the census years from 1958 to 1977; operating expenses are used here as a surrogate for operating revenues since there are no other data available.

The value of the services for wholesale agents and brokers is recorded at $6,066 million in 1977. No data are available to support an estimate for this industry for 1980.

DATA PROCESSING SERVICES[16]

The industry group "computer and data processing services" consists of four subgroups: (1) computer programming and other software services; (2) data-processing services; (3) computer facilities management; and (4) other related computer services. All elements of this industry are included in our study of the knowledge industry.

[15] See Machlup, *Production and Distribution of Knowledge,* p. 340.
[16] This is a new topic not treated by Machlup.

TABLE VIII-5B

Wholesale Agents, Brokers, and Commission Merchants:
Operating Expenses, 1958, 1963, 1967, 1972, and 1977
(millions of dollars)

Year	Establishments	Operating expenses	Payroll	Sales
1958	26,567	1,529	745	46,423
1963	25,313	1,893	990	53,245
1967	26,462	2,479	1,377	61,347
1972	32,620	3,595	1,948	85,626
1977	35,052	6,066	2,981	130,487

Sources: (1958, 1963, 1967): U.S. Bureau of the Census, *Census of Business*, quinquennial ed. (1972, 1977): U.S. Bureau of the Census, *Census of Service Industries*, quinquennial ed.

Statistics for the gross receipts of this industry have been collected by the Census Bureau since the 1972 *Census of Services*. Table VIII-5C presents that information for the years 1972, 1977, and 1980. Gross receipts of the computer and data processing services industry came to $13,365 million in 1980.

Miscellaneous Service Industries[17]

Machlup identified nine knowledge activities from among the "miscellaneous" service industries listed by the Census Bureau. This section reports on the performance of those industries over the last two decades. In addition, data are provided for one additional activity, title abstractors, for several years for which information is available.

Table VIII-5D reports the gross receipts of the miscellaneous knowledge service industries for the census years from 1958 to 1977, plus the year 1980. Data for 1958, originally reported by Machlup, have been revised to reflect later data revisions. Also, the 1980 figures are calculated using data from the Census Bureau publication, *County Business Patterns 1980: United States*.

TABLE VIII-5C

Computer and Data-Processing Services: Gross Receipts, 1972, 1977, and 1980
(millions of dollars)

Year	Gross receipts
1972	3,411
1977	7,476
1980	13,365

Sources: (1972 and 1977): U.S. Bureau of the Census, *Census of Service Industries*, quinquennial ed. (1980): U.S. Bureau of the Census, *Current Business Reports*, December 1980.

[17] See Machlup, *Production and Distribution of Knowledge*, p. 341.

TABLE VIII-5D

MISCELLANEOUS BUSINESS SERVICES: GROSS RECEIPTS, 1958, 1963, 1967, 1972, 1977, AND 1980
(millions of dollars)

Gross receipts of	1958	1963	1967	1972	1977	1980
(1) Management and public relations agencies	593	1,348	2,852	4,257	8,343	16,270
(2) Credit reporting, collection agencies	331	437	677	803*	1,238*	1,624
(3) Mailing list, steno services	192	585	772	742*	1,222*	1,920
(4) Blueprint, photocopy services	152	166	199	227*	397*	760
(5) Private employment agencies	93	138	258	505*	921*	2,260
(6) Detective agencies	85	174	261	1,420*	2,615*	1,800
(7) Interior decorating	35	91	156	241*	355*	650
(8) Auctioneers	23	56				
(9) Telephone answering services	44	85	122	205*	370*	700
(10) Title abstractors			17	40	55	80
(11) Total	1,548	3,080	5,314	8,440	15,516	26,064

SOURCES: (1958, 1963, 1967): U.S. Bureau of the Census, *Census of Business*, quinquennial ed. (1972, 1977): U.S. Bureau of the Census, *Census of Service Industries*, quinquennial ed. (1980): Author's estimates for each industry derived from ratios of annual payroll in the years 1977 and 1980. 1980 annual payroll data for detailed industries are reported in the Census Bureau publication, *County Business Patterns 1980: United States* (Washington, D.C.: Government Printing Office). This publication provides detailed statistics at the four- and five-digit SIC classification level for most service industries, but, unfortunately, does not report gross receipts. Data on title abstractors from U.S. Internal Revenue Service, *Statistics of Income*, annual ed.

* Establishments with payroll only.

Gross receipts of this group of industries came to $15,516 million in 1977 and $26,064 million in 1980.

GOVERNMENT AS KNOWLEDGE INDUSTRY[18]

Tables VIII-6 and VIII-7 report the expenditures of the federal government and state and local governments for knowledge activities not elsewhere accounted for in this book. The categories of activities set out by Machlup are followed consistently; however, changes in reporting formats have forced some changes in the categories of data originally reported by Machlup.

In 1980 federal knowledge expenditures not elsewhere reported came to $14,430 million, and similar expenditures by state and local governments came to $19,743 million.

[18] See Machlup, *Production and Distribution of Knowledge*, p. 343.

TABLE VIII-6
Federal Government Expenditures for Knowledge Production
Not Classified Elsewhere, 1956-1981
(millions of dollars)

	1956	1958	1960	1961	1962	1963	1964	1965
International affairs								
(1) Conduct of foreign affairs	120	173	217	216	249	346	297	346
(2) Information and exchange services	111	149	137	158	197	201	207	223
Natural resources								
(3) General resource surveys and administration	35	43	51	55	60	73	73	94
Commerce								
(4) Regulation of commerce and finance	41	49	59	67	74	84	91	98
General government								
(5) Legislative functions	77	88	109	118	135	131	126	142
(6) Judicial functions	38	44	49	52	57	63	66	76
(7) Executive direction and management	9	10	20	22	22	21	22	23
(8) Federal financial management	475	502	558	607	653	715	791	825
(9) General property records management	164	239	372	372	419	444	576	606
(10) Civilian weather services	34	39	54	77	100	114	126	138
(11) Protective services and alien control	188	199	263	289	300	323	335	366
(12) Other general government	238	20	88	109	136	139	189	190
Total	1,530	1,555	1,977	2,142	2,402	2,654	2,899	3,127

	1966	1967	1968	1969	1970	1971	1972	1973
International affairs								
(1) Conduct of foreign affairs	315	336	354	372	398	405	452	476
(2) Information and exchange services	227	245	253	237	235	242	274	296
Natural resources								
(3) General resource surveys and administration	89	91	100	161	122	136	153	168
Commerce								
(4) Regulation of commerce and finance	99	118	97	107	120	182	168	139
General government								
(5) Legislative functions	159	167	180	192	229	256	311	333
(6) Judicial functions	79	87	94	110	133	146	173	188
(7) Executive direction and management	24	25	27	31	37	45	68	80
(8) Federal financial management	864	968	1,024	1,094	1,271	1,414	1,715	1,729
(9) General property records management	585	617	569	568	595	613	725	918
(10) Civilian weather services	156	176	175	179	251	320	354	452

TABLE VIII-6 (*con't*)

		1956	1958	1960	1961	1962	1963	1964	1965
(11)	Protective services and alien control	385	426	452	534	666	959	1,233	1,680
(12)	Other general government	192	218	243	271	272	339	345	408
	Total	3,174	3,474	3,568	3,856	4,329	5,057	5,971	6,867

		1974	1975	1976	1977	1978	1979	1980	1981
International affairs									
(1)	Conduct of foreign affairs	606	658	1,146	981	1,241	1,310	1,367	1,347
(2)	Information and exchange services	320	348	420	386	451	465	534	525
Natural resources									
(3)	General resource surveys and administration	498	762	897	973	1,157	1,273	1,412	1,485
Commerce									
(4)	Regulation of commerce and finance	714	939	867	326	1,342	1,454	2,409	1,959
General government									
(5)	Legislative functions	521	588	837	841	900	914	1,032	1,036
(6)	Judicial functions	221	279	313	400	445	488	575	651
(7)	Executive direction and management	117	63	74	76	73	81	97	99
(8)	Federal financial management	1,329	1,752	2,130	1,930	2,124	2,330	2,522	2,600
(9)	General property records management	1,030	418	339	141	214	235	364	169
(10)	Civilian weather services	484	595	661	709	744	757	854	913
(11)	Protective services and alien control	1,274	1,593	1,852	1,990	2,171	2,389	2,689	2,901
(12)	Other general government	419	472	563	117	523	586	559	745
	Total	7,533	8,467	10,099	8,870	11,385	12,282	14,414	14,430

SOURCE: U.S. Office of Management and Budget, *The Budget of the United States Government* (Washington, D.C.: Government Printing Office, annual ed.).

NOTE: Differences in reporting categories have been reconciled in order to allow comparability across years.

TABLE VIII-7

STATE AND LOCAL GOVERNMENT EXPENDITURES FOR KNOWLEDGE PRODUCTION, 1960-1980
(millions of dollars)

Fiscal year	Total	Protective inspection and regulation	General control	Financial administration	Social insurance administration
1960	2,426		——	2,113 ——	313
1961	2,588		1,220	1,017	351
1962	2,737		1,274	1,064	399
1963	2,850		1,331	1,108	411
1964	2,993		1,387	1,180	426
1965	3,230		1,506	1,267	457
1966	3,474		1,641	1,333	500
1967	3,860		1,845	1,468	547
1968	4,253		2,037	1,610	606
1969	4,772		2,299	1,806	667
1970	5,451		2,652	2,030	769
1971	6,243		3,027	2,271	945
1972	7,023		3,407	2,480	1,136
1973	7,934		3,841	2,811	1,282
1974	8,844		4,371	3,165	1,308
1975	11,299	1,145	5,046	3,594	1,514
1976	12,447	1,250	5,711	3,960	1,526
1977	13,754	1,351	6,264	4,433	1,706
1978	15,946	1,889	7,001	5,292	1,764
1979	17,695	2,076	7,742	6,071	1,806
1980	19,743	2,318	8,698	6,719	2,008

SOURCE: U.S. Bureau of the Census, *Governmental Finances* (Washington, D.C.: Government Printing Office, annual ed.).

NOTES: "Protective Inspections and Regulations" was not reported as a separate category prior to 1974. In 1960 expenditures for "General Control" and "Financial Administration" were presented as a combined expenditure.

CHAPTER IX

Knowledge Production
and Occupational Structure[1]

Machlup offered the labor analyst a new perspective on the labor force. He proposed that "knowledge-producing" occupations have exceeded all other groups of occupations in growth since the turn of the century. In table and text, Machlup showed that growth of employment in knowledge production had proceeded more rapidly than growth in employment within the economy at large.[2]

"Knowledge-producing" occupations were defined by Machlup as those that create new knowledge and those that communicate existing knowledge to others. Among those who create new knowledge are creators of original knowledge, like research scientists, and also those who, like doctors, apply existing knowledge to new situations. The second group, knowledge communicators, includes not only teachers, aircraft controllers, and others who communicate knowledge directly, but corporate chairmen, and middle managers who transmit information indirectly, through a large supporting cast of knowledge-producing employees. Of course, Machlup recognized that some occupational groups could fall easily in both the knowledge-producing and non-knowledge-producing categories. Thus, a physician examines a patient and takes certain actions based upon the examination, but whereas the cure is not considered to be "knowledge," the diagnosis is. For this reason, Machlup proposed that physicians' work be counted as half knowledge-producing and half not.

In *The Production and Distribution of Knowledge in the United States*, Machlup examined trends in the growth of knowledge occupations for the years from 1900 to 1958. Our task is to carry Machlup's analysis forward to 1980 and to compare the trends of the past twenty years with those of the preceding six decades.

DATA PROBLEMS

A variety of problems makes it difficult to compare data on occupations and employment over time. Among these are (1) different concepts of what constitutes the "labor force"; (2) the continual appearance of new jobs and a corresponding disappearance of old jobs; and (3) different systems for classifying oc-

---

[1] Materials for this chapter were prepared by Edward Weintraub.

[2] See Fritz Machlup, *The Production and Distribution of Knowledge in the United States* (Princeton, N.J.: Princeton University Press, 1962), pp. 377-400.

cupations into major groups. Each of these difficulties is explained in more detail below, along with our approach to solving the problems.

DIFFERENT DEFINITIONS OF THE LABOR FORCE

There are at least four definitions of the "labor force" in common use. The first is simply those people who are actually employed on the day of a particular survey or census. This labor force however, is only a subset of the second, which includes all "experienced" workers who are currently employed or who are actively seeking a new job in their old occupation. The third definition of the labor force is an even larger grouping constituted by all "economically active" men and women, including persons who are seeking employment in occupations for which they have no prior work experience. A student graduating from high school or college in search of a particular type of employment is an example of the inexperienced person included in this third group. The most expansive definition of the labor force encompasses the entire "non-institutional" population of working age, i.e., all persons old enough to work who are not in prison, mental hospitals, and so on. Naturally, the concept of "working age" presents its own difficulties. Prior to 1970, fourteen year olds were included in most labor force statistics. Since the 1970 census, however, "working age" has typically been construed as sixteen years of age and above.

We have worked exclusively with the "economically active" as our definition of the labor force. Thus, in all of our tables we report on a comparable and consistently defined population for various years. The only exception to this rule is in Table IX-4, where we use the "employed" labor force to compute income in knowledge-producing occupations. The use of a more expansive definition of the labor force would have been inappropriate here, since it would overvalue the total actual earnings of this group. On working age, we are simply forced to accept the inclusion of fourteen year olds in earlier years and their exclusion later, since no other data sources are available.

CHANGES IN CLASSIFICATION SYSTEMS

In 1977 a system was developed by the Office of Federal Statistical Policy Standards that was intended to make it easier in the future to compare the occupational data provided by future decennial censuses. Such official recognition of the problems inherent in the shifting classification schemes will be very helpful to future researchers, but offers little assistance to us. The three different classification schemes used in the 1960, 1970, and 1980 censuses present the researcher with the frequent appearance of new types of jobs and the disappearance of old jobs. Moreover, in different years the occupations were rearranged into different major groupings. For example, funeral directors were sometimes listed as "professional and technical workers" and other times as "managers."

For our research we have carefully sought to bridge the various classification schemes and wherever possible, have arranged our results so that a valid comparison among years can be made.

ANALYSIS OF KNOWLEDGE-PRODUCING OCCUPATIONS

COMPOSITION OF THE KNOWLEDGE-PRODUCING OCCUPATIONS

The federal statistical agencies have long divided occupations into five general categories: (1) professional and technical workers; (2) managers, officials, and proprietors; (3) clerical workers; (4) sales workers; and (5) craftsmen and foremen. These categories vary to some degree from one source to another.

In some tabulations professional and technical workers along with nonfarm managers and administrators and sales and clerical employees are classed under the broader heading of white-collar workers. The blue-collar classification includes craftsmen, operatives, and laborers except farm workers. Service workers and farm employees are independently listed.

Table IX-1 presents a broad picture of the occupational distribution of all economically active individuals in the United States for several years between 1958 and 1980. Using the broad categories—white collar, manual and service, and farm, we see the substantial effects of the rise of technology upon the overall labor force. The number of white-collar workers has increased from 27.1 million workers in 1958 to 51.9 million workers in 1980. That is, the white-collar labor force nearly doubled in the past 22 years. In contrast, the manual and service sector has witnessed a somewhat lesser increase in employment from 30.3 million workers in 1958 to 44.7 million workers in 1980. In the farm area the trend is the reverse. Between 1958 and 1980 our economically active farm population actually dropped from 5.6 million to 2.7 million workers. Thus, the number of active farmers, including all categories of farm labor, de-

TABLE IX-1

LABOR FORCE, OR ECONOMICALLY ACTIVE CIVILIAN POPULATION, BY BROAD OCCUPATION CATEGORIES:
1958, 1963, 1967, 1972, 1977, AND 1980
(thousands of persons)

Category	1958	1963	1967	1972	1977	1980
White collar	27,056	32,378	34,232	39,092	45,187	51,887
Manual and service	30,319	34,014	36,586	39,542	42,603	44,680
Farm	5,591	4,615	3,554	3,069	2,756	2,741
Total	62,966	71,007	74,372	81,703	90,546	99,308

SOURCES: U.S. Bureau of the Census, *Statistical Abstract of the United States* (Washington, D.C.: Government Printing Office, annual ed.). Data are derived from Bureau of Labor Statistics data reported for the years cited.

creased by 2.9 million workers, or over half of the farm working population in 1958.

Table IX-2 describes the composition of the economically active labor force in percentage terms. It indicates that white-collar workers increased from 43.0 percent of the work force as a whole in 1958 to 52.2 percent in 1980.

In the manual and service areas of employment, there was first a rise and then a decline in the percent of the work force included during the period 1958 through 1972: The figures are 48.2 percent in 1958; 47.9 percent in 1963; 49.2 percent in 1967; and 48.4 percent in 1972. From 1977 to 1980 manual and service employment began to decline more sharply, going from 47.1 percent to 45.0 percent. The net effect over those 22 years is that manual and service employment had declined as a percent of the entire labor force by 3.2 percent.

The farm category declined steadily in the years 1958 through 1980. Constituting 8.8 percent of the active labor force in 1958, it fell to 2.8 percent in 1980. Over the 22-year period, there was a decrease of 6.0 percent.

OVERALL GROWTH IN THE KNOWLEDGE OCCUPATIONS

Table IX-3 portrays the overall growth of knowledge-producing and non-knowledge occupations for the period of 1960-1980.

Class I in the table contains five of the basic Census Bureau occupational classifications for each of the three decennial periods and shows the number of workers employed in knowledge-producing occupations for each classification and year. No knowledge-producing occupations occur in the remaining six basic Census Bureau classifications, which are listed for each year in Class II.

Class III shows the number of full-time students attending grades 9 and higher on the secondary school level. Our objective in this latter class is to show the potential knowledge-producing labor force. Machlup argued that students of working age should be considered "as engaged in the production of knowledge in their own minds," and presumably, "producing a value (human

TABLE IX-2

PERCENTAGE DISTRIBUTION OF LABOR FORCE, OR ECONOMICALLY ACTIVE CIVILIAN POPULATION, BY BROAD OCCUPATION CATEGORIES: 1958, 1963, 1967, 1972, 1977, AND 1980

Category	1958	1963	1967	1972	1977	1980
White collar	43.0	45.6	46.0	47.8	49.9	52.2
Manual and service	48.2	47.9	49.2	48.4	47.1	45.0
Farm	8.8	6.5	4.8	3.8	3.0	2.8
Total	100.0	100.0	100.0	100.0	100.0	100.0

SOURCE: Table IX-1 in this book.

TABLE IX-3
OCCUPATIONS OF THE ECONOMICALLY ACTIVE POPULATIONS
BY PARTICIPATION IN KNOWLEDGE-PRODUCING ACTIVITIES,
1960, 1970, AND 1980

	1960 (thousand)	1960 per cent	1970 (thousand)	1970 per cent	1980 (thousand)	1980 per ent
Class I						
Professional, technical and kindred workers	7,090		11,561		15,337	
Not knowledge-producing workers	1,844		2,610		5,370	
Knowledge-producing workers	5,246	7.72	8,951	11.22	9,967	9.54
Managers, officials, proprietors except farm	5,708		6,463		10,379	
Not knowledge-producing workers	1,577		1,358		42	
Knowledge-producing workers	4,131	6.08	5,105	6.40	10,337	9.90
Clerical and kindred workers	9,431	13.87	14,208	17.80	17,564	16.82
Sales workers	4,799		5,625		10,257	
Not knowledge-producing workers	2,731		2,967		5,500	
Knowledge-producing workers	2,068	3.04	2,658	3.33	4,757	4.55
Craftsmen, foremen and kindred workers	9,465		11,082		13,555	
Not knowledge-producing workers	9,138		10,710		13,113	
Knowledge-producing workers	327	0.48	372	0.47	442	0.42
All knowledge-producing workers	21,203	31.19	31,294	39.21	43,067	41.23
Class II						
Operatives and kindred workers	12,254		14,335		14,902	
Private household workers	1,817		1,204		627	
Service workers, except household	6,086		9,047		12,979	
Laborers, except farm and mine	3,755		3,751		5,086	
Farmers and farm managers	2,528		1,428		1,315	
Farm laborers and foremen	1,604		1,022		1,717	
Excluded from Class I	15,290		17,645		24,025	
Other, and long-term unemployed	3,453		76		732	
All not knowledge-producing	46,787	68.81	48,508	60.79	61,383	58.77
Total civilian labor force	67,990	100.0	79,802	100.0	104,450	100.0
Class III						
Full-time students in grades 9 and higher	12,816		21,554		26,871	
(A) Potential civilian labor force	80,806		101,356		131,321	
(B) Potential civilian labor force in knowledge-producing occupations (Groups I + III)	34,019		52,848		69,938	
(B) as a percentage of (A)		42.10		52.14		53.26

SOURCES: (1960-1980): U.S. Bureau of the Census, *Census of Population* (Washington, D.C.: Government Printing Office, decennial eds.).

NOTE: Because of changes in classification systems and in age groups covered, the year-to-year groupings of occupations are not directly comparable. See the text for a fuller discussion of this problem.

capital) equal or exceeding earnings," except for their academic endeavors (*Production and Distribution of Knowledge*, p. 386). Therefore, the role of potential knowledge-producing labor should be included in any analysis of knowledge-producing occupations.

We observe that there were 21.2 million knowledge-producing employees in 1960 constituting 31.19 percent of the total labor force; the number had increased by 1970 to 31.3 million or 39.21 percent of the labor force and increased further by 1980 to 43.1 million or 41.23 percent of the labor force. Consequently, the data indicated that the knowledge-producing labor force doubled from 21.2 million to 43.1 million during the 20-year period, thereby increasing from 31.19 percent to 41.23 percent of the total work force.

There were 5.2 million knowledge-producing employees in the professional category in 1960 constituting 7.72 percent of the total labor force; by 1970 this number increased to 8.95 million employees or 11.22 percent of the total labor force. By 1980 this group experienced a smaller increase to 9.97 million but decreased as a share of the overall labor force to 9.54 percent. Over the twenty years of our study this represents a net increase of 4.7 million workers, or 1.82 percent. Growth in the clerical classification was increasing similarly from 9.43 million in 1960 to 14.21 million in 1970 and 17.56 million in 1980. The overall percentages again fell, however, between 1970 and 1980: the figures are 13.87 percent in 1960, 17.80 percent in 1970, and 16.82 percent in 1980.

The manager and sales workers classifications experienced a slow growth as a percent of the total labor force but accelerated sharply in absolute numbers. Knowledge-producing managers numbered 4.13 million in 1960 or 6.08 percent, grew slightly to 5.11 million in 1970 or 6.40 percent, but more than doubled in 1980 to 10.34 million in 1980 or 9.9 percent. An overall addition of 6.21 million managerial employees joined the knowledge-producing ranks, an increase of 3.82 percent. Knowledge-producing salesworkers underwent similar growth from 2.07 million or 3.04 percent in 1960; and 2.66 million or 3.33 percent in 1970; to 4.76 million in 1980, or 4.55 percent of the total population. Thus, there was a net 20-year increase of 2.69 million employees or 1.51 percent.

The knowledge-producing craftsmen underwent a steady decline on a percentage basis. In 1960 there were 327 thousand employees, constituting 0.48 percent of the total that increased slightly in 1970 to 372 thousand but fell on a percentage basis to 0.47 percent. The year 1980 shows a rise to 442 thousand workers but drops in percentage to 0.42. As a net result, during the period 1960-1980, knowledge-producing craftsmen increased by 115 thousand but declined in the total labor force by 0.06 percent.

Class II, the nonknowledge-producing labor force, includes all occupational classifications not included in Class I. It is sufficient for our purposes to note that 46.8 million employees or 68.81 percent of the total labor force in 1960 were not knowledge-producing employees. There was a slight increase to

TABLE IX-4

INCOME FROM EMPLOYMENT IN KNOWLEDGE-PRODUCING OCCUPATION GROUPS, 1960, 1970, AND 1980

		1960 Number employed (thousands)	1960 Median earnings (in dollars)	1960 Total income (million dollars)	1970 Number employed (thousands)	1970 Median earnings (in dollars)	1970 Total income (million dollars)	1980 Number employed (thousands)	1980 Median earnings (in dollars)	1980 Total income (million dollars)
Professional, technical, and kindred workers	Male	4,303			6,517			8,904		
	Female	2,683			4,314			7,073		
Not knowledge-producing workers	Male	1,003			1,352			873		
	Female	807			1,212			2,025		
Knowledge-producing workers	Male	3,300	6,848	22,598	5,165	11,806	60,978	8,031	23,026	184,922
	Female	1,876	4,384	8,224	3,102	7,878	24,438	5,038	15,285	77,006
Total, knowledge-producing workers		5,176	11,232	30,822	8,267	19,684	85,416	13,069	38,311	261,928
Managers, officials, proprietors except farm	Male	4,797			5,126			8,219		
	Female	829			1,014			2,920		
Not knowledge-producing workers	Male	1,610			1,163			955		
	Female	306			210			458		
Knowledge-producing workers	Male	3,187	7,241	23,077	3,963	12,117	48,020	7,264	23,558	171,125
	Female	523	4,173	2,182	804	6,834	5,495	2,462	12,936	31,848
Total, knowledge-producing workers		3,710	11,414	25,259	4,767	18,951	53,515	9,726	36,494	202,973
Clerical and kindred workers	Male	2,922	5,247	15,332	3,452	8,617	29,746	3,687	18,247	67,277
	Female	6,204	3,586	22,248	9,582	5,551	53,190	14,787	10,997	162,613
Total, knowledge-producing workers		9,126	8,833	37,580	13,034	14,168	83,936	18,474	29,244	229,890
Sales workers	Male	2,986			3,268			3,450		
	Female	1,652			2,000			2,853		
Not knowledge-producing workers	Male	1,271			1,437			1,185		
	Female	1,386			1,616			2,040		

Knowledge-producing workers	Male	1,715	5,755	9,870	1,831	9,790	17,925	2,265	19,910	45,096
	Female	266	2,428	646	384	4,188	1,608	813	9,748	7,925
Total, knowledge-producing workers		1,981	8,183	10,516	2,215	13,978	19,533	3,078	29,658	53,021
Craftsmen, foremen, and kindred workers	Male	8,668			9,502			12,018		
	Female	277			495			769		
Not knowledge-producing workers	Male	8,374			9,181			11,697		
	Female	251			451			675		
Knowledge-producing workers	Male	294	5,868	1,725	321	9,254	2,971	321	18,671	5,993
	Female	26	2,934	76	44	5,089	224	94	11,701	1,100
Total, knowledge-producing workers		320	8,802	1,801	365	14,343	3,195	415	29,372	7,093
Total, all knowledge-producing workers		20,313	5,217	105,978	28,648	8,538	244,595	44,762	16,865	754,905
Total employed		64,639			77,309			99,303		

SOURCES: (1960, 1970): U.S. Bureau of the Census, *Census of Population*, 1960 and 1970. (1980): U.S. Bureau of Labor Statistics, unpublished tables.

NOTES: Total Employed figures are derived from the Bureau of Labor Statistics that are slightly lower than the previously used Bureau of the Census Total Employment figures. This has been done to remain consistent for the table as a whole and would have little or no effect upon the illustrated trends. Table IX-5 also necessarily utilizes the Bureau of Labor Statistics data for Total Employment.

48.5 million employees in 1970, but a decrease on a percentage basis to 60.79. In 1980 there was a substantial increase in number of employees to 61.4 million, but a drop to 58.77 percent of the total labor force. Over the two decades of our study, nonknowledge-producing employees increased by 14.6 million workers, but lost ground in the total labor force by 10.04 percent.

Class III constitutes the future labor force that is involved in knowledge production by attending school. Taking the secondary academic level from the ninth grade through the twelfth grade, we find that there were 12.82 million students in 1960, increasing to 21.55 million in 1970 and to 26.87 million in 1980. The potential labor force comprises the economically active labor force for the decennial year plus the number of full-time students for that year. In 1960 on that basis it follows that there was a potential labor force of 80.81 million, an increase in 1970 to 101.36 million, and for 1980 a sharply increased total of 131.32 million. Since our objective is to determine the number of potential knowledge-producing employees, the addition of the number of knowledge-producing occupations in Class I to the number of full-time students for the same year gives us the potential civilian labor force in knowledge-producing occupations (Group I plus Group III). Thus in 1960 there were potentially 34.02 million knowledge-producing workers, which increased to 52.85 million workers in 1970, and 69.94 million workers in 1980. Using the percentage of potential civilian labor force in knowledge-producing occupations of the potential labor force, i.e., III.B of III.A, we obtain 42.10 percent for 1960, 52.14 percent for 1970, and 53.26 percent in 1980.

The reader should understand that the word "potential" is the critical concept for Class III. As an example, consider the statement that there were 131.32 million potential knowledge-producing employees in 1980. Because some students will not in fact become knowledge-producing employees, the term "potential" indicates that the figure is the maximum number that may become knowledge-producing employees and not the (unknown) number of those who actually will do so. The Class I data provide the actual number of knowledge-producing employees.

INCOME IN KNOWLEDGE-PRODUCING OCCUPATIONS

Table IX-4 extends the analysis of knowledge-producing occupations to the income earned by the workers within that group. The table shows the number of workers actually employed in knowledge-producing occupations, their median income, and total income as a group for the years 1960, 1970, and 1980. It also reflects the differences of income by sex during those years.

The table shows that for 1960, 20.31 million knowledge-producing workers were employed with median earnings for both sexes of $5,217, or a total income of $105.98 billion. The 1970 figures rose substantially to 28.65 million workers employed with median earnings of $8,538, or a total income of $244.6 billion. In 1980 the number employed was slightly more than double the 1960 figure, or 44.76 million, but with the median income more than triple that of 1960 at $16,865 and a total income of $754.91 billion.

Table IX-5 compares the aggregate earnings of all workers in knowledge-producing occupations with the income earned by all workers. The table compares the relative employment and incomes from knowledge-producing employment with total employment and incomes between 1960 and 1980.

Knowledge-producing employees in 1960 numbered 20.31 million and were 31.43 percent of the total employed work force with a group income of $105.98 billion. By 1980 they underwent an increase of approximately 14 percent to 45.08 percent of the work force and increased their income sevenfold over the 20-year period, to $754.91 billion. Knowledge-producing workers' share of all employee compensation economy-wide rose to 47.28 percent in 1980, from 35.93 percent in 1960. When compared to all employees and proprietors, knowledge workers' income rose from 31.0 percent in 1960 to 43.71 percent in 1980.

TABLE IX-5
RELATIVE EMPLOYMENT AND RELATIVE INCOMES FROM
EMPLOYMENT IN KNOWLEDGE-PRODUCING OCCUPATION GROUPS, 1960, 1970, AND 1980
(millions)

	1960	1970	1980
(1) Total employed persons (thousands)	64,639	77,309	99,303
(2) Knowledge-producing persons employed (thousands)	20,313	28,648	44,762
(3) Percent of total employment [(2) ÷ (1) × 100]	31.43%	37.06%	45.08%
(4) Income of all knowledge-producing occupations	105,978	244,595	754,905
(5) Income of all employees	294,932	609,150	1,596,500
(6) Income of all employees and proprietors	341,910	674,290	1,727,200
(7) National income	412,008	798,374	2,119,500
(8) Percent of employees' income [(4) ÷ (5) × 100]	35.93%	40.15%	47.28%
(9) Percent of employees' and proprietors' income [(4) ÷ (6) × 100]	31.00%	36.27%	43.71%
(10) Percent of national income [(4) ÷ (7) × 100]	25.72%	31.64%	35.62%

SOURCES: Items (1), (2), (4): Table IX-4. Items (5), (6), (7): U.S. Bureau of Economic Analysis, *Survey of Current Businesses* (Washington, D.C.: Government Printing Office, monthly eds.).

NOTES: For Item 5 data will vary in accord with income factors which are added to the basic income; e.g., rental income, personal interest income, transfer income (social security and veterans benefits, etc.). Consequently, such additional income is variable and cited as loose estimates. The term "personal income" might also be used.

In 1960, the Bureau of Economic Analysis estimated Employees Personal Income to be 399.7 million, 801.3 million in 1970, and 2.17 billion in 1980. These figures could have been used for Item 5 of Table IX-5, and in Table IX-4.

Appendix to Chapter III

APPENDIX TABLE A
KNOWLEDGE PRODUCTION
(millions of dollars)

	1958	1963	1967	1972	1977	1980	Constant 1972 dollars					
							1958	1963	1967	1972	1977	1980
Education												
In the home	4,432	5,273	6,584	9,326	10,475	11,316	6,414	7,204	8,251	9,326	7,229	5,738
Preschool			238	1,052	1,985	3,447			299	1,052	1,449	1,937
Head Start			349	376	475	735			438	376	347	413
Elementary & secondary												
Monetary	15,648	24,482	37,008	54,000	85,500	107,100	45,225	54,164	64,474	54,000	60,768	58,879
Implicit rent	1,869	2,672	2,869	3,536	5,157	6,556	2,502	3,353	3,420	3,536	3,892	3,916
Tax exemption	351	468	645	928	1,161	1,475	629	787	940	928	892	1,108
Students' foregone earning	15,172	23,813	32,623	46,962	65,578	79,886	21,957	32,531	40,881	46,962	45,257	40,510
Transportation & clothes	455	714	979	1,409	1,967	2,397	579	877	1,137	1,409	1,517	1,572
Colleges & universities												
Monetary	4,022	7,950	14,413	20,772	31,473	41,281	11,624	17,588	25,110	20,772	22,369	22,694
Implicit rent	893	1,705	2,429	4,024	5,679	6,726	1,195	2,139	2,895	4,024	4,286	4,018
Tax exemption	168	299	547	1,057	1,732	2,355	301	503	797	1,057	1,331	1,769
Students' foregone earning	6,380	10,060	16,624	27,849	41,939	52,260	9,233	13,743	20,832	27,849	28,943	26,501
Transportation & clothes	383	604	997	1,671	2,516	3,136	487	742	1,158	1,671	1,940	2,056
Church	3,320	4,520	5,994	8,016	13,544	17,721	9,595	10,000	10,443	8,016	9,626	9,742
Military	3,410	2,226	3,697	4,257	5,684	7,299	9,855	4,925	6,441	4,257	4,040	4,013
Commercial	253	669	1,088	1,703	2,987	4,809	731	1,480	1,895	1,703	2,123	2,644
Federal programs	342	480	835	729	864	901	988	1,062	1,455	729	614	495
Public libraries	140	399	659	977	1,471	1,963	405	883	1,148	977	1,045	1,079
All education	57,238	86,334	128,578	188,644	280,187	351,363	121,722	151,980	192,014	188,644	197,669	189,085
Percent of adjusted GNP	11.79	13.31	14.74	14.79	13.66	12.45	16.61	16.82	17.44	14.79	13.40	11.97
Cost of production or omitted in official statistics	28,746	43,523	61,129	91,697	128,828	156,744	41,301	58,970	76,278	91,697	89,608	80,684

APPENDIX TABLE A (con't)

							Constant 1972 dollars					
	1958	1963	1967	1972	1977	1980	1958	1963	1967	1972	1977	1980
Research & development												
Basic research	877	1,965	3,056	3,829	5,550	8,071	1,328	2,720	3,853	3,829	3,952	4,562
Applied research	2,699	3,742	4,780	5,984	9,755	13,940	4,086	5,201	6,036	5,984	6,964	7,869
Development	7,135	11,352	15,310	18,664	27,677	40,211	10,801	15,812	19,352	18,664	19,779	22,683
All research & development	10,711	17,059	23,146	28,477	42,982	62,222	16,215	23,733	29,241	28,477	30,695	35,114
Percent of adjusted GNP	2.21	2.63	2.65	2.23	2.09	2.20	2.21	2.63	2.66	2.23	2.08	2.22
Cost of production or omitted in official statistics	3,707	5,456	8,142	11,710	19,696	30,400	5,612	7,611	10,299	11,710	14,085	17,139
Media of communication												
Books & pamphlets	1,608	2,335	3,180	4,342	7,244	9,378	2,536	3,326	4,146	4,342	5,017	5,136
Periodicals	1,803	2,215	2,941	3,676	5,914	8,699	2,844	3,155	3,834	3,831	4,096	4,764
(treated as cost)	1,056	1,294	1,738	1,889	3,250	4,949	1,666	1,843	2,266	1,889	2,251	2,710
Newspapers	3,793	4,653	6,167	8,920	13,458	18,113	5,945	6,462	7,718	8,877	9,243	9,463
(treated as cost)	2,479	3,107	4,163	6,048	9,666	13,301	3,886	4,315	5,210	6,048	6,639	6,949
Stationery, etc.	1,850	2,409	3,106	4,331	6,687	9,625	2,197	2,878	3,530	4,330	4,065	5,142
Commercial printing	3,058	3,670	4,790	6,926	11,217	15,643	4,247	4,779	5,743	6,926	7,394	7,908
(treated as final product)	27	45	89	130	258	470	37	59	107	130	170	238
Photography	1,272	1,339	3,052	7,194	12,130	17,061	1,509	1,498	3,083	7,194	9,331	9,070
Phonography	1,035	1,514	1,820	2,753	5,687	6,130	873	1,489	1,837	2,753	6,961	6,911
Theater & concerts	297	356	474	632	868	1,318	501	522	612	632	654	928
Spectator sports	249	522	802	1,211	1,753	2,284	420	765	1,035	1,211	1,320	1,608
Motion pictures	992	942	1,128	1,644	2,376	2,822	1,765	1,377	1,367	1,644	1,718	1,617
Radio stations' revenue	521	680	907	1,407	2,275	3,206	1,000	997	1,093	1,407	1,401	1,453
(treated as cost)	521	680	907	1,407	2,275	3,206	1,000	997	1,093	1,407	1,401	1,453
TV stations' revenue	1,030	1,597	2,276	3,179	5,889	8,808	1,977	2,342	2,742	3,179	3,626	3,993
(treated as cost)	1,030	1,597	2,276	3,179	5,889	8,808	1,977	2,342	2,742	3,179	3,626	3,993
Cable television			150	410	1,206	2,238			194	410	908	1,576
Radio & TV sets & repairs	1,688	2,285	4,161	5,679	7,729	9,911	1,396	2,059	3,929	5,679	7,668	9,315
Other advertising	5,000	6,000	7,537	10,415	16,774	21,914	8,157	8,475	9,293	10,415	11,521	12,236
(treated as cost)	5,000	6,000	7,537	10,415	16,774	21,914	8,157	8,475	9,293	10,415	11,521	12,236
Telephone	7,642	11,044	15,184	25,049	44,164	61,041	8,606	11,939	16,667	25,049	38,204	50,116
(treated as final product)	1,870	2,281	2,474	8,348	10,581	6,706	2,106	2,466	2,716	8,348	9,153	5,506

	1	2	3	4	5	6	7	8	9	10	11	12
Telegraph	318	385	467	659	952	1,232	358	416	513	432	824	1,011
(treated as final product)	58	59	55	144	133	77	65	64	60	144	115	63
Postal service	3,478	4,699	6,249	9,522	15,310	19,412	8,783	8,816	10,295	9,522	10,255	11,093
(treated as final product)	52	89	146	294	611	745	131	167	241	294	409	426
Conventions	1,600	2,000	2,600	2,900	5,086	8,300	2,640	3,035	3,430	2,900	3,481	3,882
All communications media	37,234	48,645	66,991	100,849	166,719	227,135	55,754	64,330	81,061	100,733	127,685	147,223
Percent of adjusted GNP	7.67	7.50	7.68	7.91	8.13	8.05	7.61	7.12	7.36	7.90	8.65	9.32
Cost of production or omitted in official statistics	10,086	12,678	16,621	22,938	37,854	52,178	16,685	17,972	20,605	22,938	25,437	27,341
Final product in official statistics	2,007	2,474	2,764	8,916	11,583	7,998	2,340	2,755	3,123	8,916	9,847	6,232
Information machines												
Broadcasting equipment	54	150	344	430	568	1,148	60	178	412	430	430	736
Printing trades machinery	311	403	656	737	1,287	2,053	523	636	859	737	840	1,051
Motion picture apparatus	148	128	194	192	178	251	176	143	196	192	137	133
Musical instruments	242	319	401	525	879	1,091	326	405	447	525	618	614
Telephone & telegraph equip.	1,079	1,632	2,459	4,247	8,125	12,979	1,256	1,969	2,938	4,247	5,097	7,004
Signaling devices	130	166	231	336	847	1,193	145	197	277	336	642	765
Measuring & control instrum.	6,509	10,079	12,806	14,815	27,005	41,358	9,365	13,602	15,504	14,815	20,123	21,941
Electronic computers	324	880	4,049	6,108	12,673	25,658	333	892	4,106	6,108	12,698	26,811
Typewriters	189	265	508	80	1,102	1,909	247	330	573	580	850	1,223
Calculators	709	970	630	694	836	1,233	709	958	626	694	873	1,233
Other office machines	183	247	418	485	918	1,337	209	272	445	485	788	851
All information machines	9,878	15,239	22,696	29,149	54,418	90,210	13,349	19,583	26,382	29,149	43,096	62,363
Percent of adjusted GNP	2.03	2.35	2.60	2.29	2.65	3.20	1.82	2.17	2.40	2.29	2.92	3.95
Information services												
Legal	3,025	4,597	6,254	10,938	18,695	23,424	6,450	8,404	9,224	10,938	12,718	13,006
Engineering & architectural	1,250	1,563	4,510	7,186	14,049	25,713	2,665	2,857	6,652	7,186	9,557	14,277
Accounting & auditing	1,409	1,615	2,547	4,126	7,990	12,625	3,004	2,952	3,757	4,126	5,435	7,010

APPENDIX TABLE A (con't)

							Constant 1972 dollars					
	1958	1963	1967	1972	1977	1980	1958	1963	1967	1972	1977	1980
Medical	2,287	3,183	4,681	7,745	14,533	23,305	4,099	5,036	6,250	7,745	9,682	12,728
Demand deposit costs	2,255	3,200	2,993	4,760	8,200	11,588	4,056	5,203	3,923	4,760	6,003	6,267
Credit card costs		725	1,158	3,288	8,409	15,240		1,241	1,924	3,299	5,632	9,961
Security & commodity brokers	2,278	916	2,520	3,533	3,334	6,876	6,011	1,568	4,186	3,533	2,233	4,494
Real estate brokers	739	2,688	4,005	4,892	10,510	15,160	1,053	3,491	4,814	4,892	7,992	9,144
Insurance agents & brokers	3,470	4,838	5,603	10,234	19,263	29,447	6,402	7,501	7,286	10,324	14,397	18,177
Wholesale agents	1,529	1,893	2,479	3,595	6,066		1,914	2,346	2,889	3,595	4,207	
Computer & data processing				3,411	7,476	13,365				3,411	7,491	13,966
Misc. business services	1,548	3,080	5,314	8,440	15,516	26,064	2,525	4,350	6,552	8,440	10,805	14,759
Federal government*	1,555	2,655	3,474	5,971	8,870	14,430	3,025	4,268	4,970	5,971	6,126	8,399
State & local government*	2,419	2,850	3,860	7,023	13,754	19,743	4,706	4,582	5,522	7,023	9,499	11,492
All information services	23,764	33,803	49,398	85,142	156,665	236,980	45,910	53,802	67,948	85,142	111,777	143,679
Percent of adjusted GNP	4.90	5.21	5.66	6.67	7.64	8.39	6.26	5.95	6.17	6.67	7.58	9.10
Final product in official statistics	3,974	5,505	7,334	12,994	22,624	34,173	7,732	8,850	10,492	12,994	15,624	19,891
Total knowledge production	138,825	201,080	290,809	432,261	700,971	967,910	252,950	313,428	396,646	432,145	510,921	577,464
Cost of production or omitted in official statistics	42,539	61,657	85,892	126,345	186,378	239,322	63,598	84,553	107,182	126,345	129,130	125,164
Final product in official statistics	5,981	7,979	10,098	21,910	34,207	42,171	10,072	11,606	13,615	21,910	25,472	26,123
Total GNP	448,881	594,738	796,312	1,171,121	1,899,500	2,626,100	679,500	830,700	1,007,700	1,171,121	1,371,700	1,480,700
Corrected GNP	485,439	648,416	872,106	1,275,556	2,051,671	2,823,251	733,026	903,647	1,101,267	1,275,556	1,475,358	1,579,741
Knowledge as percent of GNP	28.59	31.01	33.34	33.88	34.16	34.28	34.50	34.68	36.01	33.88	34.63	36.55
Other than education	16.80	17.70	18.60	19.09	20.50	21.83	17.86	18.57	18.57	19.08	21.23	24.58

* The categories "cost of production" and "final product" in the "official statistics" reconcile the production statistics with the national-income accounts because we depart from some of the conventions adopted by the official authorities. Thus, since we regard research work as final output even when it is financed as business expense, we have to enter the business expenditure in question as "cost of production in official statistics." Conversely, since we regard general expenditures of the government as operating cost of the economy, we have to enter such expenditures as "final product in official statistics."

	1958	1963	1967	1972	1977	1980	Source and comments
Education							
In the home	69.1	73.2	79.8	100	144.9	197.2	BLS wage deflator
Preschool			79.6	100	137.0	178.0	CPI
Head Start			79.6	100	137.0	178.0	
Elementary & secondary							
Monetary	34.6	45.2	57.4	100	140.7	181.9	BEA GNP deflator for education
Implicit rent	74.7	79.7	83.9	100	132.5	167.4	CPI- "residential rents"
Tax exemption	55.8	59.5	68.6	100	130.1	133.1	CPI, not available for 1958
Student's foregone earning	69.1	73.2	79.8	100	144.9	197.2	BLS wage deflator
Clothes & transportation	78.6	81.4	86.1	100	129.7	152.5	BEA output deflator, SIC 23
Colleges & universities							
Monetary	34.6	45.2	57.4	100	140.7	181.9	BEA GNP deflator for education
Implicit rent	74.7	79.7	83.9	100	132.5	167.4	CPI- "residential rents"
Tax exemption	55.8	59.5	68.6	100	130.1	133.1	CPI
Student's foregone earning	69.1	73.2	79.8	100	144.9	197.2	BLS wage deflator
Clothes & transportation	78.6	81.4	86.1	100	129.7	152.5	BEA output deflator, SIC 23
Church	34.6	45.2	57.4	100	140.7	181.9	BEA GNP deflator for education
Military	34.6	45.2	57.4	100	140.7	181.9	" " "
Commercial	34.6	45.2	57.4	100	140.7	181.9	" " "
Training on the job	34.6	45.2	57.4	100	140.7	181.9	" " "
Federal training	34.6	45.2	57.4	100	140.7	181.9	" " "
Public libraries	34.6	45.2	57.4	100	140.7	181.9	" " "
Research & development							
Basic research							
Applied research							As published by NSF
Development							
Media of communication							
Books & pamphlets	63.4	70.2	76.7	100	144.4	182.6	BEA output deflator, SIC 272-274
Periodicals	63.4	70.2	76.7	100	144.4	182.6	" " " SIC 272-274
(treated as cost)	63.4	70.2	76.7	100	144.4	182.6	" " " SIC 272-274
Newspapers	63.8	72.0	79.9	100	145.6	191.4	" " " SIC 271
(treated as cost)	63.8	72.0	79.9	100	145.6	191.4	" " " SIC 271
Stationery, etc.	84.2	83.7	88.0	100	164.5	187.2	CPI
Commercial printing	72.0	76.8	83.4	100	151.7	197.8	BEA output deflator, SIC 275-279
(treated as final product)	72.0	76.8	83.4	100	151.7	197.8	" " " SIC 275-279
Photography	84.3	89.4	99.0	100	130.0	188.1	" " " SIC 386
Phonography	118.6	101.7	99.1	100	81.7	88.7	CPI- "sound equipment"
Theater & concerts	59.3	68.2	77.5	100	132.8	142.0	BEA output deflator, SIC 79
Spectator sports	59.3	68.2	77.5	100	132.8	142.0	" " " SIC 79
Motion pictures	56.2	68.4	82.5	100	138.3	174.5	" " " SIC 78
Radio stations' revenue	52.1	68.2	83.0	100	162.4	220.6	" " " SIC 483
(treated as cost)	52.1	68.2	83.0	100	162.4	220.6	" " " SIC 483
TV stations' revenue	52.1	68.2	83.0	100	162.4	220.6	" " " SIC 483
(treated as cost)	52.1	68.2	83.0	100	162.4	220.6	" " " SIC 483
Cable television	59.3	68.2	77.5	100	132.8	142.0	" " " SIC 483
Radio & TV sets & repairs	120.9	111.0	105.9	100	100.8	106.4	" " " SIC 365
Other advertising	61.3	70.8	81.1	100	145.6	179.1	BEA output deflator, SIC 731
(treated as cost)	61.3	70.8	81.1	100	145.6	179.1	" " " SIC 731

	1958	1963	1967	1972	1977	1980	Source and comments
Telephone	88.8	92.5	91.1	100	115.6	121.8	" " " SIC 48PT
(treated as final product)	88.8	92.5	91.1	100	115.6	121.8	" " " SIC 48PT
Telegraph	88.8	92.5	91.1	100	115.6	121.8	" " " SIC 48PT
(treated as final product)	88.8	92.5	91.1	100	115.6	121.8	" " " SIC 48PT
Postal service	39.6	53.3	60.7	100	149.3	175.0	" " " SIC 43
(treated as final product)	39.6	53.3	60.7	100	149.3	175.0	" " " SIC 43
Conventions	60.6	65.9	75.8	100	146.1	213.8	" " " SIC 70, 836

Information machines

	1958	1963	1967	1972	1977	1980	Source and comments
Broadcasting equipment	89.9	84.1	83.5	100	132.0	155.9	BEA output deflator, SIC 3662
Motion picture apparatus	84.3	89.4	99.0	100	130.0	188.1	" " " SIC 386
Telephone & telegraph equip.	85.9	82.9	83.7	100	159.4	185.3	" " " SIC 3661
Signaling devices	89.9	84.1	83.5	100	132.0	155.9	" " " SIC 3662
Measuring & control instrum.	69.5	74.1	82.6	100	134.2	188.5	" " " SIC 381, 382
Electronic computers	97.2	98.6	98.6	100	99.8	95.7	" " " SIC 3573, 3574
Typewriters	76.5	80.2	88.7	100	129.7	156.1	" " " SIC 357PT
Printing trades machinery	59.5	63.4	76.4	100	153.2	195.3	Producer price index SIC 3554
Musical instruments	74.2	78.7	89.7	100	142.2	177.7	Producer price index SIC 3931
Calculators	100.0	101.3	100.7	100	95.8	100.0	Producer price index SIC 3574
Other office machines	87.4	90.7	93.9	100	116.5	157.1	Producer price index SIC 3579

Information services

	1958	1963	1967	1972	1977	1980	Source and comments
Legal	46.9	54.7	67.8	100	147.0	180.1	BEA output deflator, SIC 81, 89
Engineering & architectural	46.9	54.7	67.8	100	147.0	180.1	" " " SIC 81, 89
Accounting & auditing	46.9	54.7	67.8	100	147.0	180.1	" " " SIC 81, 89
Medical	55.8	63.2	74.9	100	150.1	183.1	" " " SIC 801-803
Demand deposit costs	55.6	61.5	76.3	100	136.6	184.9	" " " SIC 60
Credit card costs		58.4	60.2	100	149.3	153.0	" " " SIC 61, 62, 67
Security & commodity brokers	37.9	58.4	60.2	100	149.3	153.0	" " " SIC 61, 62, 67
Real estate brokers	70.2	77.0	83.2	100	131.5	165.8	" " " SIC 65, 66
Insurance agents & brokers	54.2	64.5	76.9	100	133.8	162.0	" " " SIC 63, 64
Wholesale agents	79.9	80.7	85.8	100	144.2		" " " SIC 50, 51
Computer & data processing				100	99.8	95.7	" " " SIC 3573, 3574
Misc. Business services	61.3	70.8	81.1	100	143.6	176.6	" " " SIC 731, 7396
Federal government	51.4	62.2	69.9	100	144.8	171.8	" Govt enterprise
State & local government	51.4	62.2	69.9	100	144.8	171.8	" Govt enterprise

Index

Library of Congress Cataloging-in-Publication Data
Rubin, Michael Rogers.
The knowledge industry in the United States, 1960-1980.
Includes index.
1. Learning and scholarship—United States—Statistics.
2. Education—United States—Statistics.
3. Communication—United States—Statistics.
4. Information services—United States—Statistics.
I. Huber, Mary Taylor, 1944-   II. Taylor, Elizabeth Lloyd.
III. Title.
AZ505.R83   1986   001   85-43307
ISBN 0-691-04235-7 (alk. paper)